Bomber Aircraft of World War II

Bomber Aircraft of World War II

Heavy Bombers • Light Bombers • Dive-Bombers • Torpedo Bombers

Edward Ward

amber BOOKS

This pocket edition first published in 2026

Published by
Amber Books Ltd
United House
London N7 9DP
United Kingdom
www.amberbooks.co.uk
Facebook: amberbooks
YouTube: amberbooksltd
Instagram: amberbooksltd
X(Twitter): @amberbooks

ISBN: 978-1-83886-701-0

Project editor: Michael Spilling
Design: Fredy Alexandrakis
Picture research: Terry Forshaw

Printed in China

Opposite: Boeing B-17F Flying Fortress,
US Eighth Army Air Force (Amber Books Ltd)

Contents

Introduction 6

ALLIES 10
- France
- Netherlands
- Poland
- Soviet Union
- United Kingdom
- United States

AXIS 138
- Czechoslovakia
- Germany
- Italy
- Japan
- Romania

Index 218

Picture Credits 224

2-T-8
2-T-7
2-T-9

Introduction

The bomber truly came of age during World War II as the vulnerable, slow and innaccurate machines of 1939 gave way to fast, highly capable aircraft – ushering in the subsequent age of nuclear warfare.

In the years between the wars, bombers were seen as inexorable carriers of death and destruction, feared in much the same way nuclear missiles would be during the Cold War. The phrase "the bomber will always get through", coined by British Prime Minister Stanley Baldwin in a 1932 speech, became a chilling, and widely repeated, expression of this unstoppable force. The experience of the Spanish Civil War seemed only to confirm the truth of this gloomy prediction and the horror of the German aircraft attack on Guernica in 1937 gained a particularly grim foothold in popular culture. However, World War II paradoxically showed that the bomber could be highly vulnerable when faced with effective fighter defences. It further proved – during the war's last strategic bombing campaign – that sufficiently advanced bombing aircraft, such as the B-29 Superfortress, could be virtually invincible, capable of devastating entire cities and, ultimately, doing so with a single atomic bomb.

Increased defence

The overwhelming experience of bombing aircraft in the first years of the war was one of intense vulnerability to modern fighter aircraft, which had improved greatly over the 1930s. British and French bombers attacking German targets were shot down in large numbers during daylight hours, at times suffering 100 per cent losses. Also, the later mauling of German bombers in the Battle of Britain proved that the bomber did not always get through after all. Most combatants switched to flying primarily by night, which initially worked well in terms of aircraft losses, but resulted in a drop

Left: Such was the pace of aviation development that the Douglas TBD Devastator, pictured here in the markings of Torpedo Squadron 2, was regarded as the world's most advanced torpedo bomber when it entered service in 1937. However, it was effectively obsolete by 1941 and suffered appalling losses in action.

Right: The Heinkel He 111, Germany's iconic bomber, served in various roles, including as a torpedo bomber. The He 111H-6 variant could carry two torpedoes and proved successful in operations against Allied shipping.

in accuracy. In 1941, for example, only about 20 to 30 per cent of RAF bombers were striking within 8km (5 miles) of their targets. It was decided therefore that the objectives would need to be large, leading inevitably to the area bombing of cities, an approach already seen as morally questionable at the time. The advent of radar also considerably negated the cover of night operations and Bomber Command suffered severe losses.

Daylight raids

The United States, however, took a different approach. Unwilling to give up the ideal of pinpoint accuracy, the US Army Air Forces (USAAF) equipped its bombers with such heavy armament that they were expected to repel enemy fighters and maintain a daylight offensive. This strategy proved so costly in aircrew lives and aircraft that missions over Germany were suspended in late 1943, pending the arrival of long-range fighters capable of escorting the bombers to their targets and safely back again.

While strategic bombers continued their relentless attacks on enemy cities, tactical bombers were utilized by all sides against targets near to, or on, the frontline. Meanwhile, smaller bombers undertook ground attack and close-support missions. These aircraft, particularly the light bombers, initially suffered heavy losses to enemy fighters and ground fire. Conditions improved, however, as ever more capable aircraft entered service, a process exemplified by the outstanding de Havilland Mosquito and taken to its wartime limit with the first purpose-

built jet bomber, the Arado Ar 234. To begin with, close support and ground attack were the preserve of aircraft such as the Ju 87 Stuka. Its incredible accuracy and terrifying dive-bombing assaults caused widespread panic early in the war, but the Stuka proved highly vulnerable to enemy fighters. By the war's end, most close-support bombing missions were carried out by modified fighter aircraft. By contrast, in the war at sea, the carrier-based dive bomber remained an important asset in the inventory until the conclusion of the war. Alongside torpedo bombers, it persisted as virtually the only weapon capable of striking a manoeuvring ship at sea with sufficient precision. During the latter half of the war, the first air-launched guided missiles began to appear, some achieving notable success. All of these aircraft types are described in detail in the following pages.

Allies

In 1939, Poland possessed what was arguably the world's finest medium bomber, the PZL.37, although precious few of them, while France was in the process of modernizing its air force. In Britain, the Blenheim and Wellington served as the most important light and medium bombers, later giving way to the superlative Mosquito and Lancaster. The Soviet Union, like the Axis powers, concentrated on close-support aircraft, producing the formidable Pe-2 and Il-2 in vast numbers. In contrast, the USAAF pursued a daylight strategic bombing campaign with near-singleminded determination, relying on the B-17 Flying Fortress and B-24 Liberator. Ultimately, it introduced the most fearsome bomber of the war: the B-29 Superfortress.

Opposite: The Bristol Blenheim was the RAF's most important light bomber in the early war years. Although fast by 1930s standards, it was not fast enough to escape the Luftwaffe's Messerschmitt Bf 109s and losses, especially by day, were severe.

Amiot 143

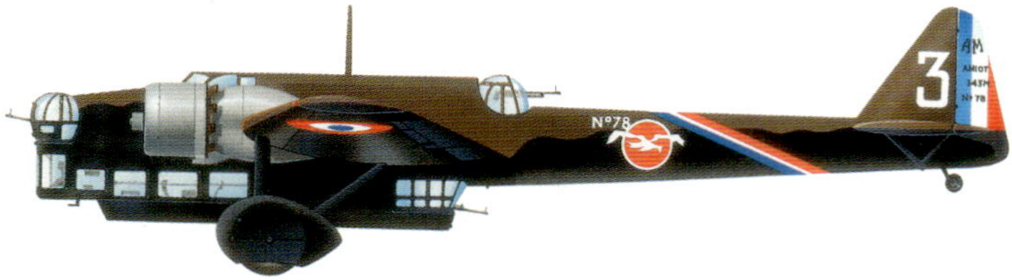

One of the oldest designs to see significant combat service during the war, the Amiot 143 performed surprisingly well when flown at night, but proved vulnerable during daylight missions.

Built to a specification issued as early as 1928, the prototype Amiot 143 had first flown in April 1931. However, changing requirements from the French Air Ministry resulted in a series of redesigns, and the aircraft eventually entered service four years later. The Amiot 143 featured all-metal construction and, although it could hardly be described as aesthetically pleasing, the aircraft boasted

Despite its undeniably cumbersome appearance, the Amiot 143 proved reliable and effective in action.

Amiot 143

Weight: 9700kg (21,383lb)
Dimensions: Length 18.25m (59ft 11in), Wingspan 24.53m (80ft 6in), Height 5.65m (18ft 8in)
Powerplant: Two 640kW (858hp) Gnome-Rhône 14K Mistral Major 14-cylinder air-cooled radial engines
Maximum speed: 310km/h (193mph)
Range: 1200km (746 miles)
Ceiling: 9000m (25,930ft)
Crew: 5
Armament: One 7.5mm (0.295in) MAC machine gun flexibly mounted in nose turret, dorsal turret and ventral position; up to 800kg (1764lb) bombload carried in bomb bay and 800kg (1764lb) externally

Opposite top:
With its undersides painted black for nocturnal operations, this Amiot 143M flew with GBA II/35 and bore the seagull emblem of the unit's 3rd Escadrille.

Above:
Striking a suitably heroic pose for the press, this Amiot 143 crew was photographed during training in 1939.

impressive structural strength, proved highly reliable and delivered an adequate performance for the era. Production of the Amiot had ceased in 1938 after 138 had been delivered, yet most remained in service by September 1939. Five units operated the Amiot in metropolitan France and another in Africa; however, by this time the design was already considered obsolete and was gradually being replaced by more modern aircraft.

Initially tasked with leaflet raids, the Amiot 143 soon began bombing missions following Germany's invasion of the Low Countries in May 1940. Over the course of nearly 200 operations, mostly flown at night, the Amiot 143 force dropped 153 tonnes (338,626lb) of bombs while losing only four aircraft. However, when conducting daylight raids during the desperate fighting just before the fall of France, the large and slow aircraft suffered at the hands of fighters and ground fire. Nonetheless, more than 70 Amiot 143s survived to enter Vichy service and some were retained in bomber service until their replacement by the LeO 451 in mid-1941. Following their withdrawal from combat service, the tough and reliable Amiots continued to be used as transport aircraft in Syria, with Vichy and then Free French forces until the last was withdrawn in 1944.

Bloch MB.174 and MB.175

Bloch's MB.174 was fast and manoeuvrable, with the potential to be a decisive bomber, but it was primarily used as a reconnaissance aircraft during the Battle for France.

One of the best aircraft produced in France before the German victory of 1940, the Bloch 174 could have been in service in much larger numbers had it not been delayed for years by prewar official dithering over its intended role. Its combat performance was remarkable yet, like several other advanced French aircraft projects, it arrived too late to make a significant impact. First flown

A Bloch 175 in service with Vichy France. The type served only briefly before production resumed under German control.

Bloch MB.174 and MB.175

Weight: 8025kg (17,962lb)
Dimensions: Length 12.23m (40ft 2in), Wingspan 17.9m (58ft 10in), Height 3.59m (11ft 8in)
Powerplant: Two 850kW (1140hp) Gnome Rhône 14N 14-cylinder air-cooled radial piston engines
Maximum speed: 540km/h (336mph)
Range: 1600km (994 miles)
Ceiling: 10,900m (35,761ft)
Crew: 3
Armament: Two 7.5mm (0.295in) MAC machine guns fixed, forward firing in wings, two flexibly mounted in rear cockpit and three fixed, rearward and downward firing under ventral fuselage; up to 600kg (1323lb) bombload

Opposite:
The white stripe combined with the fuselage roundel reveals that this Bloch 174A.3 of GR III/33 is in Vichy service. It was based at Tunis El Aouina, Tunisia.

Above:
An unmarked Bloch 174 as it appeared during the desperate fighting of May 1940. The type was an outstanding aircraft initially compromised by its insignificant bombload.

Below:
Wearing the more extensive Vichy markings adopted in late 1940, featuring vivid red and yellow stripes on engine cowlings and tail, this Bloch 175B.3 was stationed, like the aircraft opposite, at Tunis El Aouina in 1941.

in February 1938, the Bloch 174 was viewed primarily as a reconnaissance and target marking aircraft with a secondary bombing capability. A series of 50 had been completed by the time production switched to the MB.175 in May 1940, which was redesigned to allow larger bombs to be carried. The MB.174's first operational mission was flown by the pilot and author Antoine de Saint-Exupéry in March 1940. From that point until the armistice, it conducted strategic and tactical reconnaissance sorties, taking over from the Potez 637, which had been suffering heavy losses. The performance of the Bloch 174 allowed it to outrun and outmanoeuvre most enemy fighters and only three were lost to enemy action during the Battle of France. Although its bombload was limited, the aircraft's exceptional design prompted the rushed development of the Bloch 175B3 attack bomber, of which only 25 were completed before the armistice. Surviving 174 and 175 aircraft later served with Vichy forces in Tunisia, where the aircraft were modified to conduct shallow dive-bombing attacks with bombs up to 500kg (1100lb).

Bloch MB.200 and MB.210

The MB.210 was a better performing descendant of the rugged MB.200, and although both aircraft were obsolete by 1939, both were used in combat operations against German forces.

The MB.200 first flew in June 1933. Although it was modern for its time as an all-metal cantilever monoplane, its fixed undercarriage made it slow, even when it entered service in late 1934. The MB.200 entered combat in Spain with Republican forces after the first of 32 aircraft arrived in August 1936, carrying out both reconnaissance and bombing missions around Madrid. The MB.200 was also produced under

The MB.210, fitted with a retractable undercarriage, represented a notable performance upgrade over the MB.200.

Bloch MB.200 and MB.210

Weight: 10,221kg (22,533lb)
Dimensions: Length 18.83m (61ft 9in), Wingspan 22.82m (74ft 10in), Height 6.7m (22ft)
Powerplant: Two 709kW (950hp) Gnome-Rhône 14N-10/11 14-cylinder air-cooled radial piston engines
Maximum speed: 322km/h (200mph)
Range: 1700km (1100 miles)
Ceiling: 9900m (32,500ft)
Crew: 5
Armament: One 7.5mm (0.295in) MAC 1934 machine gun flexibly mounted in nose, tail and ventral turrets; up to 1600kg (3520lb) bombload

Opposite top:
The prominent fuselage stripes denote that this aircraft is a training machine. It was in use at the Air Guard Training Center in Mourmelon-le-Grand, France, in May 1940.

Above:
The slab-sided rectangular fuselage shape of the MB.210 was adopted for simplicity of manufacture and to keep production costs down.

licence in Czechoslovakia by both the Aero and Avia aircraft factories and as a result entered German service after the 1938 annexation of Czechoslovakia. Some of these aircraft were passed on to Bulgaria, which used them for coastal patrol over the Black Sea.

By September 1939, the French still possessed 92 MB.200s in frontline units and used the aircraft, albeit briefly, for unescorted daylight bombing raids before relegating them to secondary roles. Some survivors were later utilized in nocturnal bombing raids by Vichy forces in Syria. The MB.210 was a modestly upgraded version, swapping the shoulder-wing layout for a low-wing configuration and introducing a retractable undercarriage. It flew for the first time in late 1934 and entered French service two years later. Although faster than the older aircraft, the MB.210's performance could hardly be described as sprightly. Nonetheless, the aircraft was tough and extremely reliable.

At the outbreak of World War II, the MB.210s were employed to carry out a limited number of night reconnaissance sorties before being relegated to training units. However, the German advance in May 1940 saw the MB.210 thrust back into frontline service, during which they conducted nocturnal raids against targets in the Rhine region, Belgium, and occupied French territory, continuing until the armistice ended the fighting career of the Bloch MB.210.

Breguet Bre.690

Fast, manoeuvrable and easy to fly, the Bre.693 was an excellent attack aircraft although it suffered heavy losses in the desperate fighting during the Battle of France.

Originally conceived as a long-range escort fighter, the Bréguet project shifted focus to a ground-attack role due to official lack of interest in the fighter variant. However, the first prototype Bre.690 was finished as a heavy fighter, since converting it to a ground-attack configuration was believed to cause excessive delays. Ultimately, the aircraft first flew on 23 March 1938 and demonstrated

The prototype Bre.690, pictured here, made its first flight in early 1938, arriving just in time to see action before the armistice.

Bréguet 693

Weight: 4900kg (10,800lb)
Dimensions: Length 10.22m (33ft 7in), Wingspan 15.3m (50ft 5in), Height 3.4m (10ft 4in)
Powerplant: Two 522 kW (700 hp) Gnome Rhône 14M 14-cylinder air-cooled radial piston engines
Maximum speed: 490km/h (300mph)
Range: 1350km (840 miles)
Ceiling: 8500m (27,900ft)

Crew: 2
Armament: One 20mm (0.79in) Hispano 404 cannon and two 7.5mm (0.295in) MAC machine guns fixed, forward firing in nose as well as a single MAC fixed firing obliquely rearward and another flexibly mounted in rear cockpit: up to 400kg (880lb) bombload

Above and right:
Pictured as it appeared in mid-1942, this Bre.693 served with GBA I/51 of the Vichy Air Force, based at Lézignan, southern France.

Opposite top:
Serving with Groupe de Bombardement d'Assaut (GBA) I/54 at Montdidier, this Bréguet Bre.693 was lost while attacking German armour near Tongeren, Belgium, in May 1940.

outstanding handling and performance, prompting an immediate order for 100 production aircraft. Modified for the attack role, the production model was designated Bre.691. However, from the 78th aircraft onwards, the somewhat unreliable Hispano-Suiza 14AB engines were replaced with the proven Gnome-Rhône 14M, prompting a redesignation to Bre.693, which accounted for the majority of production aircraft.

The first combat mission was a disaster: seven of 11 aircraft that attacked advancing German columns were shot down, although subsequent missions were more successful. When the element of surprise was achieved, losses were minimal and the Bréguet proved to be formidable. From the start the aircraft was designed to be easy to service and maintain, and this was crucial to the high tempo of operations maintained by Bréguet units, even as they moved between airfields in the face of the German advance. By the time of the armistice, losses were significant due to the large number of operations: around 500 sorties had been flown by the end of May, with 47 aircraft lost. Following the armistice, Vichy forces kept some Bréguet aircraft in service until the German reoccupation of 1942, after which the surviving planes were transferred to Italy.

Farman F.222

This large, high wing, four-engined aircraft was one of the most powerful bombers in service at the outbreak of war and became the first aircraft of any nation to bomb Berlin.

Design work on this aircraft started in the mid-1920s but it was not until May 1932 that the prototype – designated the F.220 – took to the skies. After testing, it was used by Air France as a mail plane. Meanwhile, the initial military production variant, the F.221, switched to radial engines and ten examples were delivered to the Armee de l'Air, the last in mid-1936. Its successor was the F.222,

The small figure standing in front of this unmarked F.222 of an unknown unit highlights the aircraft's enormous size.

Farman F.222

Weight: 24,000kg (52,911lb)
Dimensions: Length 22m (72ft 2in), Wingspan 33.5m (110ft 3in), Height 5.22m (17ft 2in)
Powerplant: Four 783kW (1050hp) Hispano-Suiza 12Y-37 liquid-cooled V-12 piston engines
Maximum speed: 385km/h (239mph)
Range: 5000km (3107 miles)
Ceiling: 4000m (13120ft)
Crew: 5
Armament: One 7.5mm (0.295in) MAC machine gun flexibly mounted in nose turret and one 20mm (0.79in) Hispano 404 cannon in dorsal and ventral turrets; up to 2000kg (4400lb) bombload

Opposite top:
Wearing the bat insignia of the 2nd Escadrille, GB I/15, this Farman F.222 was based at Avord, central France in September 1939.

Above:
F-ARIN was the second NC.223.4, intended for civil transatlantic use. Named 'Jules Verne', it was the aircraft that bombed Berlin in June 1940.

which featured a retractable undercarriage for the first time and introduced pronounced dihedral on the outer wings. At the outbreak of war, more than 40 Farmans were in service and these were kept busy dropping leaflets before switching to bombing raids after the German invasion of May 1940. By this time, Farman had developed the design into the F.223, redesignated the NC.223 when Farman merged with Hanriot to become SNCAC.

The NC.223.3 was a purpose-built bomber, featuring an engine change to the V-12 Hispano-Suiza 12Y, two of which were delivered in time for installation before the aircraft took part in raids in June 1940. Farman had also developed the sleeker NC.223.4 transatlantic mail plane for Air France, of which three were built, and it was decided to convert these for military use. At first, the three aircraft were used for maritime patrol, but their role switched to heavy bombing after May 1940.

The second aircraft, named 'Jules Verne', made a single daylight raid on German forces in Belgium but was considered too vulnerable for further daytime operations. Instead, it was assigned a mission to bomb Berlin in reprisal for German attacks on Paris, becoming the first Allied aircraft to strike the German capital during a 13-hour night mission on 7/8 June. The three NC.223.4s later conducted raids against Italian targets before reverting to transport duties under Vichy control.

Liore et Olivier LeO 451

The LeO 451, the most modern and capable bomber to serve with the Armee de l'Air, was used by both Allied and Axis forces during the war and continued in service for several years afterwards.

Widely regarded as the finest French bomber of the war, the LeO 451 was also available in significant numbers before the armistice. The initial LeO 45 first flew in January 1937 and demonstrated outstanding performance, but simultaneous failures of its Hispano Suiza engines during testing resulted in a switch to Gnome-Rhône 14N engines, after which the aircraft was redesignated

This LeO 451, also from GB I/11, was photographed in early 1943, by which time it had rejoined the Allies.

LeO 451

Weight: 11,400kg (25,132lb)
Dimensions: 17.17m (56ft 4 in), Wingspan: 22.52m (73ft 11in), Height: 5.24m (17ft 2in)
Powerplant: Two 90kW (1060hp) Gnome-Rhône 14N 14-cylinder air-cooled radial piston engines
Maximum speed: 495km/h (308mph)
Range: 2900km (1800 miles)
Ceiling: 9000m (29,530ft)
Crew: 4
Armament: One 7.5mm (0.295in) MAC machine gun fixed, firing forward in nose, one 7.5mm (0.295in) MAC machine gun flexibly mounted in retractable ventral turret, and one 20mm (0.79in) Hispano 404 cannon flexibly mounted in dorsal position; up to 1568kg (3457lb) bombload

Opposite top:
The LeO 451 saw considerable service after the 1940 armistice. This Vichy Air Force example wears the black cat insignia of the 1er Escadrille of GB I/11 based at Oran-La Sénia, Morocco.

Above:
The prototype LeO 451 first took to the skies in 1937 and its design was strikingly sleek compared to the French bombers that preceded it.

LeO 451. Production machines started to be received in July 1939, although at the outbreak of the conflict just ten were in service. Initial operations were limited to reconnaissance with combat missions beginning only in May 1940, but the LeOs were subsequently involved in fierce fighting starting with an attack on German columns advancing through Belgium on 11 May. The LeO 451 units experienced heavy losses as the aircraft were being called upon to attack tactical targets at low level, rather than operate at their intended medium altitude, making them vulnerable to ground fire. Additionally, while the aircraft was fast enough to evade most fighters, the German Bf 109 and 110 were faster and could still intercept it, although at considerable risk, as the LeO's dorsal gun position was armed with a formidable 20mm (0.79in) cannon. On one occasion, a LeO 451 dorsal gunner destroyed two attacking Bf 110s using this weapon.

After the armistice, production was resumed for Vichy use. The LeO 451 was used to bomb Gibraltar in September 1940 and to attack Allied forces during the Operation Torch landings in North Africa. Surviving LeO 451s were subsequently used for training and transport duties by both Free French units under RAF control and the USAAF. The Luftwaffe also employed captured LeOs as transport aircraft. Postwar examples of the type were used as high-speed couriers and experimental testbeds, finally ending their service as air-sea rescue aircraft in 1957.

Fokker C.X

This Dutch light bomber biplane saw brief combat with its country of origin but proved highly effectively against the Soviet Union in Finland.

During the 1920s and 1930s, Fokker built nearly 1000 examples of the highly successful C.V, a remarkable figure for the period, and a number of these aircraft saw operational service in World War II with Norway, Finland and the Netherlands. The C.X was intended to replace the C.V, and although its total production was only a fraction of its predecessor's, this highly conventional – and by then

By contrast, the C.Xs in Dutch service, as shown here, were powered by a Rolls-Royce Kestrel inline engine.

Fokker C.X

Weight: 2900kg (6393lb)
Dimensions: Length 9.1m (30ft), Wingspan 12m (39ft 4in), Height 3.3m (10ft 10in)
Powerplant: One 630kW (850hp) Bristol Pegasus XII 9-cylinder air-cooled radial piston engine
Maximum speed: 340km/h (210mph)
Range: 840km (522 miles)
Ceiling: 8400m (27,600ft)
Crew: 2
Armament: Two 7.62mm (0.3in) Lahti L33/34 machine guns fixed, forward firing in forward fuselage decking and one 7.62mm (0.3in) Lahti L33/34 machine gun flexibly mounted in rear cockpit; up to 400kg (880lb) bombload, carried under wings

Opposite top:
This C.X, powered by a Bristol Pegasus engine, was one of those licence-built in Finland and features the streamlined ski landing gear used in winter operations.

Above:
The C.X was developed from the successful Fokker C.V, seen here in service with the Swedish Air Force in the mid-1930s.

essentially obsolete – aircraft saw a remarkable degree of successful operational use, remaining in frontline service until September 1944. Fokker developed the C.X during 1933 and the first prototype flew in October 1934, powered by a Rolls-Royce Kestrel engine that was also fitted to the initial batch of production aircraft. The first customer was the Netherlands East Indies, which ordered 10 for light bombing and reconnaissance, although the aircraft was replaced swiftly with the Martin 139 and relegated to target tugging and training. The Royal Netherlands Air Force ordered 20 Kestrel-powered C.Xs in 1936 and of these 11 were serviceable at the time of the German invasion. The C.X force was used almost exclusively for ground-attack missions and achieved some successes, but their limited numbers ultimately rendered their efforts largely ineffective.

The aircraft served more widely with the Finns, who employed a radial engined variant, most of which were licence-built in Finland. During the Winter War of 1940–41, the C.Xs proved effective, conducting reconnaissance missions and attacking Soviet armoured columns. The type saw further action during the Continuation War beginning in June 1941, and an additional five C.Xs were built as late as 1942 to make up for losses in the fleet. The final bombing missions were flown in September 1944, but the aircraft was retained as a trainer and target tug, serving as such until 1958.

PZL.23 Karaś

The Karaś ('Carp') was Poland's standard light bomber and ground-attack aircraft at the outbreak of war, but, like most of its contemporaries, it was highly vulnerable to fighter attacks.

A cantilever monoplane with enclosed accommodation for the crew, the PZL.23 was a highly advanced aircraft when it made its first flight in April 1934. However, rapid advances in aviation development during the late 1930s meant that by 1939, it was outclassed by modern fighters in combat. Only 40 examples of the initial PZL.23A variant were built before production switched to the PZL.23B

Photographed at Rakowice Airfield in Kraków, this Karaś served with the 22nd Battle Flight of the 2nd Air Regiment.

PZL.23 Karaś

Weight: 3526kg (7773lb)
Dimensions: Length 9.68m (31ft 9in), Wingspan 13.95m (45ft 9in), Height 3.3m (10ft 1in)
Powerplant: One 537kW (720hp) PZL Pegaz (licence-built Bristol Pegasus) VIII 9-cylinder air-cooled radial piston engine
Maximum speed: 239km/h (198mph)
Range: 1260km (780 miles)
Ceiling: 7300m (24,000ft)
Crew: 3
Armament: One 7.92 (0.31in) wz.33 machine gun fixed, forward firing in nose, one 7.92mm (0.31in) wz.36 machine gun flexibly mounted in both dorsal and ventral positions; up to 700kg (1534lb) bombload

Above and below:
The 55th Independent Bomber Squadron adopted a crouching tiger emblem. On 8 September 1939 this aircraft bombed German troops near Ostrów in Poland.

Opposite top:
The red griffon emblem denotes that this PZL.23 was in service with the 41st Reconnaissance Flight, attached to the Modlin Army, based at Toruń on 1 September 1939.

with a more powerful engine. The aircraft entered service in late 1936 and by 1939 210 PZL P.23Bs had been delivered, forming the equipment of 12 squadrons. It was already clear that the Karaś was underpowered, but its intended replacement, the PZL.46 Sum ('Catfish'), was still at the prototype stage when hostilities began. As a result, the PZL.23s were heavily deployed, suffering significant losses, although they proved effective as ground-attack aircraft when they avoided enemy interception. During the brief Polish campaign, the Karaś became the first aircraft to bomb a target in Germany during World War II when a single PZL.23 struck a factory at Ohlau in Silesia on 2 September 1939. 21 PZL.23s escaped to Romania and these entered Romanian service following the Polish surrender and saw action against the Soviet Union until their withdrawal in 1943.

A more powerful development of the PZL.23 also saw some action, the PZL.43, which was produced for Bulgaria with a Gnome Rhône Mistral Major engine in place of the Pegasus. The PZL.43 possessed notably better performance than the Karaś and although most were used for training and anti-partisan operations by Bulgaria, two that were awaiting delivery in Poland were pressed into action against the invading Germans.

PZL.37 Łoś

One of the world's finest bombers in 1939, the Łoś ('Moose') was fast, easy to fly, capable of carrying an impressive payload, and able to operate from unprepared fields.

Developed to replace the aging Fokker F.VII in bomber units, the PZL.37 was judged the most impressive of several designs presented to the Polish Department of Aeronautics, and construction of a prototype was approved in late 1934. The first flight of the new aircraft was in June 1936 and, despite a few teething problems, pilots were highly impressed. Several changes were introduced, mainly to

Łoś air and ground crews on parade in the last year of peace. The PZL.37 was likely the finest aircraft in its class in 1939.

PZL.37 Łoś

Weight: 9105kg (20,073lb)
Dimensions: Length 12.92m (42ft 5in), Wingspan 17.93m (58ft 10in), Height 5.1m (16ft 9in)
Powerplant: Two PZL Pegaz (licence-built Bristol Pegasus) XX 9-cylinder air-cooled radial piston engines
Maximum speed: 412km/h (256mph)
Range: 2600km (1600 miles)
Ceiling: 7000m (23,000ft)
Crew: 4
Armament: One 7.92mm (0.31in) wz.37 machine gun flexibly mounted in each of the nose, dorsal, and ventral positions; up to 2580kg (5690lb) bombload

Opposite top:
Profile of a typical, anonymous, Łoś as it appeared just before the outbreak of hostilities.

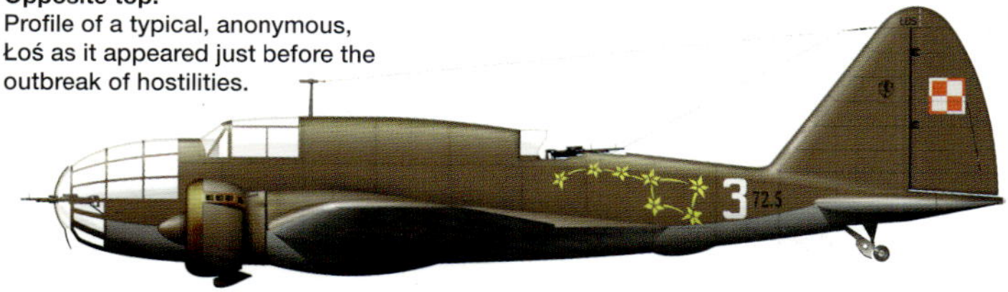

Above lower:
Romanian Air Force (Aeronautica Regală Română; ARR), 4th Bomber Group (Grupul 4 Bombardament), based at Blaj (Balázsfalva, Blasendorf) in 1940.

Above top:
This Łoś of the 212th Bomber Squadron, 1st Air Regiment, based at Okęcie wears the squadron emblem of the constellation Ursa Major.

the internal structure. While the prototype and the first 10 production PZL.37A aircraft featured a single vertical tail, the remaining 92 aircraft delivered by the outbreak of war were built as the PZL.37B variant, distinguished by a twin-tail unit and uprated engines. Displayed at aviation salons in Belgrade and Paris, the aircraft generated considerable interest and orders were placed by Yugoslavia, Bulgaria and Greece. Unfortunately, the invasion of Poland prevented any exports or licensed production. When it entered service in 1938, the Łoś was arguably the most advanced bomber in the world, but its use in combat a year later diminished many of its advantages. The PZL.37 squadrons had been dispersed from major airbases and therefore escaped destruction in the German attacks. However, the rough airstrips from which they operated prevented the aircraft from carrying their full bombloads. Moreover, they were committed to low-level ground-attack missions for which they had not been designed, and losses proved heavy.

After Poland's capitulation, more than 25 PZL.37s were seized by Romania and later used against the Soviet Union, carrying out bombing raids on Kyiv and Odessa before being withdrawn from frontline service in late 1941 for use as trainers. Interestingly, Romanian PZL.37s briefly returned to combat service for about a month in early 1944.

Ilyushin DB-3

The DB-3 gained renown through a series of long-range propaganda flights in the late 1930s and, in August 1941, became the first Soviet aircraft to bomb Berlin.

Developed from the wooden TsKB-26, the DB-3 emerged as an all-metal long-range bomber with impressive performance. Although it could carry five times the bombload of Tupolev's SB-2, it was only 24 km/h slower. It also boasted impressive manoeuvrability, demonstrated by the fact that it became the first Soviet twin-engined aircraft to perform a loop. The DB-3 incorporated

This DB-3 lacks its wheels and has been brush-painted with an improvised camouflage scheme applied over the standard silver finish.

Ilyushin DB-3

Weight: 9450kg (20,834lb)
Dimensions: Length 14.22m (46ft 8in), Wingspan 21.44m (70ft 4in), Height: 4.19m (13ft 9in)
Powerplant: Two 709kW (951hp) Nazarov M-87 9-cylinder air cooled radial engines
Maximum speed: 439km/h (273mph)

Range: 3800km (2400 miles)
Ceiling: 9600m (31,500ft)
Crew: 3
Armament: One 7.62mm ShKAS machine gun flexibly mounted in nose, one 7.62mm ShKAS machine gun in dorsal turret, one 7.62mm ShKAS flexibly mounted in ventral hatch; up to 2500kg (5500lb) bombload

Above:
The single DB-3TP floatplane, fitted with twin floats and able to carry a torpedo or 900kg (1984lb) mine, proved unsatisfactory in testing.

Opposite top:
A DB-3T of 2 MTAP (Minelaying–Torpedo Aviation Regiment) of the Black Sea Fleet.

Right:
A DB-3, modified to increase its range, attempted a nonstop flight from Moscow to New York in April 1939 but was forced to land in Canada after flying roughly 8000km (4970 miles) in just under 23 hours.

advanced features such as self-sealing fuel tanks and a crew intercom system, both included as a result of Soviet combat experience in Spain. The maximum bombload was 2500kg (5500lb) – the heaviest of any twin-engine bomber when the DB-3 entered service in 1937. Unfortunately, the aircraft's innovative construction produced a lightweight structure that was difficult to build, resulting in slow production – only 45 aircraft were completed by two factories in 1937 – delaying its planned replacement of the Tupolev TB-3 in long-range units. Eventually 1528 were built before production switched to the Il-4 in 1939.

After seeing combat over China and Finland, the DB-3 was heavily engaged fighting the German invaders from June 1941. Initially used by day, losses of the lightly defended DB-3 were considerable. In a single raid on 26 June 1941, for example, a staggering 43 DB-3s were lost, and by 1942 the aircraft had wisely switched to nocturnal operations. In Naval service, the DB-3T variant was employed as a torpedo bomber in the anti-shipping role and remained in frontline service for the duration of the war, attacking Japanese shipping in Manchuria as late as August 1945.

Ilyushin Il-2 Shturmovik

The heavily armed and armoured Il-2 Shturmovik ('Assaulter') was the most important ground-attack aircraft of the war and remains the most produced combat aircraft of all time.

Ilyushin designed the TsKB-55, which first flew in October 1939 as a two-seat, single-engine design with its entire forward structure made of armoured steel, enclosing both the engine and crew. Because the prototype was overweight and underpowered, it was redesigned as a single seater and fitted with the Mikulin AM-38 engine, optimized for low-altitude operations. In this form the

Single-seat Il-2s pictured taking off from a field airfield on a combat mission, c.1942. The foreground aircraft is equipped with long-barrel 23mm (0.91in) VYa cannons.

Ilyushin Il-2 Shturmovik

Weight: 6360kg (14,021lb)
Dimensions: Length: 11.65m (38ft 3in), Wingspan: 14.60m (47ft 11in), Height: 4.17m (13ft 8in)
Powerplant: One 1280kW (1720hp) Mikulin AM-38F liquid-cooled V12 engine
Maximum speed: 410km/h (250mph)
Range: 765km (475 miles)
Ceiling: 4525m (14,846ft)
Crew: 2
Armament: Two 23mm VYa-23 cannons and two 7.62mm ShKAS machine guns in wings, one 12.7mm Berezin UBT machine gun in rear cockpit, up to 600kg (1320lb) bombs, or four dispensers for 48 2.5kg (5.5lb) PTAB anti-armour bombs; eight RS-82 rockets or four RS-132 rockets

Opposite:
Operating on the Leningrad front, Russia, in 1944, 'White 17' is an Il-2 typical of early 1943 production.

Above:
This Il-2M3 shows the common practice of removing the rear cockpit canopy to give the gunner an unobstructed field of fire. The slogan 'mstitel' painted on the side means 'avenger'.

Below:
Flown by 3 ShAP (Attack Aviation Regiment) of the Czech mixed Air Division, this presentation airframe bears the name 'Chapaevsky' on the fuselage, honouring the workers of Chapaevsk, Russia.

Il-2 had just entered service when Germany invaded in June 1941. Although 249 Il-2s were available, the aircraft was so new that manuals had not yet been written and crews had not received training, resulting in initially high losses. At least 1000 Il-2s were field-modified with improvised rear gun positions, usually fitted with one or two 7.62mm (0.3in) ShKAS machine guns. A factory-built two-seat Il-2 entered production in September 1942, featuring a Berezin UBT 12.7mm (0.5in) gun for a rear gunner seated on a simple strap in the fuselage. In September 1943, the Il-2's wings were swept back to 15° to compensate for the rearward shift in the centre of gravity caused by the twin-seat layout. Known as the Strielka 'Arrow', this became the definitive form of the Il-2, produced until October 1945.

Il-2 attacks were usually flown at very low altitudes – sometimes so low that that aircraft were obscured by the dust they kicked up. Against armoured targets, Il-2 units often used a tactic called the 'Wheel of Death', where aircraft circled the target, made shallow dive attacks, then rejoined the circle, repeating the process until all ordnance was expended. Stalin famously described the Il-2 "as essential to the Red Army as air and bread", and the Shturmovik remains the most iconic Soviet aircraft of World War II.

Ilyushin Il-4

Initially designated the DB-3F, the Il-4 was the result of a complete redesign of the earlier bomber and served effectively for the duration of the war and beyond.

The DB-3 was the first modern, all-metal bomber in the Soviet Union, but it was hard to build and proved unreliable. Ilyushin sought to fix these problems while improving performance with the DB-3F. First flown on 21 May 1939, the aircraft featured a redesigned and simplified structure, influenced by modern US construction methods introduced to the Soviet Union through licensed production of the Douglas

Either a 12.7mm (0.5in) UBT machine gun (pictured) or 20mm (0.79in) ShVAK cannon could be fitted in the dorsal turret.

Ilyushin Il-4	
Weight: 12,120kg (26,720lb) **Dimensions:** Length: 14.76m (48ft 5in), Wingspan: 21.44m (70ft 4in), Height: 4.10m (13ft 6in) **Powerplant:** Two Tumanksy M-88B 14-cylinder air cooled radial engines **Maximum speed:** 410km/h (250mph) **Range:** 3800km (2400 miles)	**Ceiling:** 8700m (28,500ft) **Crew:** 4 **Armament:** One 7.62mm ShKAS machine gun in nose, one 12.7mm Berezin UBT machine gun in dorsal turret, one 7.62mm ShKAS machine gun in ventral hatch; up to 2700kg (6000lb) of bombs, or one 940kg (2100lb) Type 45-36 torpedo, or two BETAB-750DS 305mm rockets

Opposite:
Operating with an unknown unit over the Eastern Front in 1944,'Yellow 7' highlights the Il-4's new, streamlined design compared to the DB-3 from which it was developed.

Above:
This Il-4 is thought to have served with a Bomber Aviation Regiment and is shown here in the three-tone camouflage it wore in a 1944 Soviet newsreel.

Right:
Winter conditions in Russia were harsh, and the Soviet Air Force was better equipped to handle the freezing environment than the Luftwaffe. Here, an STZ-3 artillery tractor is serving as a tug for an Il-4 on an icy airfield.

DC-3. As a result, the time required to build the DB-3F was less than half that required for the original DB-3. Performance was improved by the adoption of a thinner wing of greater area and the use of two Tumansky M-88 in place of the M-87s of the DB-3. In an effort to alleviate the inadequate defensive armament, a fourth crew member was added, allowing a dedicated gunner for each of the three weapons and a turret in the dorsal position that allowed greater freedom of movement for the gunner. From March 1942 the Il-4, as the DB-3F had been redesignated earlier that year, gained a heavier calibre 12.7mm (0.5in) Berezin UBT machine gun in the turret.

Despite bombing Warsaw, Königsberg and Danzig the day after the invasion, the DB-3Fs – like almost every aircraft facing Operation Barbarossa – were initially used in daylight tactical missions against German ground forces, a role for which they were not designed, leaving them highly vulnerable and resulting in heavy early losses. By late 1941, missions were flown at night, with Berlin becoming a regular target from August onwards, and Il-4s carried out a largely successful strategic bombing campaign through the end of the war.

Ilyushin Il-10

Arriving too late to see major service in World War II, the Il-10 resembled its famed predecessor, the Il-2, but was a completely new design. It went on to enjoy a lengthy postwar career.

The Il-10's origins lay in a proposal for a single-seat, heavily armoured fighter, the Il-1, intended to attack bombers and transports. However, when air force enthusiasm for this concept waned, Ilyushin reworked the design as a two-seat ground-attack aircraft to replace the Il-2, and the new type flew for the first time in April 1944. Tests to decide a successor to the Il-2 resulted in the Il-10 beating two other

This wartime Il-10 was one of the first to see service with 571 ShAP in January 1945.

Ilyushin Il-10

Weight: 6535kg (14,407lb)
Dimensions: Length: 11.06m (36ft 3in), Wingspan: 13.40m (43ft 11in), Height: 4.18m (13ft 9in)
Powerplant: One 1320kW (1770hp) Mikulin AM-42 liquid-cooled V12 engine
Maximum speed: 551km/h (342mph)
Range: 800km (500 miles)
Ceiling: 5500m (18,000ft)
Crew: 2
Armament: Two 23mm Vya-23 cannon and two 7.62mm ShKAS machine guns fixed forward firing in wing, one 20mm Berezin B-20 cannon flexibly mounted in rear turret; up to 600kg (1320lb) bombs in wing bomb bays and underwing racks; eight RS-82 rockets or four RS-132 rockets

Opposite:
The Il-10's postwar career was long. Red-55 is an Il-10M dating from 1954.

Above:
'Red 1' served with the Soviet Occupation Forces in Germany in 1950. Its largely bare metal finish is unusual as Il-10s were usually painted, even after the end of hostilities.

Below:
Poland operated the Il-10 between 1949 and 1959. This example was serving with the Polish Air Force Assault Regiment in 1951.

contenders: another Ilyushin design, the larger Il-8, which was more obviously derived from the Il-2, and the rival, radial-engined Sukhoi Su-6. Production began in August 1944 and the new Il-10 featured exactly the same armament as the Il-2, applying the same concept of a heavily armoured airframe protecting both the engine and crew. Powered by a more powerful Mikulin AM-42 engine and possessing a smaller airframe, the Il-10 was around 145 km/h (90mph) faster than the older aircraft and showed near fighter-like manoeuvrability.

Il-10s entered service in January 1945 and were in action by the middle of April 1945. Il-10s were flown by three units before the end of hostilities around three weeks later, although a single unit also operated the Il-10 against rail and shipping targets in the brief Soviet campaign against Japan later in 1945. After VJ day, the Il-10 saw further combat during the Korean War and in Chinese service against Taiwan in 1955. After 1945, the Il-10 replaced the Il-2 as the standard ground-attack aircraft in Soviet service and later models featured a formidable armament of four 23mm (0.9in) Nudelman-Suranov NS-23 cannon with a 20mm (0.79in) Berezin B-20 cannon for the rear gunner. Production continued until 1954 in the USSR although the Il-10 was also built under licence in Czechoslovakia, as the Avia B-33, until 1956. The last operational Il-10s were retired by China in 1972.

Lisunov Li-2

A licence-built Douglas DC-3, more than 4000 Li-2s were built. Unlike the US C-47 equivalent, the Li-2 saw significant service not only as a transport but also as a purpose-built long-range bomber.

Originally operated by Aeroflot from 1939 as the PS-84, the Li-2 differed from its US counterpart, being powered by two Shvetsov M-62 radial engines of lower power than the Pratt & Whitney R-1830s used on the DC-3. The engines also gained a face plate with adjustable shutters to deal with cold conditions. Heavier than its progenitor – partly because the metric aluminium used for the skin was slightly thicker

Military Li-2s were often pressed into service on civil routes – aircraft 490 was photographed about to depart for Leningrad. Note dorsal turret on aircraft in background.

Lisunov Li-2

Weight: 11,280kg (24,867lb)
Dimensions: Length: 19.65m (64ft 6in), Wingspan: 28.81m (94ft 6in)
Powerplant: Two 670kW (900hp) Shvetsov M-62 9-cylinder air-cooled radial piston engines
Maximum speed: 280km/h (170mph)
Range: 2500km (1600 miles)
Ceiling: 5600m (18,400ft)
Crew: 4–6
Armament: One 12.7mm (0.50in) Berezin UBK machine gun in dorsal turret, two 7.62mm (0.3in) ShKAS machine guns flexibly mounted in port and starboard side hatches; up to 2000kg (4409lb) bombload

Opposite:
This Czech Li-2, in typical drab finish, shows the close similarity between this aircraft and the C-47 from which it was derived.

Above:
This three-colour camouflage was worn by most late-war Li-2s. 'Yellow 17' was operated by 12 GVAP at Helsinki in the winter of 1944.

Below:
This Lisunov, based at Dubrovka airfield in Ukraine, has the black-painted undersides applied to most bomber Li-2s.

than the imperial equivalent – the PS-84 also had a slightly shorter wingspan. By June 1941, 237 PS-84s had been built but production was paused while the factory was evacuated to Tashkent, restarting in January 1942. Later in the same year the aircraft was redesignated the Li-2 in accordance with the new Soviet designation system and the Li-2 ultimately became the most produced Soviet transport aircraft of the war.

Due to a shortage of bomber types in 1942, caused by heavy losses and the evacuation of aircraft factories, the decision was made to convert the Li-2 into a bomber, initially using basic conversions of transport aircraft but later in the form of the Li-2NB, a purpose-built bomber version of which several hundred were constructed. Despite lacking a bomb bay, the Li-2 could carry a maximum bombload of 2000kg (4400lb) under the centre section and was fitted with extra defensive machine guns. Mostly used to re-equip units operating the obsolete TB-3, the Li-2NB first took part in long-range bombing during the Battle of Stalingrad in 1942. It was also used in early 1944 to attack encircling forces at Leningrad, subsequently participating in raids against Helsinki.

Petlyakov Pe-2

Originally conceived as the VI-100, a turbo-supercharged high-altitude fighter with a pressurized cockpit, the aircraft that would become the Pe-2 first flew in December 1939.

However, Soviet authorities did not regard high-altitude bombers as a significant threat and, impressed by the dive-bombing capabilities of the Junkers Ju 88, instructed Petlyakov to adapt the VI-100 into a dive bomber. The conversion was completed in just 45 days, and the new aircraft was seen as so vital that tooling for mass production began before the prototype had even flown. Its maiden flight

A Soviet Pe-2 crewman is helped into his parachute on a snow-covered airfield before a mission in 1944.

Petlyakov Pe-2

Weight: 8495kg (18,728lb)
Dimensions: Length: 12.66m (41ft 6in), Wingspan: 17.16m (56ft 4in), Height: 3.5m (11ft 6in)
Powerplant: Two 903kW (1211hp) Klimov M-105PF V-12 liquid-cooled piston engines
Maximum speed: 580 km/h (360 mph)
Range: 1160km (720 miles)
Ceiling: 8800m (28,900ft)
Crew: 3
Armament: One 7.62mm (0.3in) ShKAS machine gun and one 12.7mm (0.5in) Berezin UB fixed forward firing in the nose, one 12.7mm (0.5in) Berezin UB machine gun in dorsal turret, 1 Berezin UB flexibly mounted in ventral hatch, one 7.62mm (0.3in) ShKAS interchangeable between port and starboard window mounts; up to 1000 kg (2205 lb) bombload

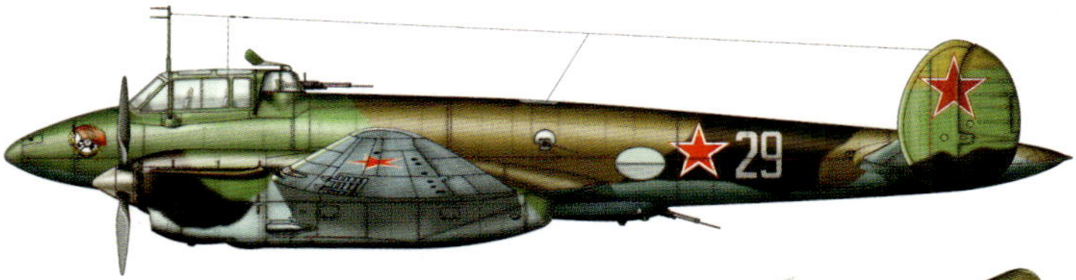

Above:
This early Pe-2FT served with 40 GvBAP (Guards Bomber Aviation Regiment) of the Black Sea Fleet in Crimea during 1944.

Opposite top:
The fuselage inscription of this Pe-2, flown by Hero of the Soviet Union NP Groshev in 1945, reads, 'Caucasus - Moscow - Riga - Berlin', the wartime progress of pilot and aircraft.

Right:
An overhead view reveals the basic simplicity of the Pe-2's design.

took place on 15 December 1940. The Pe-2 boasted impressive performance: its level speed matched that of the Messerschmitt Bf 109E fighter, and it also possessed excellent manoeuvrability. Capable of carrying an 600kg (1320lb) of bombs internally and 400kg (880lb) externally, the Pe-2's nose glazing allowed the pilot to visually acquire the target before starting a dive-bombing attack, with recovery automatic. Its service entry proved taxing, however. The aircraft was complex, early build quality was poor and performance suffered as a result. The Pe-2 also required considerable physical strength to handle – an issue that became more problematic when increasing numbers of women pilots were assigned to fly the aircraft.

Still new when the German invasion began, the Pe-2 entered combat in the hands of largely inexperienced crews and suffered heavy early losses. Even so, notable successes were achieved, including a raid on the Romanian oilfields at Ploiești that reportedly set alight a quarter of a million tonnes of oil. Production ceased in December 1945 and the final examples were retired by Poland in 1957. More than 11,000 Pe-2s were built, making it the third most produced, twin-engined combat aircraft of the war, after the Junkers Ju 88 and Vickers Wellington.

Petlyakov Pe-8

The USSR developed only one modern four-engined bomber during the war, but despite the Pe-8's impressive performance, it was sidelined due to the Soviet emphasis on smaller, tactical aircraft.

Intended as a replacement for the antiquated TB-3, the aircraft that later became the Pe-8 flew for the first time in December 1936 as the ANT-42. After modifications, the aircraft entered production as the TB-7, subsequently renamed Pe-8 in honour of its chief designer Alexander Petlyakov. The first four production aircraft had a complex supercharging system, with a 750kW (1006hp) Klimov

This rare view of the Pe-8 used to fly Soviet minister Molotov to the UK and US in May 1942 shows its black and green camouflage.

Petlyakov Pe-8

Weight: 35,000kg (77,162lb)
Dimensions: Length: 23.2m (76ft 1in), Wingspan: 39.13m (128ft 5in), Height: 6.2m (20ft 4in)
Powerplant: Four 999kW (1340hp) Mikulin AM-35A V-12 liquid-cooled piston engines
Maximum speed: 443km/h (275mph)
Range: 3700km (2300 miles)
Ceiling: 9300m (30,500ft)
Crew: 11
Armament: Two 7.62mm (0.3in) ShKAS machine guns in nose turret, one 12.7mm (0.5in) Berezin UBT in port and starboard inner engine nacelle turret, one 20mm (0.8in) ShVAK in dorsal turret, one 20mm (0.8in) ShVAK in rear turret; up to Up to 5000kg (11,000lb) bombload

Opposite top:
Based at Kratovo airfield near Moscow in March 1943, this AM-35A-powered Pe-8 served with 746 APDD (Long Range Aviation Regiment).

Above and right:
In prewar finish, this is another AM-35A-powered example. The deep inner engine nacelles house the main wheels as well as a manned rear gun position on each side.

M-100 engine mounted in the fuselage to drive the superchargers for the four Mikulin AM-34FRN engines. While capable of impressive results, this system was overly complicated and difficult to manufacture, and was eventually abandoned. Subsequent development of the Pe-8 largely focused on finding a suitable alternative powerplant for the aircraft, and although only 93 were built, four different engine types were fitted during its limited production. After several were built with the Mikulin AM-35A engine, attention moved to the Charomskiy M-30 diesel, which offered exceptional range, but proved unreliable in service. The last Pe-8s featured Shvetsov M-82 radials with better power, but inferior range to the efficient diesels.

Always an uncommon aircraft – never more than 30 operational at any one time – the Pe-8 flew long-range missions throughout the war, including its first bombing of Berlin on 10 August 1941. Early in its service life, the Pe-8 possessed excellent performance compared to its contemporaries and was hard to intercept, but as the war progressed and German defences improved, losses more than doubled by 1944.

Polikarpov Po-2

The Po-2, the most-produced biplane in history, was first designed as a trainer but saw extensive use as a night harassment bomber, often flown by women, where it had a deep psychological impact.

A typical aircraft of its era, the U-2 first flew in June 1927 and entered service as a basic trainer, although its excellent STOL performance made it widely useful as a liaison aircraft. Nicknamed 'Kukuruznik' in Russia, a slang term for a collective farm worker, because of its agricultural use, the Polikarpov was called the 'Nähmaschine' (sewing machine) by the Germans for its distinctive engine

The Polikarpov biplane was hugely versatile; this U-2S ambulance variant, built from 1934, could carry a stretcher and a medical orderly.

Polikarpov Po-2

Weight: 1350kg (2976lb)
Dimensions: Length: 8.17m (26ft 10in), Wingspan: 11.4m (37ft 5in), Height: 3.1m (10ft 2in)
Powerplant: One 93kW (125hp) Shvetsov M-11D 5-cylinder air-cooled radial piston engine
Maximum speed: 152km/h (94mph)
Range: 630km (390 miles)
Ceiling: 3000m (9800ft)
Crew: 2
Armament: One 7.62mm (0.3in) ShKAS machine gun flexibly mounted in rear cockpit; up to six 50kg (110lb) bombs

Below:
In typical mid-war three-colour camouflage, this U-2 belonged to 46 ZAP (Reserve Aviation Regiment) in July 1943.

Opposite top:
The square marking on the forward fuselage reveals this aircraft served in one of the two Polish Light Night Harassment units, probably the 2nd 'Kraków' Night Bomber Regiment.

Right:
Two members of the famed 588th Night Bomber Regiment, an all-female unit, nicknamed the 'Night Witches' by the Germans, which became known for their relentless low-altitude nocturnal attacks on Axis ground positions.

sound. Its female pilots earned the fearsome nickname 'Nachthexen' (Night Witches). The U-2's use as a bomber began with field conversions but later the purpose-built U-2LNB appeared, carrying up to 300kg (660lb) of bombs.

Operating from their bases to forward airfields at dusk, U-2 missions were significantly short-range and sorties could be flown in rapid succession. In one extreme example, U-2 crew members Yekaterina Ryabova and Nadezhda Popova, flew 18 missions in a single night. Although these raids caused little material damage, their psychological effect cannot be overstated: approaching through the darkness silently, with the engine throttled back or even switched off, the U-2 could strike at any moment with practically no warning. The aircraft was almost immune to interception: its maximum speed was slower than the stalling speed of most contemporary fighters, and flak was largely ineffective. German gunners discovered that firing on a U-2 often served only to reveal their own positions, inviting a counterattack. After designer Nikolai Polikarpov's death in 1944, the U-2 was renamed Po-2 in his honour. Although the total number of U-2/Po-2s constructed is unknown, it is believed to be between 30,000 and 40,000.

Polikarpov R-5 and R-Z

The Polikarov R-5 was the standard Soviet light bomber in the 1930s and continued in widespread service during World War II, complemented by the more powerful and streamlined R-Z variant.

The R-5 was a conventional single engine, two-seat biplane powered by the M-17 engine – a licence-built BMW VI. First flown during the autumn of 1928, the R-5 entered service with the V-VS in 1930, proving dependable and popular. It saw combat throughout the mid-to-late 1930s, including the Spanish Civil War, the Battle of Khalkhin-Gol and the Sino-Japanese War. It served both as a standard light

This heavily retouched 1930s photo shows a typical R-5, unusually numerous for its era with several thousand built.

Polikarpov R-5 and R-Z

Weight: 3247kg (7158lb)
Dimensions: Length: 10.56m (34ft 8in), Wingspan: 15.5m (50ft 10in), Height: 3.25m (10ft 8in)
Powerplant: One 507kW (680hp) Mikulin M-17B V-12 liquid-cooled piston engine
Maximum speed: 228km/h (142mph)
Range: 800km (500 miles)
Ceiling: 6400m (21,000ft)
Crew: 2
Armament: One 7.62mm (0.3in) PV-1 machine gun fixed forward firing in upper cowling, one 7.62mm (0.3in) Degtyaryov DA machine gun flexibly mounted in rear cockpit

Above:
This Polikarpov, serving with 719 LBAP in late 1941, was operating at night, as the R-Z had become too vulnerable for daytime missions.

Opposite top:
The R-5SSS was a rare upgraded model with improved performance and heavier armament. This example was serving near Kyiv in 1936.

Right:
An early, civil-registered R-5 is manhandled into position on a prewar airfield.

bomber and as the R-5Sh, the Shturmovik variant, which featured four PV-1 7.62mm (0.3in) machine guns mounted in two pods under the lower wing. Heavily used during the Winter War with Finland (1939–40), the R-5 was obsolete by 1941 but, like the more famous Polikarpov Po-2, continued to serve as a nocturnal harassment bomber, remaining in frontline service until at least early 1944. Around 7000 were built.

A variant of the R-5, the R-5-SSS featured improved aerodynamics and heavier armament, with around 100 built. This design further evolved into the mass-produced R-Z. Powered by the more powerful Mikulin M-34, the maximum speed was raised to 316km/h (196mph) along with an increased bombload of 400kg (880lb). Produced until spring 1937, 1031 R-Zs were built and saw extensive action in Spain and the Far East, later participating in the invasion of Poland and the war against Finland in 1939. By November 1941, only five regiments remained operational with the R-Z, compared to 27 with the R-5, and by the end of 1942 the R-Z's combat career had effectively ended.

Sukhoi Su-2

The Su-2 was a light bomber that, like many of its contemporaries, proved vulnerable in its intended role but later enjoyed success as a reconnaissance platform.

The Su-2 was designed to meet the 'Ivanov' requirement for a multirole aircraft capable of performing tactical reconnaissance and then attacking targets it had located. Pavel Sukhoi, who was working within the Tupolev design bureau at the time, designated it the ANT-51 when it made its first flight in August 1937. The first prototype was slower than the specification demanded, but the overall design

Wearing a heated engine cover to prevent the oil from freezing, this Su-2 stands ready amid the harsh conditions of a typical Soviet winter.

Sukhoi Su-2

Weight: 4620kg (10,185lb)
Dimensions: Length: 14.30m (46ft 11in), Wingspan: 14.30m (46ft 11in), Height: 3.75m (12ft 4in)
Powerplant: One 992kW (1330hp) Shvetsov M-82 14-cylinder two-row air-cooled radial engine

Maximum speed: 486km/h (302mph)
Range: 910km (565 miles)
Ceiling: 8400m (27,560ft)
Crew: 2
Armament: Four 7.62mm (0.3in) ShKAS fixed in wings, one 7.62mm (0.3in) ShKAS in rear turret; up to 600kg bombload, or ten RS-82 rockets

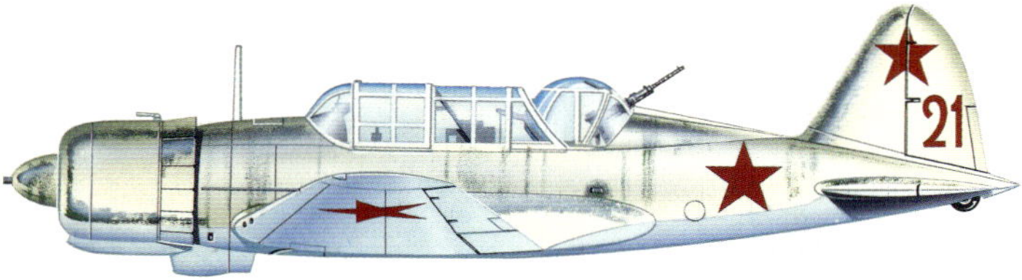

Above and right:
In the winter of 1941–42, many Soviet aircraft adopted a temporary white scheme to camouflage the aircraft against snow. This was water-soluble and wore off quickly, producing a weathered appearance, as can be seen beginning to develop on this Su-2.

Opposite top:
This SU-2 was assigned to 226 BAP on the Southwestern Front in July 1941. It still retains its basic prewar colours. Later, nearly all Soviet combat aircraft were painted in a disruptive black and green scheme.

was considered sound. A switch from the Shvetsov M-62 engine to the more powerful Tumansky M-87 improved matters, resulting in a respectable top speed of 468km/h (291mph). In this form, the aircraft was accepted for production and designated as the BB-1 – BB standing for 'Blizhniy Bombardirovshchik' (short-range bomber). Unfortunately, the M-87 engine proved unreliable and a further change to the Tumansky M-88 did not massively improve matters because this engine was also suffering teething issues. However, the final Su-2s of the 910 constructed were built with the highly reliable Shvetsov M-82, which considerably improved performance.

In combat, the Su-2 was vulnerable to fighter attack and the cannon-armed and heavily armoured Il-2 and the larger, faster Pe-2 proved far superior for the attack- and light-bomber roles. Although little used for bombing missions after the Battle of Stalingrad in late 1942, the Su-2 was instead employed for reconnaissance. It excelled in this role, often flying in weather conditions that grounded other aircraft, and continued to serve in this capacity until early 1944.

Tupolev SB-2 and Arkhangelsky Ar-2

Despite being one of the world's most advanced bombers when it entered service in 1936, the SB-2 was already obsolete by the time of the German invasion.

The SB-2's origin lay with a requirement for a bomber aircraft fast enough to be able to operate without a fighter escort. In response Andrei Tupolev and his associate Aleksander Arkhangelsky designed the first Soviet aircraft to feature a stressed skin construction, the ANT-40. Originally fitted with two Wright Cyclone radials, an engine change in the second prototype to two Hispano-Suiza 12Ybrs V-12 engines

The diminutive size of the Ar-2 is illustrated by the German serviceman posing with this captured example in 1941.

Tupolev SB-2

Weight: 7880kg (17,372lb)
Dimensions: Length: 12.57m (41ft 3in), Wingspan: 20.33m (66ft 8in), Height: 3.6m (11ft 10in)
Powerplant: Two 716kW (960hp) Klimov M-103 V-12 liquid-cooled piston engines
Maximum speed: 450km/h (280mph)
Range: 2300km (1400 miles)
Ceiling: 9300m (30,500ft)
Crew: 3
Armament: Two 7.62mm (0.3in) ShKAS machine guns in nose, one 7.62mm ShKAS machine gun in dorsal position and one 7.62mm ShKAS machine gun in ventral hatch; six 100kg (220lb) or six 50g (110lb) bombs in bomb bay, two 250kg (550lb) bombs on wing racks

Above and right:
'White 8' was an early SB-2 with radiators directly behind the propellers, later updated with the 1940 green and blue livery and fitted with an MV-3 dorsal turret.

Opposite top:
Found abandoned by German troops in the Kyiv district, this Ar-2 was probably on the strength of 33 BAP (Bomber Aviation Regiment) in the summer of 1941.

led to a jump in performance to 430km/h (267mph), exceeding the specification by a spectacular 100 km/h (60mph). Production of the SB-2 began in early 1936, and later that year it entered combat over Spain. Initially, its high speed made it largely immune to interception, although losses increased once the Messerschmitt Bf 109 was introduced. SB-2 production ramped up in 1940 due to the lack of a viable replacement, making it by far the most numerous Soviet bomber when Germany invaded in June 1941, with between 1500 and 2000 deployed along the western border of the USSR. Large numbers were destroyed on the ground and losses were heavy during attempts to halt the German advance. After only a few days, operations switched to nocturnal missions, with the SB-2 heavily employed against German positions during the defence of Moscow and Leningrad in the latter half of 1941.

Following Tupolev's arrest in 1937, Arkhangelsky oversaw the development of a new, faster SB variant optimized for dive bombing. The first examples of the aircraft, now known as the Ar-2, were built in December 1940. However, production lasted only three months before the factory switched to the Pe-2.

Tupolev TB-3

The TB-3, the world's first four-engined cantilever monoplane heavy bomber, was completely obsolete by 1941. Nonetheless, it saw considerable action during the initial stages of the conflict.

Essentially a stretched version of Tuopolev's earlier twin-engined TB-1, the TB-3 first flew in December 1930, entering service during 1932. The TB-3 set several payload to altitude records in the early 1930s, as well as an endurance record achieved by staying aloft for more than 18 hours. Initial production aircraft were fitted with Mikulin M-17 V-12 engines, a licence-built BMW VI, but later production TB-

The TB-3 was also used as a paratroop transport, as pictured here during a prewar exercise.

Tupolev TB-3

Weight: 19,300kg (42,549lb
Dimensions: Length: 24.4m (80ft 1in), Wingspan: 41.8m (137ft 2in), Height: 8.5m (27ft 11in)
Powerplant: Four 526kW (705hp) Mikulin M-17F V-12 liquid-cooled piston engines
Maximum speed: 212km/h (132mph)
Range: 2000km (1200 miles)
Ceiling: 4800m (15,700ft)
Crew: 8–10
Armament: Two paired 7.62mm (0.3in) Degtyaryov DA machine guns in nose, two paired 7.62mm (0.3in) DA machine guns in port and starboard dorsal gun positions, one 7.62mm (0.3in) DA machine gun in ventral 'dustbin' turret; up to 5000kg (11,000lb) bombload

Opposite top:
This modified TB-3, operational in mid-1942, has been fitted with two MV-3 turrets, each armed with a 7.62mm (0.3in) ShKAS machine gun in the staggered dorsal gun position.

Above (both images):
'Red 3' was flown by the 2nd Squadron of 1 TBAP (Heavy Bomber Aviation Regiment) based at Novocherkassk in the Rostov region during June 1941.

3s utilized the more powerful Mikulin AM-34. The TB-3 was never a fast aircraft and early M-17 powered aircraft struggled to exceed even 200 km/h (120mph). It is unsurprising therefore that the defensive armament was comprehensive by mid-1930s standards, featuring twin-gun positions in the nose and two amidships as well as two underwing 'dustbin' turrets; later aircraft featured a tail position in place of the underwing turrets. Bombload throughout the TB-3's service life remained 2000kg (4400lb).

More than 500 TB-3s remained active at the time of the German attack, despite having been officially withdrawn in 1939. As they were based well behind the frontline, the TB-3s escaped the widespread destruction wrought in the initial stages of Operation Barbarossa. The TB-3s were returned to front-line service, mostly at night, as daylight raids were nearly suicidal for the huge, painfully slow bomber. However, several were used in daylight as part of the unique 'Zveno' (Link) composite aircraft, carrying two Polikarpov I-16 parasite dive bombers –one under each wing – to successfully attack targets in Romania. During the first two years of the war, the TB-3s were heavily committed: crews sometimes flew three missions a night, and the aircraft was also used as a paratroop transport. By the end of 1943, the TB-3 was no longer used in combat and was operating primarily in the transport role. Of the 818 TB-3s built, ten were still flying in July 1945.

Tupolev Tu-2

Designed in prison by Andrei Tupolev, the Tu-2 was a superb aircraft that enjoyed both a highly successful combat career and a long production life.

The three-seat aircraft was designed to an impossibly ambitious specification: a maximum level speed of 700–740km/h (435–460mph) and a surface ceiling of 13,000– 14,000m (42,650–46,000ft), while also being capable of both level and dive bombing. Construction of 'Aircraft 103' (the project not initially linked to the disgraced and imprisoned Tupolev) began in May 1940 and the first flight took place on 29 January

The Tu-2's extensive nose glazing delivered excellent downward visibility for the pilot and bomb aimer.

Tupolev Tu-2

Weight: 11,768kg (25,944lb)
Dimensions: Length: 13.8m (45ft 3in), Wingspan: 18.86m (61ft 11in), Height: 4.13m (13ft 7in)
Powerplant: Two 1380kW (1850hp) Shvetsov ASh-82 14-cylinder air-cooled radial piston engines
Maximum speed: 528km/h (328mph)
Range: 2020km (1260 miles)
Ceiling: 9000m (30,000ft)
Crew: 4
Armament: Two fixed forward firing 20mm (0.8in) ShVAK cannon in the wings, three 7.62 mm (0.3in) ShKAS machine guns in rear cockpit canopy, dorsal and ventral hatches: up to 1500kg (3300lb) in bomb bay

Opposite:
Wartime Tu-2s were invariably finished in a camouflage pattern. The uniform Soviet green upper surfaces of this anonymous example suggest that it was produced in the postwar era. The Tu-2 remained in production until 1952.

Below:
The Tu-2 was more complex and took longer to build than the highly successful Pe-2 so was slow to enter production.

Above:
This Tu-2S of 88 BAD was flown by A. Pushkin, the commander of the unit. This aircraft was lost during the huge Soviet advance in early 1945.

1941. The aircraft demonstrated excellent performance, outpacing nearly all operational fighters of the time. However, Soviet authorities required the crew size to be increased to four – following the example of an early Junkers Ju 88 that was acquired by the USSR in 1940 – necessitating substantial alterations to the cockpit. Furthermore, development of the Mikulin AM-37 V-12 engine ran into insuperable problems and the only readily available alternative was the Shvetsov M-82 radial, which, although dependable, led to a further reduction in maximum speed. In July 1941, Tupolev was released and the aircraft was officially renamed Tu-2.

Despite being widely considered the finest medium bomber available to the Soviet Union, the Tu-2 did not reach significant numbers until the last year of the war. During 1942 there was a critical shortage of fighters and Tu-2 production was halted to concentrate on the Yak-9 fighter. Following enthusiastic reports from frontline Tu-2 crew, production restarted in mid-1943. In service from early 1944, the ASh-82FN powered Tu-2S proved popular and effective. Easy to handle even when carrying its maximum bombload, the Tu-2 possessed strong defensive armament and was fast enough to be difficult to intercept. Postwar, production of the Tu-2 continued until 1948.

Yakovlev Yak-2 and Yak-4

The Yak-2's performance caused a sensation when it first flew in 1939, but production models failed to match the prototype's potential. Both the Yak-2 and its successor, the Yak-4, saw only brief service.

The Yak-2 was designed as a versatile platform for a cannon-armed twin-engined fighter, short-range bomber, and tactical reconnaissance aircraft, all sharing the same airframe. It was built for maximum speed, and the prototype became one of the fastest military aircraft in the world, famously showcased during a dramatic May Day flypast over Red Square in 1939. Stalin ordered production to begin,

Photographed just before the outbreak of hostilities, this Yak-4 was undergoing engine maintenance in the open.

Yakovlev Yak-2

Weight: 5660kg (12,477lb)
Dimensions: Length: 9.34m (30ft 8in), Wingspan: 14m (45ft 11in), Height: 4.18m (13ft 9in)
Powerplant: Two 716kW (960hp) Klimov M-103 V-12 liquid-cooled piston engines
Maximum speed: 515km/h (320mph)
Range: 800km (500 miles)
Ceiling: 8900m (29,200ft)
Crew: 3
Armament: One 7.62mm (0.3in) ShKAS machine gun fixed forward firing in nose, one ShKAS machine gun flexibly mounted in rear cockpit; up to 600kg (1300lb) bombload

Opposite:
Lieutenant I.M Agarkov, commander of 316 RAP, flew this Yak-2 on operations over the Southwestern Front during July and August 1941.

Above:
Still in its prewar overall green scheme, 'Yellow 3' was a Yak-4 that was destroyed on the ground at Grodno airfield in Belarus in the opening stages of Operation Barbarossa, June 1941.

as the BB-22 'Blizhniy Bombardirovshchik' (short-range bomber), before the prototype had completed testing. This proved premature, as the aircraft soon suffered from engine overheating, instability, and general unpopularity, not least because escape in the event of an emergency was practically impossible. Weight growth caused by the installation of military equipment coupled with poor quality workmanship meant that production BB-22s had much the same speed as the earlier SB-2, which could carry twice the bombload nearly three times as far. In service, crews joked that BB stood for 'Bespoleznyy Bombardirovshchik' (Useless Bomber).

Service use, primarily as a reconnaissance platform, was very brief and most were destroyed during the first month of combat, with only one remaining airworthy by 18 July. Keen to improve upon the Yak-2, Yakovlev re-engined the aircraft with more powerful Klimov M-105s and increased the bombload to 400kg (880lb). Yet, even this modest load had a negative effect on the aircraft's centre of gravity leading to handling issues, a problem that had also afflicted the earlier Yak-2.

The first Yak-4s, then known as the BB-22bis, began to appear in October 1940. However, a mere 90 examples had been constructed by the time production ceased. Given the success of the considerably more formidable Pe-2, no argument could be made to continue development of the Yak twin. In combat, the Yak-4 was found to be impressively fast but virtually all were destroyed by the end of 1941.

Yermolaev Yer-2

Although little known today, the Yermolaev Yer-2 was an intriguing design that returned to production more than two years after initial manufacturing had ceased.

The Yer-2 was derived from the advanced Stal-7 prototype airliner, originally designed by Italian aeronautical engineer Roberto Bartini. Development passed to his deputy, Vladimir Yermolaev, after Bartini was imprisoned on contrived espionage charges in 1938. Under Yermolaev, the airliner was redesigned as the DB-240 – 'DB' standing for 'Dalny Bombardirovshcik' (long-range

A heavily retouched official photo shows a Yer-2, with the extensive nose glazing visible on this M-105-powered example.

Yermolaev Yer-2

Weight: 18,580kg (40,962lb)
Dimensions: Length: 16.42m (53ft 10in), Wingspan: 23m (75ft 6in), Height: 4.82m (15ft 10in)
Powerplant: Two 1100kW (1500hp) Charomskiy ACh-30B V-12 liquid-cooled diesel piston engines
Maximum speed: 507km/h (315mph)
Range: 5500km (3417 miles)
Ceiling: 7200m (23,600ft)
Crew: 4
Armament: One 12.7mm (0.5in) Berezin UBT flexibly mounted in nose, one 12.7mm Berezin UBT on flexible ventral mount, one 20mm (0.8in) ShVAK cannon in dorsal turret; up to 5000 kg (11,023lb) bombload

Right:
Posing in 1945 on a snow-covered airfield, this Yer-2 was a testbed for the 24-cylinder X-pattern Dobrotvorskii MB-100F engine that delivered a colossal 2390kW (3200hp) for take off.

Opposite top and below:
'White 5' was assigned to 421 DBAP (Long-Range Bomber Regiment), based at Rostov-on-Don, in October 1941.

bomber) – and flew for the first time in May 1940. Performance fell slightly short of initial estimates because the aircraft had to use two Klimov M-105s instead of the higher-powered M-106s it was designed for, as the M-106 suffered from unresolved cooling problems. On the other hand, the DB-240 offered excellent range and decent defensive armament, and it entered production as the Yer-2 in March 1941. Its initial production life was short, however, with only 128 built before the factory switched in August 1941 to building the more urgently required Il-2.

In the same month, the Yer-2 entered combat for the first time when three aircraft bombed Berlin, although one was mistakenly shot down by Polikarpov I-16s on its return to Soviet airspace. Later, tasked with interdicting the German advance on Moscow, the Yer-2s suffered severe losses during desperate low-level tactical missions for which they were ill-suited. The survivors remained in frontline service until August 1943, when remaining aircraft were transferred to training units. Although initial production had ceased, development of the design continued, and Yer-2 production was resumed towards the end of 1943 with efficient Charomskiy ACh-30 diesel engines. Production difficulties delayed service entry, which meant the first bombing mission of the updated Yer-2 occurred only around a month before VE day, and the aircraft subsequently remained in service until the late 1940s.

Armstrong-Whitworth Albemarle

The Albemarle, designed to match contemporary RAF medium bombers with non-strategic materials, saw limited bomber use and was mainly employed as a glider tug.

Intended as a backup to conventional aircraft if aluminium and light alloys became scarce during wartime, the Albemarle was a commendable attempt to solve a problem that ultimately never arose. Had the war progressed differently, the Albemarle might have proved a significant aircraft but as it transpired, the bomber operated in its intended role on only one occasion and remains obscure.

Forty-nine examples of the Albemarle ST Mk.V were built, specifically modified for troop carrying and glider tug duties.

Armstrong Whitworth Albemarle ST Mk I

Weight: 16,570kg (36,500lb)
Dimensions: Length 18.25m (59ft 11in), Wingspan 23.47m (77ft), Height 4.75m (15ft 7in)
Powerplant: Two 1190kW (1590hp) Bristol Hercules XI 14-cylinder air-cooled radial piston engines

Maximum speed: 426km/h (265mph)
Range: 2092km (1300 miles)
Ceiling: 5486m (18,000ft)
Crew: 4
Armament: Four 7.7mm (0.303in) Browning machine guns in dorsal turret; up to 2041kg (4500lb) bombload

Opposite top:
This aircraft is shown as it appeared during testing in the USSR in March and April 1943, still wearing its RAF serial and night bomber camouflage. The Soviet opinion of the Albemarle was not enthusiastic.

Above:
This aircraft, serial number V1599, was the last Albemarle to be built in the original bomber configuration and the first to be modified for 'Special Transport' (ST) duties.

The first British production aircraft to feature a retractable tricycle undercarriage, 200 of the Albemarle were ordered 'off the drawing board' in late 1938. The aircraft was almost entirely constructed of steel and wood, and flew for the first time on 20 March 1940, demonstrating a decent performance for a medium bomber of its era. The organization required to build it consisted of more than 1000 engineering and woodworking firms – car manufacturer Rover supplied wing centre sections, while furniture maker Harris Lebus made the tailplanes – on the assumption that such a widely distributed production network would be resilient to enemy bombing. Unfortunately, service entry of the new aircraft was seriously delayed by redesign work to address weight and aerodynamic issues, and by the time the aircraft reached RAF service its performance was inferior to that of other bombers already in service.

Only 32 Albemarles were constructed in the original BI bomber configuration, taking part in one leaflet drop and a single night bombing raid in May 1943. The remaining 602 aircraft were completed as transports and glider tugs, playing a significant role in the invasion of Sicily, the D-Day landings in June 1944 and Operation Market Garden in September 1944), and continuing in this capacity until the end of the war.

Armstrong-Whitworth Whitley

Designed from the outset for nocturnal operations, the Whitley was heavily used in the early years of the war before its increasingly outdated performance saw it relegated to less demanding roles.

Of the three medium bombers in RAF service at the outbreak of war, only the Whitley was intended for night operations. It equipped Bomber Command's No.4 Group, the world's only fully trained night bomber force at that time. The Whitley itself had first flown in January 1936 and was a curious mix of the old and new. The aircraft featured a semi-monocoque metal fuselage – the first of its kind in

Early Whitleys, equipped with hand-operated turrets, featured a small emergency exit hatch beneath the turret, as seen here.

Armstrong-Whitworth Whitley V

Weight: 15,195kg (33,500lb)
Dimensions: Length 21.49m (70ft 6in), Wingspan 25.6m (84ft), Height 4.57m (15ft)
Powerplant: Two 854kW (1154hp) Rolls-Royce Merlin X liquid-cooled V-12 piston engines
Maximum speed: 370km/h (230mph)
Range: 2660km (1650 miles)
Ceiling: 7900m (26,000ft)
Crew: 5
Armament: One 7.7mm (0.303in) Vickers K Machine gun flexibly mounted in nose turret and four 7.7mm (0.303in) flexibly mounted in rear turret; up to 3175kg (7000lb) bombload

Opposite:
Serving with No. 10 Squadron, this Whitley I was based at Dishforth, Yorkshire in 1937.

Above:
Standard Whitley finish featured black undersides but on some aircraft the black was extended to the fuselage sides. This Whitley V belonged to 77 Squadron at Linton-on-Ouse, Yorkshire, October 1940.

Below:
The towing yoke on the rear fuselage reveals that this Whitley V – wearing day camouflage but no squadron codes – was used on glider tug duties in 1943.

RAF service – but was also originally designed without wing flaps, then a relatively new technology. To compensate, its wings were set at a high level of incidence to provide reasonable take off and landing performance. This configuration remained unchanged even after flaps were added, giving the Whitley its distinctive – and somewhat alarming – nose-down attitude in flight. Early variants were powered by Armstrong-Whitworth's own Tiger radial engine, however, a switch to the Rolls-Royce Merlin improved performance and most of the 1814 constructed were Merlin powered.

Early wartime operations were mostly concerned with dropping leaflets and Whitleys roved as far as Berlin on these duties. The first bombing raid on German soil was carried out in conjunction with Hampden bombers against the seaplane base at Sylt in March 1940. The Whitley also became the first British aircraft to penetrate Italian airspace, bombing Turin just hours after Italy declared war. Later, the Whitley was heavily used in Bomber Command's night bombing offensive until April 1942 when it was withdrawn to other roles after having delivered 8931 tonnes (19,689,485lb) of bombs over the course of 8996 operations. In addition to its bombing role, the Whitley served as a paratroop transport, glider tug and maritime patrol aircraft with Coastal Command, where it sank five U-boats.

Avro Anson

The Anson was mainly used for training and utility roles, but at the start of the war it was a major part of Coastal Command, though largely ineffective in action.

The RAF's first retractable undercarriage monoplane to enter service, the Anson was at the vanguard of British military aviation development when it made its squadron debut in March 1936. The aircraft had been developed to a specification for a comparatively cheap land-based maritime patrol aircraft to supplement the RAF's highly capable, but expensive flying boat squadrons. Avro proposed a version of their 652

The Anson primarily flew convoy patrols, as shown here. It was mostly withdrawn from frontline service by the end of 1940.

Avro Anson

Weight: 3629kg (8000lb)
Dimensions: Length 12.88m (42ft 3in), Wingspan 17.22m (56ft 6in), Height 3.99m (13ft 1in)
Powerplant: Two 250kW (350hp) Armstrong-Siddeley Cheetah IX 7-cylinder air-cooled radial piston engines
Maximum speed: 303km/h (188mph)
Range: 1060km (660 miles)
Ceiling: 5800m (19,000ft)
Crew: 3–4
Armament: One 7.7mm (0.303in) Browning machine gun fixed, firing forward in starboard fuselage nose, one 78.7mm (0.303in) Vickers K machine gun flexibly mounted in dorsal turret; up to 160kg (360lb) bombload

Opposite:
Resplendent in the prewar, all-silver scheme adopted by Coastal Command, this Anson I served with No. 220 Squadron at Thornaby, Yorkshire, in 1937.

Above:
This Anson served with No. 206 Squadron Coastal Command at Manston, Kent, in 1940.

Below:
No. 321 (Dutch) Squadron consisted of personnel from the Royal Netherlands Naval Air Service operating under RAF control, hence the orange triangle national marking on the fin. This unit flew Ansons on maritime patrols before transitioning to Catalina flying boats.

airliner (only two of which were built for Imperial Airways) and this proved superior to de Havilland's rival design. From the start of the Anson's service, Bomber Command employed it exclusively as a training aircraft, whereas in Coastal Command it fulfilled its intended purpose as a maritime patrol aircraft. In 1937 the Anson became the first aircraft to use ASV radar during exercises, a technology that later proved invaluable in the war at sea.

Even before the war began, it was recognized that the Anson was ill-suited for Coastal Command due to its limited range and light armament. In 1938, a decision was made to acquire the Lockheed Hudson for land-based Coastal Command squadrons; however, by September 1939 only a few Hudsons had been received, and the Anson remained in heavy use during the first year of the war. By the end of 1940, the Anson had disappeared from frontline squadrons, but it continued to play a vital role as a training aircraft throughout the war, ultimately becoming the fourth most numerous British aircraft in history, with 11,020 built.

Avro Lancaster

The most famous British bomber of World War II, the Lancaster was also one of the most effective, capable of carrying remarkably heavy bombloads to targets deep within German territory.

Rising phoenix-like from the ashes of the Manchester debacle, the Lancaster proved to be the finest heavy bomber fielded by the RAF during the war. The Manchester was a decent aircraft plagued by engine problems and a redesign to a four Merlin engine layout was underway at Avro by mid-1940, utilizing the combined engine and cowling 'power egg' units developed for the Bristol Beaufighter in a wing

This Lancaster I was photographed on a test flight from Castle Bromwich in 1945 and has yet to be issued to an operational squadron.

Avro Lancaster B.I

Weight: 30,844kg (68,000lb)
Dimensions: Length 21.13m (69ft 4in), Wingspan 31.09m (102ft), Height 6.25m (20ft 6in)
Powerplant: Four 950kW (1280hp) Rolls-Royce Merlin XX liquid-cooled V-12 piston engines
Maximum speed: 454km/h (282mph)
Range: 4070km (2530 miles)
Ceiling: 6500m (21,400ft)
Crew: 7
Armament: Two 7.7mm (0.303) Browning machine guns in both nose and dorsal turrets and four 7.7mm (0.303) Browning machine guns in rear turret; up to 8200kg (18,000lb) bombload

Opposite:
R5543, assigned to No. 61 Squadron, was lost on its 18th operation on 20 August 1942, after being intercepted by a Ju 88, ultimately crashing in Spain.

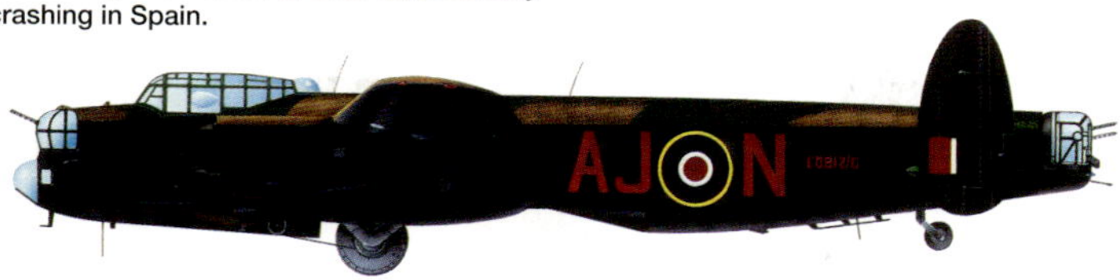

Above:
Fitted with the 'Bouncing Bomb' under the fuselage, this 617 Squadron aircraft breached the Eder dam during the famous "Dambusters" raid of May 1943. The dorsal turret has been removed as a weight saving measure.

Below:
Serving with 44 Squadron aircraft in November 1944, LM560 features fin and rudders painted overall red. These markings were adopted as a visual identification for flight leaders in squadrons in 5 Group, which undertook daylight raids as well as nocturnal missions.

of increased span. First flown on 9 January 1941, the Manchester Mk III – its initial designation – demonstrated such promising performance that all remaining fuselages on the production line were completed to the new standard and redesignated Lancaster I. The initial order was for 1070 aircraft, with deliveries beginning in late 1941, allowing the type to carry out its first bombing raid on Essen in March 1942. Lancaster production soon ramped up, and over the next three years it became the backbone of Bomber Command. By May 1942, during Operation Millennium – the first 1000-bomber raid on Cologne – more Lancasters were in service than the total production run of Manchesters. A total of 7377 Lancasters were built, the majority being the initial B.I variant or the B.III.

In addition, 300 Lancaster B.IIs were produced with Bristol Hercules engines as an alternative to the Merlin. The Lancaster earned renown during its service for its exceptional lifting capability. Inheriting a large bomb bay from the Manchester, it could carry bombloads of up to 8200kg (18,000 b), and in modified form, it could carry the 10-tonne (22,000lb) 'Grand Slam', the heaviest conventional bomb used during the war.

Avro Manchester

A disappointing aircraft, the Manchester's performance was compromised by its catastrophically unreliable Vulture engines, but the basic design ultimately evolved into the superlative Lancaster.

The Manchester was designed in response to Specification P.13/36 – which also led to the Handley-Page Halifax – calling for a monoplane medium bomber capable of carrying up to 8000lb (3600kg) of bombs and performing shallow dive-bombing attacks. Avro's response to the requirement took shape as a twin-engined aircraft powered by the promising new Rolls-Royce Vulture

The Manchester IA introduced a larger-span tail with enlarged vertical surfaces, as shown on this 207 Squadron example.

Avro Manchester I

Weight: 22,680kg (50,000lb)
Dimensions: Length 21m (70ft)
Wingspan 27.46m (90ft 1in), Height 5.94m (19ft 6in)
Powerplant: Two 1310kW (1750hp) Rolls-Royce Vulture liquid cooled X-24 piston engines
Maximum speed: 426km/h (265mph)
Range: 1900km (1200 miles)
Ceiling: 5900m (19,200ft)
Crew: 7
Armament: Two 7.7mm (0.303) Browning machine guns in both nose and dorsal turrets and four 7.7mm (0.303) Browning machine guns in rear turret; up to 4695kg (10,350lb) bombload

Opposite top:
The first 20 Manchester Is had small vertical tail surfaces, requiring the addition of the central fin, as seen here on Q for Queenie of No. 83 Squadron in March 1942.

Above and right:
Q for Queenie was lost on its 15th mission, a raid on the Blohm and Voss shipyard in Hamburg on 9 April 1942. From all angles, the family resemblance to the far more successful Lancaster is obvious.

engine, with 24 cylinders arranged in an X configuration and rated at an impressive 1310kW (1750hp). The first flight of the aircraft took place in July 1939 and initial testing revealed a greater tail area was required. A distinctive central fin was fitted to the fuselage pending a tailplane redesign, and the first 20 production aircraft also sported this modification.

Meanwhile, problems with the Vulture were already apparent: the engine was proving unreliable and was seldom able to deliver its rated power. Despite its shortcomings, the Manchester was accepted for service, with the first aircraft delivered to No. 207 Squadron in November 1940. Slow production, however, meant that it did not make its combat debut until February 1941, when Manchesters participated in a raid on Brest. The Manchester quickly suffered from hydraulic and propeller issues, but its biggest problem was the unreliable Vulture engines, which lacked power and prevented the aircraft from maintaining altitude on one engine. Production ended in November 1941 after 202 were built, with the last operation flown in June 1942. Avro then developed the Manchester Mk III, replacing the Vultures with four Rolls-Royce Merlin engines, effectively resolving its major flaws. By the time this version entered production, it had been redesignated the Lancaster.

Bristol Beaufort

Coastal Command's standard torpedo bomber of the early war period, the Beaufort was also manufactured in large numbers in Australia.

A derivative of the Blenheim first flown in October 1938, the Beaufort was larger, carried an extra crew member, and was heavier, requiring more powerful Taurus engines in place of the Blenheim's Mercuries. The first operational mission flew in April 1940 when nine aircraft dropped magnetic mines in the approaches to Wilhelmshaven. Beaufort units were initially engaged in minelaying and

This 217 Squadron Beaufort was pictured flying from its base at St Eval in Cornwall. The squadron moved to Malta in late 1942.

Bristol Beaufort I

Weight: 9629kg (21,230lb)
Dimensions: Length 13.46m (44ft 2in), Wingspan 17.63m (57ft 10in), Height 4.34m (14ft 3in)
Powerplant: Two 840kW (1130hp) Bristol Taurus II 14-cylinder air-cooled radial piston engines
Maximum speed: 437km/h (272mph)
Range: 2600km (1600 miles)
Ceiling: 5000m (16,500ft)
Crew: 4
Armament: One 7.7mm (0.303in) Vickers GO machine gun fixed, forward firing in port wing, two 7.7mm (0.303in) Vickers GO machine guns in dorsal turret, and optional 7.7mm (0.303in) Browning machine gun in rearward firing chin turret; up to 907kg (2000lb) bombload

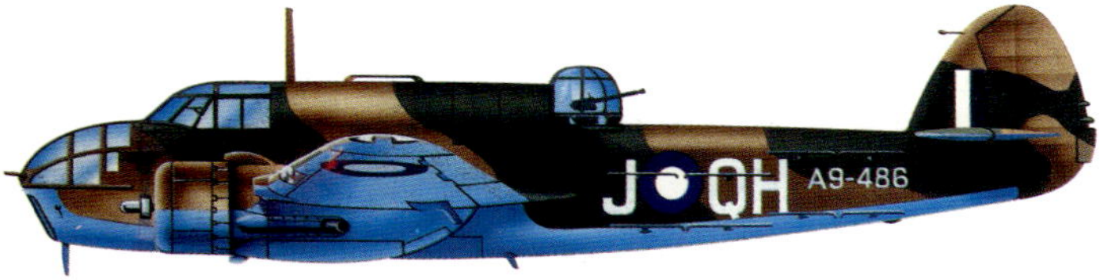

Above:
The Australian-built Beaufort VIII was fitted with American Pratt & Whitney Twin Wasp engines and served exclusively in the South West Pacific.

Opposite top:
An early production example, this Beaufort was serving with the first unit to operate the type, No. 22 Squadron Coastal Command, in December 1939.

Right:
This interior shot shows the view looking forward past the pilot on the left to the navigator seated at his station in the nose.

conventional bombing, with a Beaufort becoming the first British aircraft to drop the new 2000lb (910kg) bomb in May 1940. The type made its first torpedo attack in September 1940, targeting German merchant ships off the Dutch coast, and later attacked the battlecruisers *Scharnhorst* off Norway and *Gneisenau* in Brest harbour. By mid-1942, frontline Beaufort squadrons had moved to other theatres, proving effective in the Mediterranean against Italian shipping and later in the Pacific.

The structure was built in easily transportable modular sections, enabling assembly by widely distributed subcontractors, facilitating licence production in Australia by the Department of Aircraft Production (DAP). The first Australian-built Beaufort flew in May 1941, with 700 produced using locally made Pratt & Whitney Twin Wasp engines. Both British-supplied and Australian-built Beauforts served with 19 RAAF squadrons, seeing extensive action from early 1942, particularly around New Guinea.

Bristol Blenheim

The first RAF aircraft to enter German airspace during the war, the Blenheim was faster than most fighters, but by 1940 its performance advantage had evaporated and it suffered appalling losses.

Derived from the high-speed Bristol Type 142 civil aircraft, which outperformed contemporary RAF fighters, the Blenheim first flew in June 1936 and entered service the following year. During 1939 the improved Blenheim IV variant appeared, which featured an extended nose containing improved accommodation for the navigator. At the start of the war, Blenheims equipped 13 squadrons

Three Blenheim IVs of 53 Squadron, Coastal Command, just before the outbreak of war in 1939. This squadron would operate the Blenheim before re-equipping with Hudsons in 1941.

Bristol Blenheim IV

Weight: 7120kg (15,682lb)
Dimensions: Length 12.98m (42ft 7in), Wingspan 17.17m (56ft 4in), Height 3m (9ft 10in)
Powerplant: Two 690kW (920hp) Bristol Mercury XV 9-cylinder air-cooled radial piston engines
Maximum speed: 428km/h (266mph)
Range: 2350km (1460 miles)
Ceiling: 8310m (27,260ft)
Crew: 3
Armament: One 7.7mm (0.303in) Browning machine gun fixed, firing forward in port wing, two 7.7mm (0.303in) Browning machine guns mounted in dorsal turret and one in optional chin turret; up to 540kg (1200lb) bombload

Opposite:
Serving with No. 56 Squadron in France during 1940, this Mk I features the blunt nose design of earlier production machines.

Above:
Based at Plivot, France, in April 1940, this Blenheim IV was on the strength of No. 139 Squadron. Blenheims suffered severe losses to fighters when the Germans invaded France.

Below:
The revised nose and two gun Bristol BX turret identify this aircraft as a Blenheim V, the last production variant.

and on the same day that Britain declared war a reconnaissance flight over Wilhelmshaven harbour was made by a single Blenheim, becoming the first British aircraft to penetrate enemy airspace. Blenheim squadrons based in France were heavily used following the German invasion, but proved extremely vulnerable to both enemy fighters and ground fire, and surviving aircraft had been withdrawn to Britain by the time of the Dunkirk evacuation. Attacks continued to be made against targets in Europe but losses continued to be prohibitively high. For example, during a raid against Aalborg in Denmark in August 1940 all 11 aircraft that attacked the target were destroyed. During this period, the Blenheim was also heavily employed in anti-shipping attacks, and again suffered significant losses.

Operations in the Middle East and Mediterranean were more successful due to less intense fighter opposition. It was in this theatre that the final variant, the Mk V – sometimes called the 'Bisley' – was introduced in mid-1942 as a more heavily armoured version optimized for ground attack, although the existence of the superior Beaufighter and Mosquito meant the Bisley's service life was short.

de Havilland Mosquito

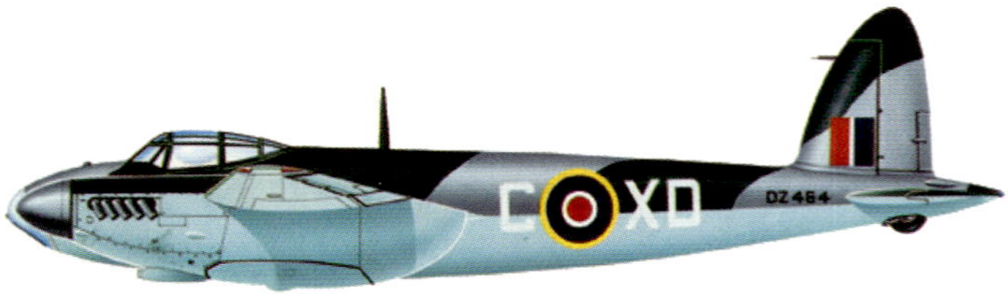

The bomber variants of the multirole Mosquito carried no defensive weapons, relying on the aircraft's phenomenal performance to avoid interception and proved to be outstandingly successful.

Constructed almost entirely of wood, the Mosquito used minimal strategic materials but was one of the fastest production aircraft in the world.

The concept of rejecting any sort of defensive gun armament in the name of greater performance proved too radical for many officials and it was only due to the foresight of Wilfred Freeman, chief of Research and Development at the Air Ministry that the aircraft

A line up of 139 Squadron Mosquito B Mk.IVs about to depart on a mission from their base at Marham, Norfolk, in mid-1943.

De Havilland Mosquito B.Mk XVI

Weight: 11,340kg (25,000lb)
Dimensions: Length 13.56m (44ft 6in), Wingspan 16.51m (54ft 2in), Height 5.31m (17ft 5in)
Powerplant: Two 1280kW (1710hp) Rolls-Royce Merlin 76/77 liquid-cooled V-12 piston engines

Maximum speed: 668km/h (415mph)
Range: 2100km (1300 miles)
Ceiling: 11,000m (37,000ft)
Crew: 2
Armament: up to 1800kg (4000lb) bombload

Opposite:
A B Mk.IV of 139 Squadron, this Mosquito was heavily engaged on daylight missions over occupied Europe until it was shot down by flak on the French coast in May 1943.

Below:
The FB Mk.VI combined bombs and a gun armament in the same airframe. In June 1944, this Mosquito of 248 Squadron took part in an attack on U-821 off Ushant resulting in the crew of the U-boat abandoning ship.

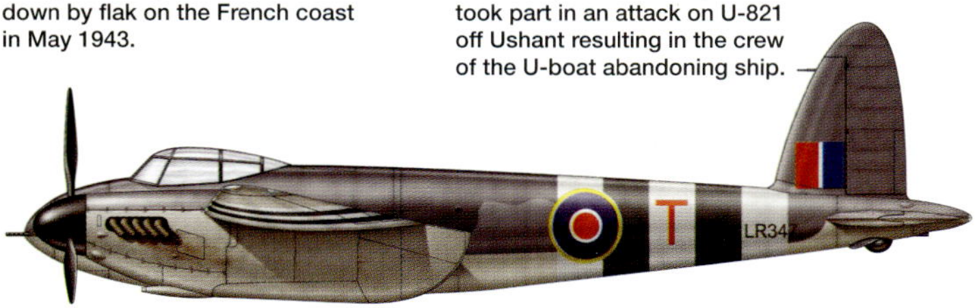

Below:
This daylight camouflaged B Mk.IV was on strength with No. 105 Squadron based at Horsham St Faith in Norfolk in late 1942. 105 Squadron was the first bomber unit to operate the Mosquito.

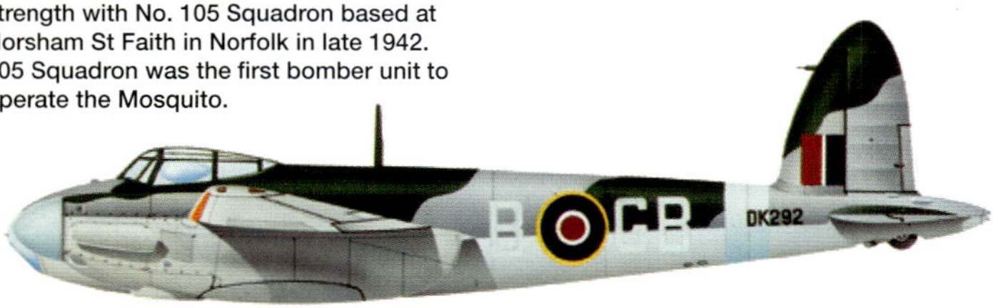

made it to the hardware stage. The first prototype flew in November 1940 and in tests proved to be 51km/h (32mph) faster than a Spitfire Mk II. Operational flights began in July 1941 when one of the prototypes was used on reconnaissance missions, but the first service examples were of the B.Mk IV bomber variant, delivered in November of the same year.

Initial bombing missions took place in May 1942 and the aircraft proved popular with crews as its speed rendered it nearly impossible to intercept. In the course of the war, Mosquito loss rates were just a tenth of those suffered by the Lancaster. Over the following year, Mosquito squadrons gained a reputation for precise, low-level attacks on high-value targets: for example, in January 1943 they destroyed the main broadcasting station in Berlin just before Reichsmarshal Goering was due to deliver a speech marking ten years of Nazi rule. The Mosquito B.Mk IV (special) introduced bulged bomb bay doors, later standardized on the B.Mk XVI allowing a 4000lb (1800kg) bomb to be carried to Berlin, the same payload that a B-17 Flying Fortress could carry to the same target.

Fairey Albacore

The Albacore saw intense action and proved effective in several demanding roles and theatres, but it never fully replaced its famous predecessor, the Swordfish.

Although it was stipulated that the crew of the Navy's new torpedo bomber were to be housed in an enclosed, heated cockpit, the demanding needs of carrier operation were still thought to be best served by the strong, high lift biplane, and so the Albacore became the last combat biplane design to enter British service. The prototype first flew in December 1938 and testing revealed few problems. The Albacore proved

Photographed at the point of releasing its torpedo, the Albacore was originally designed to replace the Swordfish.

Fairey Albacore

Weight: 5820kg (12,830lb)
Dimensions: Length: 12.13m (39ft 10in), Wingspan: 15.24m (50ft), Height: 4.65m (15ft 3in)
Powerplant: One 794kW (1065hp) Bristol Taurus II or one 840kW (1130hp) Bristol Taurus XII 14-cylinder, air-cooled, radial piston engine
Maximum speed: 272km/h (169mph)
Range: 1497km (930 miles)
Ceiling: 6309m (20,700ft)
Crew: 2 or 3
Armament: One 7.7mm (0.303in) Browning machine gun fixed forward firing in starboard wing, one or two 7.7mm (0.303in) Vickers K machine guns flexibly mounted in rear cockpit; up to 907kg (2000lb) bombload or one 730kg (1610lb) torpedo

Opposite top:
Embarked on the carrier HMS *Formidable* for convoy escort duty in the winter of 1940–41, this Albacore was serving with 826 Naval Air Squadron. 826 would later operate its Albacores in the Western desert of North Africa.

Above:
Wings folded, Albacores await their next duty, circa 1942. The aircraft's official name of Albacore (a type of tuna fish) led to its popular nickname of 'Applecore'.

generally pleasant to fly with a superb view for the pilot and good deck landing characteristics. Initial deliveries to service units began in December 1939 and the Albacore's operational use commenced during March 1940.

The first combat use of the Albacore occurred during the evacuation from Dunkirk and the aircraft was subsequently used as a dive bomber to attack shore targets and German shipping, perform convoy escort duties and drop mines. The Albacore first went to sea in November 1940 aboard HMS *Formidable* for convoy escort duty before proving decisive during the Battle of Cape Matapan where Albacores crippled the Italian battleship *Vittorio Veneto* and three cruisers. Albacores were later kept busy in actions ranging from Norway to Malaya, including making the only torpedo attack on the *Tirpitz* at sea, attacking Vichy French airfields during Operation Torch, and flying nocturnal dive-bombing missions in the Western Desert. The bomber persisted in frontline use into 1945. The last unit to operate the Albacore was 119 Squadron RAF, which used it to make radar-guided attacks on E-boats by night. Ironically, in March 1945 the squadron replaced their Albacores with the Fairey Swordfish – the very aircraft the Albacore had been designed to replace.

Fairey Barracuda

Although underpowered and introduced late, the Barracuda proved effective in multiple demanding roles and became one of Britain's most important carrier aircraft in the final two years of the war.

Developed as a monoplane replacement for the Albacore, the Barracuda was intended to perform torpedo and dive bombing, as well as reconnaissance and spotting duties. Three hundred examples were ordered 'off the drawing board' in August 1939 and the first prototype flew in December 1940, but delays during testing slowed production. Fewer than 30 Mk Is were built before production

The Barracuda was often derided for its clumsy appearance, evident here, but it performed well in several difficult roles.

Fairey Barracuda II

Weight: 6396kg (14,100lb)
Dimensions: Length: 12.12m (39ft 9in), Wingspan: 14.99m (49ft 2in), Height: 4.62m (15ft 2in)
Powerplant: One 1220kW (1640hp) Rolls-Royce Merlin 32 V-12 liquid-cooled piston engine
Maximum speed: 390km/h (240mph)
Range: 1850km (1150 miles)
Ceiling: 4900m (16,000ft)
Crew: 3
Armament: Two 7.7mm (0.303in) Vickers K machine guns flexibly mounted in rear cockpit; one 735kg (1620lb) torpedo or four 205kg (450lb) depth charges or up to 660kg (1500lb) bombload

Opposite top:
This Barracuda II was one of 42 Barracudas that flew from HMS *Victorious* to dive-bomb and seriously damage the battleship *Tirpitz* in Kaafjord, Norway, during April 1944.

Above:
Photographed after the war, these Barracuda Mk IIIs were developed specifically for anti-submarine warfare.

switched to the much improved Mk II and this became the first variant to enter service in January 1943. The Barracuda's first combat operations came in early 1944, with mixed torpedo- and bomb-armed flights striking shipping along the Norwegian coast. By the end of May, they had sunk 14 ships and damaged 18. During Operation Tungsten, four Barracuda squadrons attacked the German battleship *Tirpitz*, inflicting heavy damage. However, the majority of the Barracuda's operational career took place in the Far East, beginning with the successful strikes on refineries in Sabang, Sumatra. Unfortunately, the high local temperatures degraded the Barracuda's performance, with combat range being reduced by as much as 30 per cent and the decision was taken to re-equip squadrons in the Pacific with the Grumman Avenger. This process was ongoing at the end of the conflict and the final Barracuda combat sorties took place on 1 September (after the surrender), attacking Japanese shipping that defied the ceasefire.

Efforts to optimize the Barracuda for anti-submarine warfare resulted in the Mk.III, which mounted an ASV III radar in a semi-retractable blister under the rear fuselage. A more thorough redesign was undertaken to deal with the Barracuda's acknowledged lack of power when a Mk.II was fitted with a Rolls-Royce Griffon to become the prototype Mk.IV that first flew in November 1944.

Fairey Battle

Although a huge improvement over earlier aircraft, by 1940 the Battle was too slow, too lightly armed and insufficiently manoeuvrable to survive against modern fighters.

Even before its first flight, concerns about the Battle's performance were being raised, with Fairey proposing alternative designs for a twin-engined alternative before the design was finalized. Nonetheless, despite being an anachronism even before the outbreak of war, the Battle was produced in far larger numbers than its performance justified. First flown in March 1936, the Battle replaced the biplane Hawker

Photographed during the 'phoney war' period, these three Battles were part of 218 Squadron stationed in France in early 1940.

Fairey Battle I

Weight: 5307kg (11,700lb)
Dimensions: Length 12.93m (42ft 5in), Wingspan 16.45m (54ft), Height 4.57m (15ft)
Powerplant: One 770kW (1030hp) Rolls-Royce Merlin II liquid-cooled V-12 piston engine
Maximum speed: 406km/h (252mph)
Range: 1714km (1065 miles)
Ceiling: 7925m (26,000ft)
Crew: 2
Armament: One 7.7mm (0.303in) Browning machine gun fixed, forward firing in starboard wing and one 7.7mm (0.303in) Vickers K machine gun flexibly mounted in rear cockpit; up to 450kg (1000lb) bombload with optional wing racks for a further 220kg (500lb) externally

Opposite:
This aircraft was flown by Donald Garland of 12 Squadron on a mission to attack the bridge over the Albert Canal.

Above:
The same aircraft as in the foreground of the photo opposite, this aircraft was lost to ground fire on 12 May 1940 while attacking German columns near Bouillon, Belgium.

Below:
The Belgian Aeronautique Militaire took delivery of 16 Battles, most of which were destroyed in combat in May 1940. This example was based at Evere-Bruxelles.

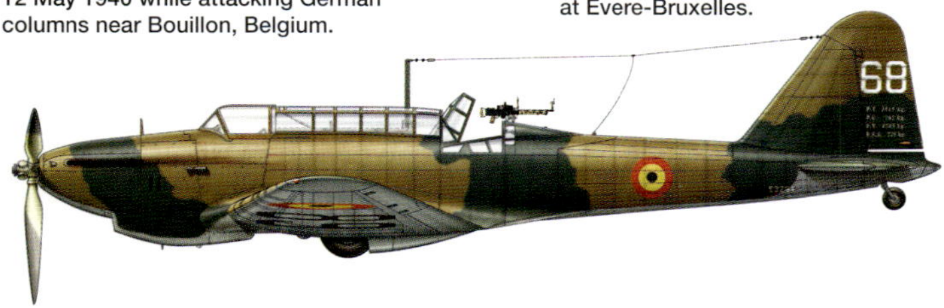

Hart in the light bomber role and it was, at least, significantly more capable than the earlier aircraft. It was also the first aircraft to enter service powered by the famous Rolls-Royce Merlin engine, but by the late 1930s it was clear that it was obsolescent. Despite this, the intense political pressure to expand the RAF saw large numbers constructed.

When war was declared, 18 squadrons were operating the Battle and by 1940 no fewer than 2201 had been built, many of which formed part of the Advanced Air Striking Force that moved to France during the 'phoney war' period. Although replacement by the Blenheim had begun by the German invasion, 110 Battles remained operational and were soon in the thick of the fighting. Losses went from severe – 13 of 36 attacking aircraft were lost in the Battle's first bombing operation – to catastrophic, 35 were lost from a force of 62 attacking pontoon bridges at Sedan, including 10 of the 11 aircraft of 218 squadron. As a result, the Battle was only used at night but its overly light bombload saw it soon replaced. The last operations flew against German invasion barges in October 1940. The Battle was used a little longer on reconnaissance and from Reykjavik as a convoy escort, before all were relegated to training, a role in which the aircraft excelled.

Fairey Swordfish

The Swordfish sank a greater tonnage of Axis shipping than any other Allied aircraft despite its obvious obsolescence and absurdly low speed.

First flown in April 1934, the Swordfish I entered service with 825 Squadron aboard HMS *Glorious* in July 1936, replacing the Fairey Seal and Blackburn Baffin. By the outbreak of war the Fleet Air Arm operated 13 squadrons. Early wartime operations brought several notable firsts: in April 1940 Swordfish carried out the war's first aerial torpedo attack, striking German destroyers off Trondheim, and later that

The Deck Landing Control Officer (DLCO) signals this rocket-armed Swordfish pilot to cut the engine and catch an arrestor wire.

Fairey Swordfish II

Weight: 4196kg (9251lb)
Dimensions: Length 11.12m (36ft 6in), Wingspan 13.92m (45ft 8in), Height 3.93m (12ft 11in)
Powerplant: One 560kW (750hp) Bristol Pegasus 30 9-cylinder air-cooled radial piston engine
Maximum speed: 224km/h (139mph)
Range: 1658km (1030 miles)
Ceiling: 3260m (10,695ft)
Crew: 3
Armament: One fixed forward firing 7.7mm (0.303in) Browning machine gun in nose, one 7.7mm (0.303in) Vickers K gun in rear cockpit; one 730kg (1670lb) torpedo, up to 700kg (1500lb) bombload or eight 27kg (60lb) rockets

Opposite top:
This Swordfish of 810 Naval Air Squadron, operating from HMS *Ark Royal*, was one of the aircraft that attacked and disabled the battleship *Bismarck* on 26 May 1941.

Above and right:
Seen from above, the Swordfish's three-seat configuration becomes apparent with a space for the observer and the gunner's position at the rear. The middle seat was frequently swapped for a long-range fuel tank.

month a floatplane from HMS *Warspite* sank the submarine U-64, the first U-boat destroyed by a naval aircraft.

The Swordfish reached the height of its fame during the Taranto raid of November 1940, when 21 aircraft crippled half of Italy's Mediterranean fleet in harbour. However, the Swordfish's most famous action occurred in May 1941, when aircraft from HMS *Ark Royal* attacked the German battleship *Bismarck*, crippling her rudder and rendering her unable to escape her pursuers, which ultimately led to her sinking.

The Mk II entered service in November 1941, but by then the Swordfish was too vulnerable to contemporary fighters. Its excellent short take-off performance made it ideal for escort carriers in the anti-submarine role, often equipped with rockets and ASV radar; the first U-boat destroyed by rocket-armed Swordfish was sunk in May 1943. The aircraft remained in service until VE Day, outliving its intended replacement, the Albacore, and earned the nickname 'Stringbag' for its ability to carry almost anything.

Handley Page Halifax

The second of the RAF's four-engined 'heavies' to enter service, the Halifax overcame its disappointing initial performance to become a highly effective and versatile aircraft.

Designed to the same specification as the Manchester, the Halifax was originally intended to use the same pair of Vulture engines as the Avro aircraft. However, by mid-1937, the Air Ministry was concerned about the Vulture's problematic development, and advised Handley-Page to study alternative engine arrangements. A four Merlin configuration appeared so promising that the Ministry immediately altered

This Halifax C.VIII transport variant featured a ventral cargo pannier.

Handley Page Halifax III

Weight: 29,484kg (65,000lb)
Dimensions: Length 21.82m (71ft 7in), Wingspan 31.75m (104ft 2in), Height 6.32m (20ft 9in)
Powerplant: four 1204kW (1615hp) Bristol Hercules XVI 14-cylinder air-cooled radial piston engines
Maximum speed: 454km/h (282mph)
Range: 2990km (1860 miles)
Ceiling: 7300m (24,000ft)
Crew: 7
Armament: One 7.7mm (0.303in) Vickers K machine gun flexibly mounted in nose, four 7.7mm (0.303in) Browning machine guns flexibly mounted in both dorsal and rear turrets; up to 5900kg (13,000lb) bombload

Opposite:
A late war Halifax, this Mk III, O for Oscar, served with 640 Squadron based at RAF Leconfield in Yorkshire.

Above:
The two large aerial masts signify that this Halifax III was equipped with 'Airborne Cigar' radio jamming equipment to disrupt Luftwaffe ground-to-air radio transmissions. It was operated by 462 Squadron RAAF in early 1945.

Below:
A Merlin-powered Halifax II Series IA of 78 Squadron. This aircraft was based at Breighton, Yorkshire, in September 1943.

the contract and the prototype Halifax appeared in this form. It made its first flight in October 1939, entering service just over a year later. The first operational mission was a bombing raid on port installations at Le Havre in March 1941 and in July the aircraft was used on a daylight raid on the battleship *Scharnhorst* at La Pallice. Initial performance fell short of Handley Page's predictions due to higher-than-expected drag, prompting extensive efforts that ultimately succeeded in improving the aircraft's performance. The front turret was removed and replaced with a fairing and the dorsal turret was also removed. Later aircraft featured a more streamlined nose with perspex fairing featuring a gimbal-mounted nose gun. The performance issues were finally resolved by the adoption of the Bristol Hercules engine in the Mk III and later aircraft boasted a performance equal to the Lancaster. However, the roominess of the Halifax's fuselage made it more amenable to other tasks beyond strategic bombing. Many aircraft served as long-range maritime patrol aircraft in Coastal Command, regularly undertaking missions of 13 hours or longer. The Halifax was also used as a glider tug, paratroop transport and freighter.

Handley Page Hampden

A highly distinctive design, with its slender, tadpole-shaped fuselage, the Hampden was noted for excellent handling but lacked the versatility and payload of the contemporary Wellington.

The Hampden had first flown in June 1936 and its impressive performance and manoeuvrability led to it being described as a 'fighting bomber' with the pilot provided with a fixed forward-firing gun. When it entered service in September 1938, the extremely narrow and slab-sided fuselage earned it the nickname of the 'Flying Suitcase'. However, the limited width of the aircraft would later prove a severe

The distinctive profile of the Hampden in flight. The aircraft handled beautifully but proved highly vulnerable to enemy fighters.

Handley Page Hampden

Weight: 10,206kg (22,500lb)
Dimensions: Length 16.33m (53ft 7in), Wingspan 21.08m (69ft 2in), Height 4.55m (14ft 11in)
Powerplant: Two 750kW (1000hp) Bristol Pegasus XVIII 9-cylinder air-cooled piston engines
Maximum speed: 398km/h (247mph)
Range: 2770km (1720 miles)
Ceiling: 5800m (19,000ft)
Crew: 4
Armament: One 7.7mm (0.303in) Browning machine gun fixed, forward firing in nose, one 7.7mm (0.303in) Vickers K machine gun mounted in nose, and one or two 7.7mm (0.303in) Vickers K machine gun in both dorsal and ventral positions; up to 1800kg (4000lb) bombload or one 728kg (1605lb) Mk XII torpedo

Opposite:
Based at RAF Leuchars in Scotland in late 1942 for daylight operations in the torpedo bombing role, this Hampden of 489 Squadron RNZAF wears an unusually light grey finish.

Below:
The Soviet Union also used the Hampden in the torpedo bombing role for a time. This TB I of the Northern Fleet Air Force was based at Vaenga, near Murmansk, in October 1942.

Below:
The yellow ring of the fuselage roundel has been painted over and unusual code letters have been applied to this Hampden I of 106 Squadron at Finningley, Yorkshire, in April 1940.

handicap in combat as it was near impossible for the crew to move between positions in flight. Any notion that the aircraft was a true 'fighting bomber' was quickly dispelled during the type's first wartime operations: a series of daytime reconnaissance missions in which the Hampden proved no match for contemporary Luftwaffe fighters, leading to the vast majority of its service being conducted at night. After a period carrying out leaflet raids and minelaying, the Hampden took part in the first bombing raid on German soil, attacking the seaplane base on the island of Sylt, in March 1940. Over the next two years the Hampden formed an important part of Bomber Command's nocturnal campaign against German targets, participating in operations including the first RAF raid on Berlin in August 1940 and Operation Millenium, the first 1000 bomber raid, on Cologne, in May 1942. From April 1942 the Hampden began undertaking a secondary role as a long-range torpedo bomber with Coastal Command, continuing to serve in this capacity until the end of 1943. Twenty aircraft were flown in the same role by the Soviet Navy, using aircraft passed on to them by RAF units who operated from Vaenga in Russia during September 1942, covering convoys in the Arctic Sea. After its withdrawal from operations, the Hampden was employed as a trainer.

Short Stirling

The Short Stirling, the first of the RAF's four-engined 'heavies', was truly colossal and carried an unprecedented bombload, but its performance at high altitude was poor.

The specification that led to the construction of the Stirling was unusually demanding: it called for a four-engined aircraft capable of carrying a 14,000lb (6400kg) bombload for 2000 miles (3220km) at 230mph (370km/h), but with a wingspan less than 100ft (30.5m). The latter requirement was added to restrict the size of modern aircraft, which was then seen as growing excessively. Unusually,

Photographed at Waterbeach, Cambridgeshire, the crew of this Stirling of 1651 Heavy Conversion Unit receives a last-minute briefing. Note the distinctive twin tailwheels.

Short Stirling I

Weight: 31,751kg (70,000lb)
Dimensions: Length 26.59m (87ft 3in), Wingspan 30.2m (99ft 1in), Height 6.93m (22ft 9in)
Powerplant: Four 1100kW (1500hp) Bristol Hercules XI 14-cylinder air-cooled radial piston engines
Maximum speed: 454km/h (282mph)
Range: 3750km (2330 miles)
Ceiling: 5000m (16,500ft)
Crew: 7
Armament: Two 7.7mm (0.303in) Browning machine guns flexibly mounted in both nose and dorsal turrets and four 7.7mm (0.303in) Browning machine guns flexibly mounted in tail turret; up to 6400kg (14,000lb) bombload

Opposite:
No. 620 Squadron flew the Stirling from its formation in June 1943 to VE day and beyond. Initially a bombing unit, it switched to glider tugging and paratroop transport duties by the end of that year.

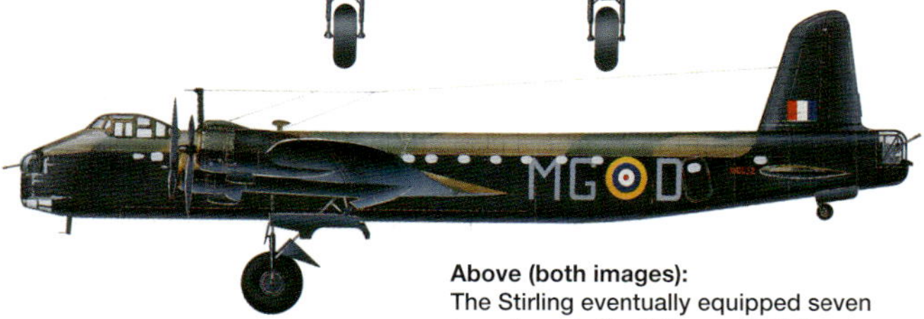

Above (both images):
The Stirling eventually equipped seven squadrons in No. 3 Group, RAF Bomber Command. No. 7 Sqn was the first of these to receive Stirling Mk Is in August 1940.

the design was tested on a half-scale piloted model, which demonstrated excellent handling. Its take-off run was considered overlong, however, and the full-size prototype was fitted with a taller undercarriage to increase the wing's angle of incidence. This proved immediately problematic when the prototype's undercarriage collapsed on landing after its first flight in May 1939 and had to be strengthened for production examples.

The first production aircraft was delivered in August 1940, and its first mission took place in February 1941, attacking fuel storage facilities in the Netherlands. Pilots found that the immense bomber was surprisingly manoeuvrable, proving able to outturn both the Ju 88 and Bf 110. The bombload was in a class of its own for early 1941 but unfortunately the design of the bomb bay, with structural members running fore and aft, prevented the aircraft from carrying any bomb bigger than a 2000 pounder (1814kg). Most serious, however, was the short wingspan, which limited the Stirling's ceiling to 5000m (16,500ft), placing it within range of accurate anti-aircraft fire. As the Halifax and Lancaster became available in larger numbers, both of which could carry a wider range of munitions and had better performance, the Stirling was gradually withdrawn from bombing operations. By 1944 it was operating as a minelayer, glider tug and transport.

Vickers Vildebeest and Vincent

The last biplane bomber to see service with the RAF, the Vildebeest and its Vincent derivative were obsolete at the start of the war, but saw intense action in Malaya and East Africa.

Vickers had flown the prototype Vildebeest torpedo bomber as early as April 1928, making it one of the oldest designs to undertake significant combat service in World War II. Early aircraft used the Bristol Jupiter engine, but the Mk III, delivered to the RAF from 1935, switched to the more powerful Pegasus and added a dedicated navigator/bomb-aimer as a third crew member. Meanwhile,

This Vildebeest Mk IV features a more powerful Bristol Perseus engine replacing the Pegasus, along with a streamlined cowling.

Vickers Vildebeest III

Weight: 3856kg (8500lb)
Dimensions: Length 11.18m (36ft 8in), Wingspan 14.94m (49ft), Height 4.47m (14ft in)
Powerplant: One 474kW (635hp) Bristol Pegasus II nine-cylinder air-cooled radial piston engine
Maximum speed: 230km/h (143mph)
Range: 2010km (1250 miles)
Ceiling: 5800m (19,000ft)
Crew: 3
Armament: One 7.7mm (0.303in) Vickers machine gun, fixed firing forward in fuselage nose decking and one 7.7mm (0.303in) Lewis machine gun flexibly mounted in dorsal position; up to 500kg (1100lb) bombload or one 728kg (1605lb) Mk XII torpedo

Above:
The Vincent enjoyed a long career in New Zealand. This example was serving with No. 2 SFTS (Service Flying Training School) at Woodbourne on New Zealand's South Island in January 1941.

Opposite top:
This Vildebeest III was operated by 273 Squadron RAF based at China Bay in British Ceylon (modern-day Sri Lanka), which operated the aircraft until converting to the Fairey Fulmar fighter.

the Vincent, a derivative of the Vildebeest intended for bombing and general purpose duties, had entered service in Aden in 1934. The Vildebeest was also produced under licence in Spain and around 20 saw service on the Republican side during the Spanish Civil War.

Although both the Vildebeest and Vincent were operational in 1939, the Vildebeest was replaced in UK-based squadrons by the Bristol Beaufort during 1940. However, two Vildebeest squadrons based in Singapore were still awaiting their Beaufort replacements when the Japanese offensive began in December 1941 and they were plunged into action. The aircraft repeatedly attacked shipping and suffered heavy losses, even when provided with fighter escort, but inflicted significant damage on Japanese vessels, including claiming eight ships sunk on 31 January, by which time surviving Vildebeests had retreated to Java.

The last operational RAF Vildebeests, based in Ceylon (modern-day Sri Lanka), were withdrawn in March 1942. The type continued in service slightly longer in New Zealand, where it was used for maritime patrol before switching to training duties. The Vincent persisted longer in service; 84 examples remained on RAF strength in September 1939 and were kept busy bombing Italian positions in the East African campaign. In addition the type undertook coastal patrols, during the course of which one aircraft attacked the Italian submarine *Galileo Galilei*, and also bombed Iraqi targets during the brief Anglo-Iraqi War in 1941. Eventually withdrawn from frontline service in 1943, survivors were used in secondary roles until 1944.

Vickers Warwick

Intended to replace the Wellington, the Warwick was delayed by engine issues and, by the time it entered production, was already obsolete, seeing no operational use in its intended role.

The Warwick was developed to a 1934 Air Ministry specification for a twin-engined strategic bomber to complement the yet-to-fly Wellington, featuring larger engines for greater speed, range, and payload. Before construction began, the specification was revised to demand greater fuel capacity and payload, making it clear that the originally chosen Bristol Hercules engines would not provide

British Overseas Airways Corporation used 14 Warwick C Mk. Is to fly mail, freight and passengers, mainly between Bathurst (modern-day Banjul, Gambia) and Cairo, Egypt.

Vickers Warwick GR.V

Weight: 22,680kg (50,000lb)
Dimensions: Length 22.25m (73ft), Wingspan 29.48m (96ft 9in), Height 5.64m (18ft 6in)
Powerplant: Two 1879kW (2520hp) Bristol Centaurus VII 18-cylinder air-cooled radial piston engines
Maximum speed: 475km/h (295mph)
Range: 4911km (3052 miles)
Ceiling: 5790m (19,000ft)
Crew: 6
Armament: One 12.7mm (0.5in) Browning machine gun flexibly mounted in nose and both waist positions and four 7.7mm (0.303in) machine guns flexibly mounted in tail turret; up to 6917kg (15,250lb) bombload

Opposite:
Much of the Warwick's service use was in the transport role. The C Mk.III introduced the large ventral freight pannier seen here, considerably improving the aircraft's usefulness.

Above:
The GR Mk.V entered service a few months before the end of the war. This example was flown by 179 Squadron based at St Eval in Cornwall.

Right:
For the air-sea rescue role, the Warwick ASR carried an airborne lifeboat under the fuselage to be dropped by parachute. The lifeboat was equipped with an engine, sails, food and a radio.

sufficient power. The prototype Warwick eventually emerged in 1939 fitted with Rolls-Royce Vulture engines and made its first flight in August that year. The Avro Manchester had priority for the Vulture engine, although it was also clear by this time that the engine was running into serious difficulties and alternatives were sought. All production aircraft were eventually fitted with Bristol Centaurus or Pratt & Whitney Twin Wasps.

The first production Warwick B.Mk Is appeared in July 1942. Ultimately, 846 Warwicks were built, which performed valuable service in a variety of roles, not least from 1943 as air-sea rescue aircraft, carrying an airborne lifeboat, fitted with both sails and an engine, and provisioned with food and emergency equipment. This was mounted flush under the fuselage to be parachuted to the surface. Hundreds more served as transports, both for passengers and freight, and a dedicated long-range maritime patrol variant, the GR.V flew its first patrol in December 1944, serving until the end of the conflict.

Vickers Wellesley

A single-engined light bomber of unusual appearance, the Wellesley was coming to the end of its career at the start of war, though saw considerable action for the first two years of the conflict.

Although obscure today, the Wellesley gained considerable fame in 1938 when three examples, serving with the RAF Long-Range Development Unit, set off in formation from Ismailia, Egypt. One was forced to land at Koepang in the Dutch East Indies (modern-day Indonesia) but the other two pressed on to Darwin, Australia, a distance of 11,526km (7,162 miles) and a new world record.

The Wellesley's impressive span becomes apparent when viewed from above. This is the 14th production airframe.

Vickers Wellesley I

Weight: 5670kg (12,500lb)
Dimensions: Length 11.96m (39ft 3in), Wingspan 22.66m (74ft 4in), Height m (ft in)
Powerplant: One 690kW (925hp) Bristol Pegasus XX nine-cylinder air-cooled radial piston engine
Maximum speed: 367km/h (228mph)
Range: 1960km (1220 miles)
Ceiling: 7800m (25,500ft)
Crew: 3
Armament: One 7.7 mm (0.303in) Vickers machine gun fixed, forward firing in starboard wing and one 7.7mm (0.303in) Vickers K machine gun flexibly mounted in rear cockpit; up to 910kg (2000lb) bombload

Opposite top:
The Wellesley had disappeared from UK squadrons by the outbreak of war. This 76 Squadron example was based at Finningley in Yorkshire in April 1937.

Above:
Flying in Palestine just before the start of the war, these two Wellesleys were serving with 14 Squadron.

Nonetheless, the Wellesley was regarded as obsolete by September 1939 and although withdrawn from UK-based units it played an important role in East Africa. The aircraft itself was the first Vickers production aircraft to use the geodetic construction method, in which a fabric covering was stretched over an aluminium latticework spaceframe, resulting in a very light but immensely strong structure. It had been designed in response to an Air Ministry specification for a general purpose reconnaissance bomber along with a biplane design, which won the contract. Despite this, Vickers built the monoplane as a private venture and its performance proved so superior that the RAF ordered it into production. The first aircraft entered squadron service in early 1937. The Wellesley's combat career began the day after the 10 June 1940 declaration of war by Italy, with a raid on Asmara in Eritrea, following up by a devastatingly successful attack on the port of Massawa. The latter mission destroyed 10,000 tons of fuel oil, effectively delaying the planned Italian invasion of Sudan and buying time for reinforcements to arrive, thus turning the tide of the entire campaign. Subsequently used for maritime patrol, a Wellesley depth-charged the submarine U-559 in October 1942. The U-boat sunk after further attacks from destroyers but not before Enigma code books were recovered, allowing code breakers to decrypt 4-rotor Enigma messages for the first time.

Vickers Wellington

The Wellington, the principal British bomber of the conflict's first four years, was produced from the first day of war to the last and became the most-produced multi-engined British aircraft in history.

Affectionately known as 'Wimpey' by its crews, after the Popeye comic strip character 'J Wellington Wimpey', the Wellington was a crucial combat aircraft. First flown in June 1936 and originally intended, like the Hampden, as a day bomber, the Wellington was the best of the three medium bombers available to the RAF in 1939, combining adequate performance with a respectable payload. Production

This Wellington IA was in use with the CGS (Central Gunnery School) based at Sutton Bridge, Lincolnshire, in 1943.

Vickers Wellington IC

Weight: 12,927kg (28,500lb)
Dimensions: Length 19.69m (64ft 7in), Wingspan 26.26m (86ft 2in), Height 5.31m (17ft 5in)
Powerplant: Two 780kw (1050hp) Bristol Pegasus XVIII 9-cylinder air-cooled radial piston engines
Maximum speed: 378km/h (235mph)
Range: 4100km (2550 miles)
Ceiling: 5500m (18,000ft)
Crew: 5 or 6
Armament: Two 7.7mm (0.303in) Browning machine guns in both nose and tail turrets and one 7.7mm (0.303in) Browning machine guns flexibly mounted in each waist position; up to 1814kg (4000lb) bombload

Opposite:
Operated by the Polish manned 301 Squadron, this Wellington IC was shot down just after midnight on 4 July 1941 by night fighter ace Helmut Lent. Five of the six crew survived to become prisoners of war.

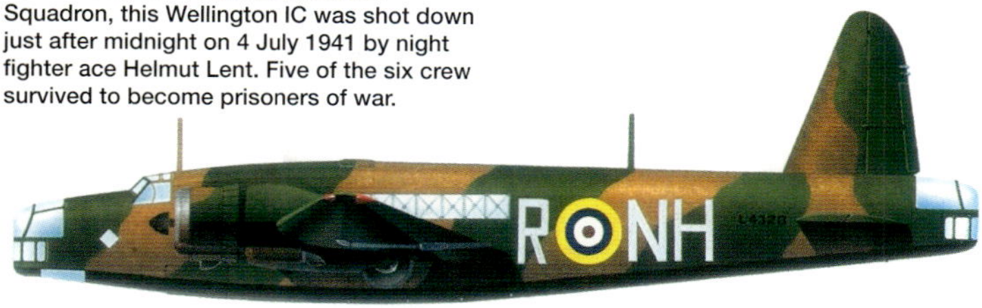

Above:
One of the first production aircraft, this Wellington I was based at RAF Marham in Norfolk when it was serving with 38 Squadron in mid-1938.

Below:
By April 1940, when this Wellington IA was on the strength of 37 Squadron at Feltwell, Norfolk, powered gun turrets had replaced the manual gun positions originally fitted.

increased until Vickers were building one Wellington daily by the end of the year, a tempo that grew as more factories joined the production effort. When production ceased in October 1945, a staggering 11,462 examples had been built. Eight squadrons were Wellington-equipped in September 1939 and the aircraft was soon in action, bombing enemy shipping within 24 hours of the declaration of war. Initial aircraft were powered by the Bristol Pegasus but in October 1940 deliveries began of the Rolls-Royce Merlin powered Mk.II, although the definitive engine would be the Bristol Hercules in the Mk.III onwards.

From 1940 to early 1943 the Wellington was the most numerous bomber in RAF service and bore the brunt of early operations as the bombing campaign developed. In the first 1000 bomber raid in May 1942, Wellingtons accounted for more than half of all the aircraft used, but the introduction of the four-engined 'heavies' saw the aircraft fly its last European bombing mission in October 1943. The Wellington remained an important bomber elsewhere and was used in the maritime patrol role, sinking at least 27 enemy submarines before the end of hostilities.

Boeing B-17 Flying Fortress

Probably the best-known bomber of World War II, the B-17 achieved lasting fame with the Eighth Air Force in England, although the Fortress served across the globe in various roles.

Designed to fulfill a USAAC specification for a 'multi-engine' bomber, the Boeing Model 299 represented a gamble for the then-struggling company but proved to be an astounding success. In July 1935 the aircraft was described as a '15-ton flying fortress' in the *Seattle Times* and Boeing swiftly trademarked the Flying Fortress name. A service test batch of 13 aircraft was ordered in 1936, leading

Early aircraft are known as 'shark fin' B-17s due to the shape of the vertical tail. This is a B-17C of which 38 were constructed.

Boeing B-17G Flying Fortress

Weight: 29,700kg (65,500lb)
Dimensions: Length: 22.66m (74ft 4in), Wingspan: 32.6m (103ft 9in), Height: 5.82m (19ft 1in)
Powerplant: Four 895kW (1200hp) Wright R-1820-97 Cyclone radial nine-cylinder air-cooled piston engines
Maximum speed: 462km/h (287mph)
Range: 3219km (2000 miles)
Ceiling: 10,850m (35,600ft)
Crew: 10
Armament: One 12.7mm (0.5in) M2 Browning machine gun, two 12.7mm (0.5in) M2 Browning machine guns in dorsal and ventral ball turrets and two in tail position; 7,983kg (17,600lb) bombload

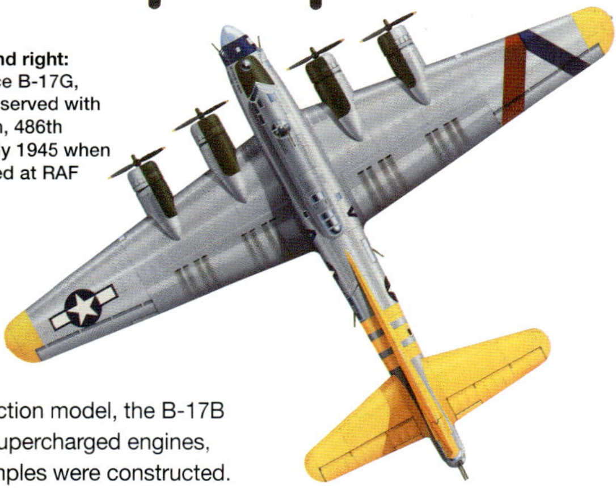

Opposite, above and right: This Eighth Air Force B-17G, named 'Short Arm' served with the 883rd Squadron, 486th Bomb Group in early 1945 when the group was based at RAF Sudbury, Suffolk.

to the first production model, the B-17B featuring turbo-supercharged engines, of which 39 examples were constructed. Growing political tensions overseas led to an order for more than 500 B-17s in July 1940. The B-17C featured more powerful engines and introduced a ventral gondola gun position and was the first variant to see combat use, with the RAF in July 1941. The first mass-produced model of the Flying Fortress was the B-17E, which introduced the distinctive large vertical tail surfaces, and was first used in combat in April 1942 to bomb Japanese positions in the Andaman islands. The B-17E also became the first USAAF Flying Fortress variant to arrive in Europe, which became the type's primary theatre.

On 17 August 1942, 12 B-17Es of the Eighth Air Force bombed marshalling yards at Rouen in France, kickstarting the daylight bombing campaign with which the B-17 would forever be associated. The B-17F was the first Fortress variant to strike Germany itself on 27 January 1943, when Wilhelmshaven and Emden were attacked. Raids on German targets at increasing distances and strength caused mounting losses, and although the B-17G added a chin turret for extra protection, significant reductions in losses only came with the introduction of long-range escort fighters. In total, 12,731 B-17s were built and by mid-1944 the despatch of 1000 Fortresses on a single raid had become relatively common.

Boeing B-29 Superfortress

The only aircraft to drop a nuclear weapon in combat, the B-29 was both the war's most expensive single arms programme and the most advanced bomber to see service.

In December 1939 the Air Corps issued a challenging specification for a so-called 'superbomber' that could deliver 9100kg (20,000lb) of bombs to a target more than 2500 miles (4023km) away at a speed of 400mph (640km/h). Boeing were already working on just such an aircraft, the Model 345, which was built as the prototype XB-29 and made its first flight on 21 September 1942. The advanced XB-29

B-29s release their bombloads during an attack on Mingaladon Air Field, Burma (modern-day Myanmar), on 28 February 1945.

Boeing B-29 Superfortress

Weight: 61,000kg (135,000lb)
Dimensions: Length: 30.18m (99ft), Wingspan: 43.05m (141ft 3in), Height: 8.46m (27ft 9in)
Powerplant: Four 1600kW (2200hp) Wright R-3350-23 Duplex-Cyclone 18-cylinder air-cooled radial piston engines
Maximum speed: 575km/h (357mph)
Range: 5230km (3250 miles)
Ceiling: 9710m (31,850ft)
Crew: 11
Armament: Two 12.7mm (0.5in) Browning M2/AN machine guns in each of four remotely controlled turrets, one 20mm (0.79in) M2 cannon and two 12.7mm (0.5in) Browning M2/AN machine guns in rear turret; up to 9071kg (20,000lb) bombload

Opposite top:
When the B-29 switched to nocturnal operations, the 444th Bomb Group adopted black undersides. This unit flew the longest bombing raid of the war, successfully attacking the George V dry dock in Singapore from bases in India.

Above:
Based on Saipan in 1945, this B-29 was assigned to the 500th Bomb Squadron, a component of the 73rd Bomb Wing. The 73rd was the first unit to operate from bases in the Mariana Islands.

adopted pressurization and remotely controlled defensive armament managed by an electromechanical computer system. It also featured an untried engine, the powerful Wright R-3350 Duplex-Cyclone, which became the design's most troublesome aspect when it entered service, regularly suffering from inflight fires. Production of such a complex machine proved difficult, but after delays the B-29's first mission was flown on 5 June 1944, when aircraft from Indian bases attacked the marshalling yard at Bangkok. Mainland Japan was bombed on 15 June, when 75 Superfortresses attacked the steelworks at Yawata from bases in China. Airbases on the captured Mariana Islands brought more targets within range and culminated in the fire bombing of Tokyo on the night of 9/10 March 1945, the single deadliest raid of the war. A quarter of the city was destroyed and 100,000 civilians were killed.

A radically new era in warfare began, however, when the B-29 'Enola Gay' dropped the first 'Little Boy' atomic weapon over Hiroshima on 6 August 1945. The bomb exploded 580m (1900ft) above the city, immediately killing 60–90,000 people. A second more powerful bomb, was dropped on Nagasaki three days later. Within a week, the Japanese surrender brought World War II to an end.

Consolidated B-24 Liberator

The B-24 was a more versatile machine than the more famous Flying Fortress, and more Liberators were built than any other US combat aircraft in history.

A later design than the B-17, the Liberator emerged after the Air Corps requested Consolidated build B-17s under licence. Consolidated felt they could produce a better aircraft, resulting in the XB-24. First flown in December 1939, the XB-24 immediately attracted export interest and orders were placed before the aircraft had even flown. France ordered 120 aircraft and the UK took 164. The

Photographed during testing in the USA, this is a factory fresh B-24J, the single most-produced Liberator variant.

Consolidated B-24J Liberator

Weight: 32,295kg (71,200lb)
Dimensions: Length: 20.47m (67ft 2in), Wingspan: 33.52m (110ft), Height: 5.48m (18ft)
Powerplant: Four 895kW (1200hp) Pratt & Whitney R-1830-35 Twin Wasp, R-1830-41 or R-1830-65 14-cylinder radial piston engines
Maximum speed: 483km/h (300mph)
Range: 2480km (1540 miles)
Ceiling: 8534m (28,000ft)
Crew: 10
Armament: Two 12.7mm (0.5in) Browning machine guns in nose, upper, ventral and tail turrets, one 12.7mm (0.5in) Browning machine gun in each waist position; maximum short-range bombload of 5806kg (12,800lb); normal offensive bombload of 2268kg (5000lb)

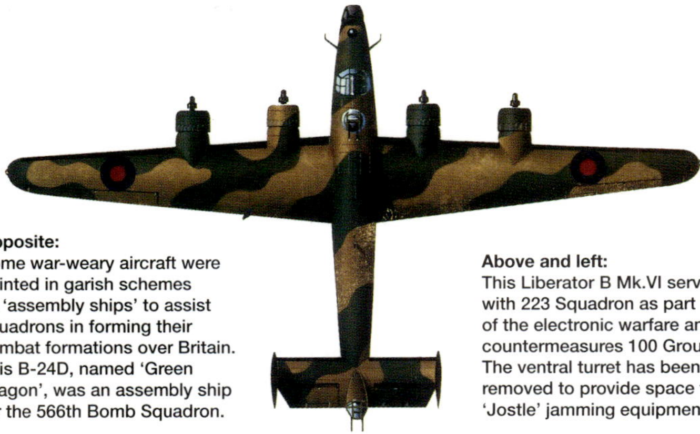

Opposite:
Some war-weary aircraft were painted in garish schemes as 'assembly ships' to assist squadrons in forming their combat formations over Britain. This B-24D, named 'Green Dragon', was an assembly ship for the 566th Bomb Squadron.

Above and left:
This Liberator B Mk.VI served with 223 Squadron as part of the electronic warfare and countermeasures 100 Group. The ventral turret has been removed to provide space for 'Jostle' jamming equipment.

latter became the first to use the Liberator operationally, utilizing its enormous range for maritime patrol over the Atlantic. Meanwhile, development continued and the B-24C introduced turbo-superchargers and a tail turret. The B-24D was the first to be built in serious numbers, becoming the first USAAF heavy bomber to attack Europe when around a dozen aircraft bombed Ploiești oil refinery in Romania on 12 June 1942. The first use of the B-24 by the Eighth Air Force began in October when B-24D and Es attacked Lille, France.

Initial B-24 losses were heavy, and the aircraft was generally not as popular with aircrew as the B-17 since it was less resilient to battle damage, possessed a lower ceiling, and was trickier to fly, especially at low speed. The problem of vulnerability to frontal attack was addressed in the B-24H, which adopted an Emerson electrically operated nose turret and the B-24J, which differed only in featuring a Consolidated hydraulically powered nose turret. By the end of the war, the B-24 was serving in vast numbers in Europe and the Far East as a heavy bomber, maritime patrol aircraft, transport, fuel-tanker, and even as an airliner. A total of 18,188 examples of this remarkable aircraft were built.

Consolidated B-32 Dominator

The B-32 was ordered as a backup to the B-29 but its development was plagued with delays. Consequently, the Dominator only entered service in small numbers in the last months of the war.

The USAAC requested Consolidated design a similar aircraft to the B-29 in June 1940, which was around two years after work had begun at Boeing on the Superfortress. Work proceeded swiftly and the Consolidated Model 33 took shape as a larger iteration of the highly successful B-24, featuring a similar high aspect ratio Davis wing and with twin tails but equipped with a larger, more streamlined fuselage. Both

The strikingly enormous vertical tail was adopted to deal with stability problems encountered by the twin-tailed prototype.

Consolidated B-32A Dominator

Weight: 55,905kg (123,250lb)
Dimensions: Length: 25.02m (82ft 1in), Wingspan: 41.15m (135ft), Height: 9.8m (32ft 2in)
Powerplant: Four 1600kW (2200hp) Wright R-3350-23A Duplex Cyclone eighteen-cylinder air-cooled radial piston engines

Maximum speed: 575km/h (375mph)
Range: 6100km (3800 miles)
Ceiling: 9400m (30,700ft)
Crew: 10
Armament: Two 12.7mm (0.5in) Browning M2 machine guns each in nose, tail, ventral and two dorsal turrets; up to 9072kg (20,000lb) bombload

Opposite top:
This aircraft 'Hobo Queen II' took part in the last known aerial combat of World War II, when it was attacked by Japanese fighters over Tokyo three days after the Japanese surrender.

Above:
The B-32 production line at Fort Worth, Texas, in June 1944. Although it suffered development issues and was always in the shadow of the B-29, the Dominator still performed impressively.

cabin pressurization and remotely controlled defensive armament were planned but neither was ready when the prototype XB-32 first flew on 7 September 1942. Remarkably, this was two weeks before the B-29 first took to the air. Unfortunately, the XB-32 quickly ran into serious problems. The pressurization system never functioned properly and was abandoned, and the remote gun turrets, sighted by a Sperry analogue computer, were subject to severe problems and replaced with conventional manned gun turrets. Stability problems saw the twin tails replaced by a huge single fin and rudder of a similar design to that fitted to the Privateer.

Serial production began slowly but by May 1945 sufficient numbers had been delivered for the first combat mission to take place in the Philippines. Several more bombing missions took place before the B-32s switched to photographic reconnaissance duties, a role it continued to perform beyond VJ-day as the Allies gained more information about Japanese mainland facilities in preparation for occupation. During one of these missions, a B-32 became involved in the last aerial combat of World War II, when on 18 August 1945 it was engaged by 17 Japanese fighters over Tokyo in the mistaken belief that it was going to bomb the city. Although no aircraft were lost on either side, one of the B-32's crew was fatally wounded and became the last US casualty of World War II.

Consolidated PB4Y-1 Liberator & PB4Y-2 Privateer

As well as being a key heavy bomber, the Liberator became the most successful anti-submarine aircraft of the war and was developed into a dedicated maritime patrol aircraft, the Privateer.

Just under a 1000 Liberators were supplied to the US Navy, which designated the aircraft the PB4Y-1 and followed its successful service as a maritime patrol aircraft with the RAF. The aircraft was primarily of interest to the Navy due to its prodigious range, which allowed it to close the so-called 'Mid-Atlantic Gap' beyond the range of aircraft flying from either the United Kingdom or the United States,

The Privateer was the first aircraft to carry the ASM-N-2 Bat guided missile in combat, shown here under the wings of this PB4Y-2.

Consolidated PB4Y-2 Privateer

Weight: 29,484kg (65,000lb)
Dimensions: Length 22.73m (74ft 7in), Wingspan 33.53m (110ft), Height 9.17m (30ft 1in)
Powerplant: Four 1010kW (1350hp) Pratt & Whitney R-1830-94 Twin Wasp 14-cylinder air-cooled radial piston engines
Maximum speed: 398km/h (247mph)
Range: 4230km (2630 miles)
Ceiling: 6400m (21,000ft)
Crew: 11
Armament: Two 12.7mm (0.5in) M2 Browning machine guns flexibly mounted in nose, tail and two dorsal turrets and two 12.7mm (0.5in) M2 Browning machine guns flexibly mounted in both waist blisters; up to 3600kg (8000lb) of bombs, depth charges, or torpedoes

Opposite top:
This PB4Y-1 was based in Devon, UK, during the winter of 1944, conducting long-range maritime patrols over the Atlantic.

Above:
The Privateer remained an important frontline type for several years. This example from Patrol Squadron 23 (VP-23) was photographed over Florida in July 1949.

where U-boats could operate with impunity. The PB4Y was a relatively minimal conversion from the B-24, featuring a spherical Erco turret in the nose and with the ventral ball turret removed to allow a retractable radar radome to be fitted in its place. The Liberator ultimately accounted for 93 U-boats sunk, some aongside other aircraft or surface vessels, more than any other aircraft type.

The success of the PB4Y-1 spurred the development of a more fully navalized variant, the PB4Y-2, instantly recognizable by its enormous single vertical tail replacing the Liberator's twin fins, and its significantly lengthened forward fuselage. The Privateer became operational during late 1944 and arrived in theatre only in early 1945, making the PB4Y-2's WWII service life relatively brief. By this stage of the war, advances in electronics meant that the Privateer possessed a versatile electronic suite that could be tailored to suit a variety of roles such as anti-shipping search and destroy, radar and radio-station hunter-killing, or even acting as their own standoff anti-radar jamming unit. The Privateer also made history by becoming the first aircraft to launch a fully automated guided missile in action, the ASM-N-2 'Bat' radar-guided glide bomb. Several ships were sunk with this revolutionary weapon and others put out of action, most notably the coastal defence ship *Akugi*.

Curtiss SB2C Helldiver

The Curtiss SB2C Helldiver faced long delays, a problematic introduction and a poor reputation among aircrew, but it eventually became a highly successful naval aircraft.

Intended as a replacement for the SBD Dauntless, the XSB2C first flew on 18 December 1940. Unfortunately, the aircraft possessed poor handling characteristics and a high stalling speed and it took nearly three years of modifications before the aircraft was put, prematurely, into service. The problems were mostly due to the fact that the SB2C's dimensions were dictated by the need for it to fit on an

This SB2C-5 from USS *Intrepid* overflies Tientsin, China, as the city is reoccupied by Allied forces in September 1945.

Curtiss SB2C-4

Weight: 7710kg (16,997lb)
Dimensions: Length: 11.18m (36ft 8in), Wingspan: 15.16m (49ft 9in), Height: 4.01m (13ft 2in)
Powerplant: One 1400kW (1900hp) Wright R-2600-20 Twin Cyclone 14-cylinder air-cooled radial piston engine
Maximum speed: 475km/h (295mph)
Range: 1875km (1165 miles)
Ceiling: 8900m (29,100ft)
Crew: 2
Armament: Two 20mm (0.79in) AN/M2 cannon in wings, two 7.62mm (0.3in) M1919 Browning machine guns in rear cockpit: 910kg (2000lb) bombload or one 910kg (2000lb) Mark XIII torpedo in internal bomb bay

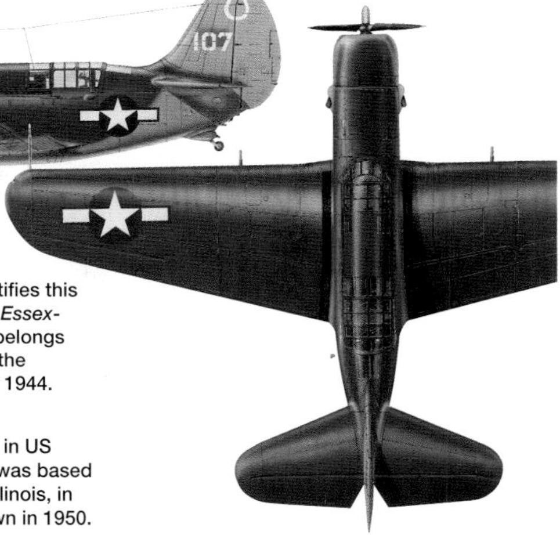

Above and right:
The horseshoe on the tail identifies this SB2C-3 as serving aboard the *Essex*-class carrier USS *Hancock*. It belongs to VB-3, which participated in the Battle of Leyte Gulf in October 1944.

Opposite top:
The SB2C did not survive long in US service postwar. This SB2C-5 was based at Glenview naval air station, Illinois, in 1948 but all would be withdrawn in 1950.

Essex-class carrier's deck lift. The aircraft was essentially too small for its weight and the prototype showed structural weaknesses, poor handling, directional instability and stall characteristics. These issues prompted the Navy to demand an unprecedented 880 design changes, delaying the appearance of the aircraft.

The initial SB2C-1 production version was built in limited numbers due to combat shortcomings, with most retained in the USA for training – though the SB2C-1C became the first version to see combat when VB-17 Helldivers from USS *Bunker Hill* attacked Rabaul on 11 November 1943.

The aircraft initially proved unpopular with crews who compared it to the SBD Dauntless it replaced, joking that SB2C stood for 'Son of a Bitch 2nd Class' and nicknamed the aircraft 'the Beast'. The SB2C-3 featured a more powerful R-2600-20 engine and four-bladed propeller, largely mitigating the handling issues and increasing the top speed and dive-bombing accuracy. By June 1944, squadrons on five carriers were equipped with the SB2C and in the same month it played a significant part in the Battle of the Philippine Sea, proving highly formidable. The SB2C-4, the most numerous Helldiver model produced, incorporated every improvement of the SB2C-3 and added eight zero-length rocket launchers under the wings to deal with increasingly shore-based targets. The final variant to see production, the SB2C-5, differed principally in possessing increased fuel capacity.

Douglas A-20 Boston

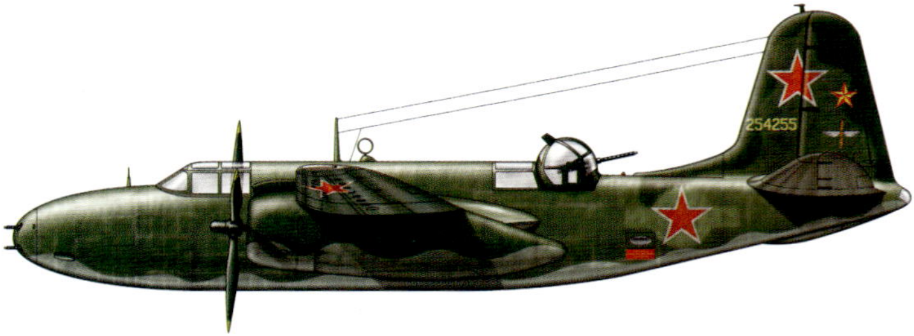

The fast and agile A-20 proved to be an outstanding attack bomber and saw widespread service with several nations.

Built at Douglas's own expense, the Model 7B first flew on 26 October 1938 and immediately demonstrated excellent handling and performance. The aircraft attracted the interest of France even before testing was complete and 100 production examples were ordered. The French stipulated many changes and the aircraft was redesignated the DB-7, with a few seeing combat just

This USAAF A-20G was photographed in the United States when it was serving as an advanced trainer.

Douglas A-20 Boston

Weight: 13,608kg (30,000lb)
Dimensions: Length 14.63m (48ft), Wingspan 18.69m (61ft 4in), Height 5.51m (18ft 1in)
Powerplant: Two 1194kW (1600hp) Wright R-2600-23 Twin Cyclone 14-cylinder air-cooled radial piston engines
Maximum speed: 523km/h (325mph)
Range: 1521km (945 miles)
Ceiling: 7200m (23,700ft)
Crew: 3
Armament: Six 12.7mm (0.5in) Browning M2 machine guns in nose, two 12.7mm (0.5in) Browning M2 machine guns in dorsal turret, one 12.7mm (0.5in) Browning M2 machine gun, flexibly in ventral position mounted behind bomb bay: up to 900kg (2000lb) of bombload

Right:
In an unusual field-applied camouflage scheme, this was one of the relatively few A-20Bs to serve with the USAAF. It was used by the 47th BG at Mediouna, Morocco in December 1942.

Opposite:
The Soviet Union was the largest user of the A-20, receiving 3414 examples, and it proved highly popular with Soviet crews. This A-20G has been modified with a Soviet UTK-1 turret.

before the French surrender. The DB-7 order was taken over by the British: the aircraft was named 'Boston' when used as a bomber and 'Havoc' if adapted for the night fighter role. Meanwhile, the first production aircraft ordered by the Americans were built as the A-20. The first variant ordered in large numbers (999) was the A-20B, although as it was based on an earlier export production standard, the A-20B lacked self-sealing fuel tanks and carried little armour protection. Following experience in the Pacific with other, better protected A-20 variants, most A-20Bs were supplied to the USSR instead. The A-20C was intended as a standardized aircraft for use by both the USA and UK, which the RAF employed extensively as the Boston III. Many more were supplied to the Soviet Union where its ability to carry a torpedo was regularly employed for anti-shipping operations.

The A-20G, however, was built in larger numbers than any other subtype with 2850 constructed. It introduced a solid nose armed with four 20mm (0.79in) M2 cannon and two 12.7mm (0.5in) machine guns. Later production A-20Gs featured a powered dorsal turret and the majority were supplied to the USSR for use in low-level attacks against German targets, resulting in heavy losses to flak. USAAF A-20Gs were used in a similar fashion by the 9th Air Force in France and also suffered severe losses, The A-20J reintroduced a perspex bombardier nose and was intended to operate as a 'lead ship' for formations of solid-nose A-20s. Although in the process of withdrawal by the end of the war, many A-20s remained in frontline service as hostilities ended.

Douglas A-26 Invader

Representing a technological leap in this class of aircraft, the A-26 entered service only late in the war but proved highly effective. It remained in frontline USAF service until 1972.

The A-26 took shape as a larger and more powerful replacement for the highly successful A-20. First flown on 10 July 1942, flight testing revealed that the XA-26 possessed excellent performance and handling. Overall, testing went smoothly, although the sighting and control system for the dorsal and ventral remotely operated turrets – both managed by the same crewman – was difficult to develop,

A formation of A-26Bs heads to the target in the Pacific during 1945.

Douglas A-26B Invader

Weight: 15,876kg (35,000lb)
Dimensions: Length: 15.24m (50ft), Wingspan: 21.34m (70ft), Height: 5.64m (18ft 6in)
Powerplant: Two 1491kW (2000hp) Pratt & Whitney R-2800-71 Double Wasp 18-cylinder air-cooled radial piston engines
Maximum speed: 578 km/h (359mph)
Range: 4184km (2600 miles)
Ceiling: 8687m (28,500ft)
Crew: 3
Armament: Six or eight 12.7mm (0.5in) Browning M2 machine guns fixed forward in the nose; two 12.7mm (0.5in) in each remote dorsal and ventral turret; plus up to eight 12.7mm (0.5in) in four underwing pods or three 12.7mm (0.5in) in each wing; 1800kg (4000lb) in bomb bay plus 910kg (2000lb) on underwing hardpoints

Opposite:
Based at Beaumont-sur-Oise, north of Paris, in April 1945, this Ninth Air Force A-26 'Stinky' served with the 552nd BS in the 386th BG.

Above:
Douglas A-26 bombers dropping their munitions on an ammunition dump in Bonn, Germany.

operate effectively, and later maintain in the field. The first production aircraft was delivered to the USAAF in September 1943 and a batch of early A-26s was sent to the South West Pacific for evaluation under combat conditions. All these aircraft were examples of the initial A-26B variant, the first to enter production. The first mission flew on 23 June 1944 when four aircraft bombed Japanese positions in the Netherlands East Indies (modern-day Indonesia). The A-26B proved unpopular in the Pacific due to the position of the engines obscuring the downward view and rendering it unsuitable for its intended ground-attack role. This led General George Kenney, commander of Far East AIr Forces to state: "We do not want the A-26 under any circumstances as a replacement for anything".

In Europe, the situation proved radically different after the first 18 evaluation aircraft arrived in the summer of 1944, flying their first mission on 6 September. In the course of eight test missions, no aircraft were lost and the Ninth Air Force undertook to replace both the A-20 and B-26 with the new aircraft. A-26s undertook bombing, strafing, tactical reconnaissance and night interdiction missions, proving highly effective. In marked contrast to the experience in the Pacific, the A-26 was well received by pilots and crew alike, and by VE-Day, A-26s had dropped 18,054 tons of bombs. The aircraft subsequently served in the Korean and Vietnam wars.

Douglas B-18 Bolo

Although rapidly superseded by more capable aircraft, the Douglas B-18 Bolo delivered reliable service in several roles, including as a tactical bomber and submarine hunter.

Derived from the DC-2 airliner, the B-18 beat the prototype Flying Fortress to be declared the winner in a 1935 competition to select a new bomber for the US Army Air Corps (largely due to its comparatively low price). Ordered into production as the B-18 'Bolo', named after a type of Filipino knife, the aircraft entered US service in early 1937. The first B-18s featured a gun turret mounted above the bombardier's

This immaculate USAAC B-10, belonging to the 23rd Bombardment Squadron, was engaged in exercises over Oahu, Hawaii, in 1941.

Douglas B-18 Bolo

Weight: 12,552kg (27,672lb)
Dimensions: Length: 17.62m (57ft 10in), Wingspan: 27.28m (89ft 6in), Height: 4.62m (15ft 2in)
Powerplant: Two 746kW (1000hp) Wright R-1820-53 Cyclone nine-cylinder air-cooled radial piston engines
Maximum speed: 346km/h (215mph)
Range: 3380km (2100 miles)
Ceiling: 7285m (23,900ft)
Crew: 6
Armament: One 7.62mm (0.3in) Browning machine gun flexibly mounted in nose, dorsal and ventral positions; up to 2948kg (4400lb) of bombs or depth charges

Opposite:
Martin B-10B of the 28th Bomb Squadron of the US Army Air Corps, based at Camp Nichols, Luzon (Philippines) between 1937 and 1941.

Above:
Resplendent in prewar Air Corps blue, this B-10 was one of a formation that flew from Washington DC to Alaska in 1934.

Right:
Two USAAC B-18 bombers overfly infantry during a road march in the Philippines on 24 July 1941.

position, but this turned out to be cramped and difficult to use, and therefore the final 217 aircraft were completed to B-18A standard with the turret mounted in the lower nose and the bombardier provided with an enlarged position in a distinctive pointed nose.

With war in Europe appearing increasingly likely, Douglas expected to sell large numbers of B-18s to export customers, but the Bolo's performance was simply too pedestrian to survive in the skies over Western Europe and the sole overseas order was for 20 examples, named 'Digby', for Canada. Many B-18s were destroyed on the ground during the Pearl Harbor attack and in the Philippines, where the aircraft saw considerable use as an armed transport but the aircraft was destined never to operate in its intended role as a strategic bomber. By mid-1942, the B-18 was being used primarily in the anti-submarine role, and accounted for three U-boats confirmed sunk, one by an RCAF Digby. An attempt to improve the Bolo resulted in the redesigned B-23 'Dragon' with much better performance than the B-18, but it could not compete with later designs such as the B-24 and B-25.

Douglas SBD Dauntless

Obsolete, slow and seemingly vulnerable, the SBD Dauntless nonetheless enjoyed a spectacularly successful career, arguably turning the tide of the Pacific war at Midway.

Derived from the underwhelming Northrop BT-1, the improved BT-2 became the SBD after Northrop was taken over by Douglas. Unlike its predecessor, the SBD (Scout Bomber Douglas) was easy to land on carriers and possessed excellent diving characteristics, though by contemporary standards it was slow – prompting crews to joke that SBD stood for 'Slow But Deadly.' The US Marine

Pictured in prewar markings, this SBD-2 is shown flying from USS *Enterprise* near Hawaii in October 1941.

Douglas SBD-5

Weight: 4853kg (10700lb)
Dimensions: Length 10.09m (33ft 1in), Wingspan 12.66m (41ft 6in), Height 4.14m (13ft 7in)
Powerplant: One 890kW (1200hp) Wright R-1820-60 Cyclone 9-cylinder air-cooled radial engine
Maximum speed: 410km/h (255mph)
Range: 1794km (1115 miles)
Ceiling: 7780m (25,530ft)
Crew: 2
Armament: Two 12.7mm (0.5in) M2 Browning machine guns fixed forward firing in cowling, two 7.62mm (0.30in) M1919 Browning machine guns flexibly mounted in rear cockpit; up to 1020kg (2250lb) bombload

Opposite:
This Marine Corps' SBD-5 of VMSB-231 was flown by the unit commander Major Elmer G. Glidden in February 1944, the same month that the squadron attacked the Japanese base at Truk.

Above:
The USAAF also operated the Dauntless, designating it the A-24 Banshee. This A-24B of the 312th BG (Dive) was based on Makin Island in December 1943.

Below:
Both the Armee de l'Air and the Aéronavale flew the Dauntless intensively against the last pockets of German resistance in western Europe. This is a naval SBD-5 of Flotille 4FB based at Cognac, France, in January 1945.

Corps received the first aircraft in late 1940, and by the end of 1941 SBDs were operating from the carriers USS *Enterprise* and USS *Lexington*. Although the newer SB2C Helldiver was already in development and the Dauntless was intended only as a stopgap, delays to its replacement kept the SBD in production and service far longer than expected. The externally similar SBD-4, introduced in late 1942, featured improvements to its electrical system and defensive armament, while the later SBD-5 mounted a more powerful R-1820-60 Cyclone engine.

By the time the SBD-5 appeared on carrier decks, the Dauntless had already played a decisive role in the Pacific War, helping destroy six Japanese carriers – three of them at the Battle of Midway, often regarded as the conflict's most decisive naval engagement. SBDs also took part in Operation Torch in North Africa and sank five ships at Bodø harbour in Norway during Operation Leader. The type's final major action came at the Battle of the Philippine Sea in June 1944.

Douglas TBD Devastator

The rapid pace of 1930s aviation development meant the TBD Devastator, among the world's most advanced carrier aircraft in 1937, had become dangerously vulnerable by 1942.

First flown in April 1935, the XTBD-1 was simultaneously the US Navy's first mass-produced carrier-based monoplane, its first all-metal aircraft and its first with a fully enclosed cockpit and hydraulically folding wings. Designed to perform torpedo and conventional bombing attacks, the aircraft was fitted with a Norden bombsight for level bombing, aimed through a window just behind the

Pictured during exercises in October 1941, this TBD has just released a Mark 13 torpedo. This weapon proved highly unreliable in actual combat.

Douglas TBD-1

Weight: 4624kg (10194lb)
Dimensions: Length: 10.67m (35ft), Wingspan: 15.24m (50ft), Height: 4.6m (15ft 1in)
Powerplant: One 670kW (900hp) Pratt & Whitney R-1830-64 Twin Wasp 14-cylinder air cooled radial engines
Maximum speed: 332km/h (206mph)
Range: 1152km (715 miles)
Ceiling: 5900m (19,500ft)
Crew: 3
Armament: One 7.62mm (0.30in) Browning M1919 machine gun in cowling, one 7.62mm (0.30in) Browning M1919 machine gun in rear cockpit; up to 453kg (1000lb) bombload or one 907kg (2000lb) Mk XIII torpedo

Opposite top:
Torpedo Squadron 6 (VT-6) operated TBDs from 1938 until just after the Battle of Midway in 1942. The colourful prewar markings were enhanced by the entire upper surface of the wing being painted bright yellow.

Above:
The same aircraft portrayed in the profile opposite, this TBD was photographed flying over the USA in 1938 when VT-6 was embarked on USS *Enterprise*. This aircraft was lost after it stalled on take off from the carrier in March 1939 and ditched in the sea.

engine cowling, and operated from a prone position. The XTBD-1 featured a semi-retractable undercarriage and, with its large wing area and flaps, had a low landing speed of 95km/h (59mph), making deck landings easy. It sailed through acceptance trials and only minor changes were specified for the production TBD-1, most notably a taller canopy allowing for the inclusion of a rollover bar. A total of 110 TBD-1s were ordered in early 1935, then the largest aircraft order placed by the US Navy during peacetime.

The first examples were delivered to frontline units in October 1937, beginning with VT-3 aboard USS *Saratoga*. By December 1941, the TBD was already slated for replacement by the Grumman TBF but none had been delivered by the time of Pearl Harbor. Initially the TBD proved effective, damaging the carrier *Shokaku* and sinking the carrier *Shoho* in concert with SBDs at the Battle of the Coral Sea. However, the June 1942 Battle of Midway exposed the vulnerability of the TBD and the unreliability of the Mark XIII torpedo. Of 41 aircraft committed, only six came back (and one of these was forced to ditch due to lack of fuel) and not a single torpedo struck its target. After Midway, remaining TBDs were quickly withdrawn in favour of TBFs and transferred to training units.

Grumman TBF Avenger

The versatile TBF Avenger was likely the best aircraft in its class, as well as being the heaviest single-engined aircraft to see service during the war.

By 1939 it was becoming increasingly clear that the Douglas TBD was already falling behind international standards and a replacement would be needed as a matter of urgency. Ordered in March 1940, the first of two prototype Grumman XBTF-1s flew for the first time on 7 August 1941. Broadly resembling a scaled-up F4F Wildcat, the XTBF utilized Grumman's patented sto-wing system, which effectively reduced the

The Avenger was an excellent deck-landing aircraft. This training TBF has landed on an unidentified escort carrier in mid-1943.

Grumman TBF-1 Avenger

Weight: 8115kg (17,895lb)
Dimensions: Length: 12.2m (40ft), Wingspan: 16.51m (54ft 2in), Height: 5m (16ft 5in)
Powerplant: One 1300kW (1700hp) Wright R-2600-8 Twin Cyclone 14-cylinder air-cooled radial piston engine
Maximum speed: 447km/h (278mph)
Range: 1456km (905 miles)
Ceiling: 6900m (22,600ft)
Crew: 3
Armament: One 7.62mm (0.3in) M1919 Browning machine gun in nose, one 12.7mm (0.5in) M2 Browning machine gun in rear turret, one 7.62mm (0.3in) M1919 Browning machine gun in ventral position; 907kg (2000lbs) bombload or one 907kg (2000lb) Mark XIII torpedo

Opposite:
The British initially named the TBF 'Tarpon' but swiftly adopted the American name. This aircraft was based at RNAS Donibristle, Scotland, in June 1944 and wears full D-day stripes.

Right and below:
New Zealand used the TBF as a land-based bomber; this example was flown by 31 Squadron RNZAF against Japanese positions during the Bougainville campaign in 1944.

size of this large aircraft for efficient storage aboard ship. It also featured a powered turret for defence, a first on a US carrier aircraft. The first TBF-1s rolled off the assembly line in January 1942.

The Avenger's combat debut was a disaster. Flying without fighter escort from Midway Island, five of the six Avengers were shot down and the sixth was badly damaged, but later combat proved more successful. Avengers sunk their first enemy ship, the battleship *Hiei* in November of 1942 and their wartime career culminated in the destruction, in partnership with the SB2C Helldiver dive bombers, of the Japanese super battleships *Musashi* and *Yamato* in October 1944 and August 1945 respectively. The TBF was also capable of operating from smaller escort carriers on convoy escort work and proved to be one of the most successful anti-submarine aircraft of the war, credited with sinking or assisting in sinking 39 U-boats and Japanese submarines. In addition to US use, nearly 1000 were supplied to both the Royal Navy, seeing considerable action in both the Atlantic and Pacific, and the RNZAF, flying in support of the Bougainville campaign in 1944.

Lockheed A-28/A-29 Hudson

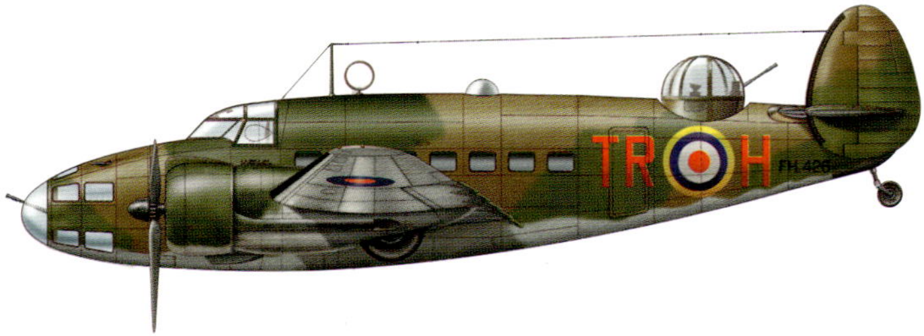

Although little used by US forces, the Hudson was operated in large numbers by the RAF and became the first US aircraft to sink a U-boat during World War II.

In late 1937, Lockheed sent details of its new Model 14 Super Electra airliner to the British Purchasing Commission, and it was seen as a useful supplement to the barely adequate Avro Anson in the maritime patrol role. Two hundred were ordered, entering British service in February 1939, and on 8 October 1939 a Hudson shot down a Dornier Do 18 flying boat over Jutland – the first enemy aircraft destroyed by a British-based

Pictured at a typically low level over the featureless ocean, the Hudson was a mainstay of Coastal Command during the first half of the war.

Lockheed A-29

Weight: 9662kg (21,300lb)
Dimensions: Length 13.51m (44ft 4in), Wingspan 19.96m (65ft 6in), Height 3.62m (10ft 11in)
Powerplant: Two 895kW (1200hp) Wright R-1820-87 Cyclone nine cylinder air-cooled radial piston engines
Maximum speed: 407km/h (253mph)
Range: 2490km (1550 miles)
Ceiling: 8077m (26,500ft)
Crew: 5
Armament: Two 7.7mm (0.303in) Browning machine guns fixed forward firing in the upper nose, two 7.7mm (0.303in) Browning machine guns in dorsal turret; up to 454kg (1000lb) bombload

Opposite:
This Hudson IIIA served with No. 59 Squadron in August 1942. It was severely damaged while conducting an anti-shipping patrol along the Dutch coast, but managed to return to base at North Coates with a large hole in the starboard wing.

Below:
233 Squadron Coastal Command operated Hudsons from 1939 to 1944, attacking U-boats, maritime and land targets, and shooting down an He 111 and an Fw 200 in 1941. This Mk III joined the squadron that year.

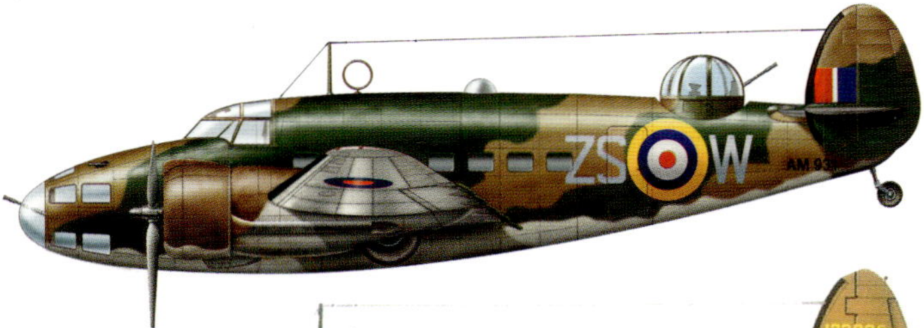

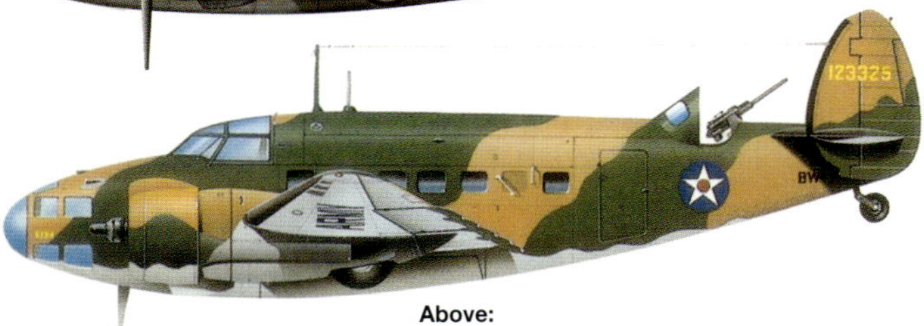

Above:
This USAAF A-29 was based at Portland, Oregon, for anti-submarine patrol duties in April 1942.

aircraft in the war. Subsequently, Hudsons played an important role as a maritime patrol aircraft in RAF Coastal Command and were credited with the sinking of 21 U-boats. In addition to their primary role Hudsons also performed reconnaissance flights over occupied Europe as well as clandestine operations in both Europe and Burma. The Hudson became the first aircraft to sink an enemy submarine by rocket attack and in August 1941 a Hudson bombed U-570 forcing it to surrender, the only instance of an enemy vessel surrendering to an Allied aircraft during the war.

After Pearl Harbor, Hudsons were requisitioned for US use as the A-28, or A-29 for those examples fitted with 890kW (1200hp) R-1830 engines. The first 20 A-29s were issued to the US Navy, which designated them the PBO-1 and used them, like the RAF, for maritime patrol. On 1 March 1942, a PBO-1 depth charged and sank U-656 off Cape Race, Newfoundland, the first German U-boat to be sunk by the US Navy. Hudsons would also be responsible for the first submarines to be sunk by both New Zealand and Brazil. In total, 2941 examples were built by the end of production in 1943.

Lockheed PV-1 Ventura

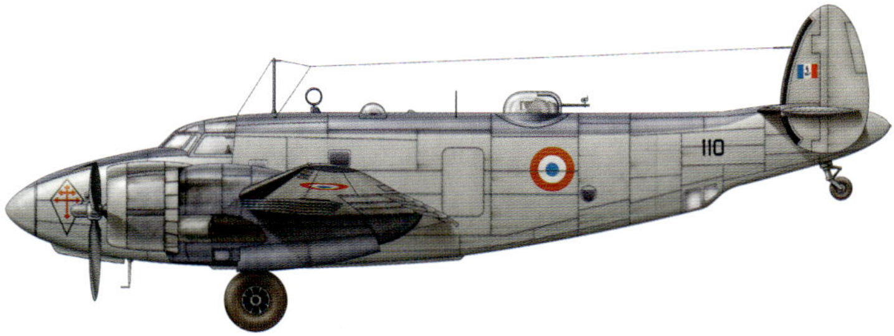

The Ventura proved to be a mediocre medium bomber, but enjoyed greater success as a maritime patrol aircraft, and, strangely, as a night fighter.

Following the great success of the Hudson, derived from the Super Electra airliner, Lockheed proposed a variant of its higher performance Model 18 Lodestar airliner for British use as a replacement for both the Hudson and the Bristol Blenheim. The proposal was met with enthusiasm and contracts were placed for 675 aircraft. Deliveries began in mid-1942 and Venturas were used for daylight raids over Europe

An early PV-1 is bombed up in the Aleutians in mid-1943. Note the national markings simply painted over the nose glazing.

Lockheed PV-1 Ventura

Weight: 14,096kg (31,077lb)
Dimensions: Length 15.8m (51ft 9in), Wingspan 20m (65ft 6in), Height 3.6m (11ft 10in)
Powerplant: Two 1,492kW (2,000hp) Pratt & Whitney R-2800-31 Double Wasp 18-cylinder air-cooled radial piston engines
Maximum speed: 502km/h (312mph)
Range: 2671km (1660 miles)
Ceiling: 8016m (26,300ft)
Crew: 6
Armament: Two 12.7mm (0.5in) Browning M2 MGs in nose, two 7.62mm (0.3in) Browning M1919 MGs flexibly mounted in nose, two 7.62mm (0.3in) Browning M1919 MGs in rear ventral position; two Browning M1919 MGs in dorsal turret; up to 1134kg (2,500lb) bombload

Opposite:
The Ventura proved popular with several nations. This example served with 6 Flotille d'Exploration (6FE) of the Forces navale françaises libres (Free French Navy) at Casablanca, Algeria, in 1944.

Above:
The PV-1 replaced PBO-1s in VB-135 in December 1942. This example operated over the Pacific in 1944. The much cleaner Martin turret helped boost the PV-1's maximum speed to 502km/h (312mph) at 4200m (13,800ft).

Below:
This Ventura Mk II of No. 21 Sqn operated from Methwold airfield, Norfolk, in late 1942. It took part in the large-scale daylight raid against the Philips factory at Eindhoven on 6 December 1942.

but they proved vulnerable without fighter escort, which was not then available. A particular low point occurred when 10 Venturas of 487 Squadron RNZAF attacked a power station in Amsterdam, and all were shot down.

Replaced by the considerably superior de Havilland Mosquito, the Ventura was transferred to patrol duties with Coastal Command, and Venturas ultimately sank seven U-boats. The USAAF received more than 200 Venturas and while a few were used for anti-submarine patrol, designated the B-34 Lexington, most were used for training. However, in 1942, as part of a deal to secure the Naval plant at Renton for B-29 production, the USAAF signed rights to the B-34 design to the US Navy, which subsequently emerged in navalized form as the PV-1 Ventura and entered service in February 1943. Navy Venturas flew medium bombing missions against Japanese targets and, as one of the first radar-equipped land-based naval aircraft, often acted as a lead ship for Liberator heavy bombers. In the absence of any other more suitable aircraft, the PV-1 also became the Marine Corps' first radar-equipped night fighter, scoring its first victory in the early hours of 13 November 1943.

Martin B-10, Model 139 & Model 166

Although incredibly advanced and hugely influential when it first flew, the Martin B-10 (also known as the Model 123) was nearing retirement when World War II began.

The private venture Martin Model 123 caused a sensation when it first flew in February 1932, because, at a time when virtually all military aircraft were biplanes, it was an all-metal monoplane featuring enclosed cockpits, a rotating gun turret, retractable landing gear and an internal bomb bay. Although historically important, the B-10 – designated Model 123 by the Army – was numerically insignificant compared to later bomber

This USAAC B-10 was engaged in exercises over Oahu, Hawaii, in 1941. The aircraft belonged to the 23rd Bombardment Squadron.

Martin B-10

Weight: 7439kg (16,400lb)
Dimensions: Length 13.6m (44ft 9in), Wingspan 21.5m (70ft 6in), Height 4.7m (15ft 5in)
Powerplant: Length 13.64m (44ft 9in), Wingspan 21.49m (70ft 6in), Height 4.7m (15ft 5in)
Maximum speed: 343km/h (213mph)
Range: 2000km (1240 miles)
Ceiling: 7400m (24,200ft)
Crew: 3
Armament: One 7.62mm (0.3in) Browning M1919 machine guns flexibly mounted in nose, ventral and dorsal positions; up to 1025kg (2260lb) of bombs

Opposite:
Martin B-10B of the 28th Bomb Squadron of the US Army Air Corps, based at Camp Nichols, Luzon (Philippines) between 1937 and 1941.

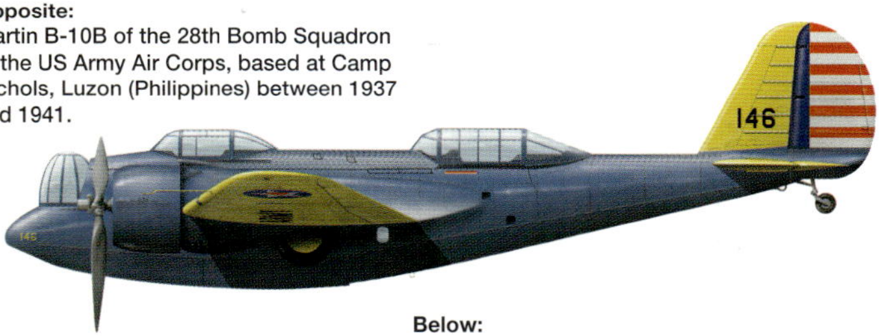

Above:
Resplendent in prewar Air Corps blue, this B-10 was one of a formation that flew from Washington DC to Alaska in 1934.

Below:
The B-10s of the 25th Bomb Squadron pictured in a lineup at France Field (now Enrique Adolfo Jiménez Airport) in the Panama Canal Zone in 1935. This unit converted to the B-18 Bolo in December 1939.

fleets, with just 166 built for US use and deliveries to Air Corps units starting in July 1935. The relentless pace of aviation development meant the B-10 was obsolete by 1939 and the last few in US hands were withdrawn during 1940. Martin was permitted to export the design during 1936 and orders were received from Argentina, Turkey, Siam (Thailand from 1939), China and the Netherlands.

The Martin bomber was employed in action by China, which used its Model 139WCs against the Japanese during the Second Sino-Japanese War from 1937 onwards, including the Taihoku airstrike, a daring unescorted leaflet raid in 1938, the first air raid to target mainland Japan. Thai aircraft were used in the brief Franco-Thai war to bomb Vichy French targets in December of 1940 and January 1941 but the Netherlands East Indies (NEI) was the biggest export customer. The NEI flew both the Model 139WH and improved Model 166, which featured uprated engines, a long 'greenhouse' canopy, and redesigned wings and both were used to combat the Japanese invasion in the NEI (modern-day Indonesia) itself and in Singapore.

Martin B-26 Marauder

The Marauder was an advanced design that overcame a problematic reputation to become the USAAF's most successful tactical bomber in Europe.

The Marauder was ordered 'off the drawing board' after Martin submitted its Model 179 design in response to the March 1939 USAAC Circular Proposal 39-640, calling for a twin-engined medium bomber with a maximum speed of 560km/h (350 mph), 4800km (3000 miles) range and a bombload of 910kg (2000lb). This was a challenging specification and the Martin design team responded with an advanced

The PN squadron code of these two B-26Bs identifies them as belonging to the 449th Bomb Squadron, 322nd Bomb Group in 1943.

Martin B-26B Marauder

Weight: 16,783kg (37,000lb) **Dimensions:** Length: 17.75m (58ft 3in), Wingspan: 21.64m (71ft), Height: 6.05m (19ft 10in) **Powerplant:** Two 1491kW (2000hp) Pratt & Whitney R-2800-43 Double Wasp air-cooled radial piston engines **Maximum speed:** 454km/h (282mph) **Range:** 1850km (1150 miles) **Ceiling:** 6614m (21,700ft)	**Crew:** 7 **Armament:** One 12.7mm (0.5in) Browning M2 machine gun in nose position, four 12.7mm (0.5in) Browning M2 machine gun in blisters, two 12.7mm (0.5in) Browning M2 machine guns in dorsal turret, two 12.7mm (0.5in) Browning M2 machine guns in tail turret, two 12.7mm (0.5in) Browning M2 machine gun in waist position; up to 1814kg (4000lb) bombload

Opposite:
'Baby Bumps II' was an invasion-striped B-26C of the 557th Bombardment Squadron, 387th BG. On D-Day, 6 June 1944, the 387th bombed defences at Utah beach before switching to enemy troop concentrations and strong points.

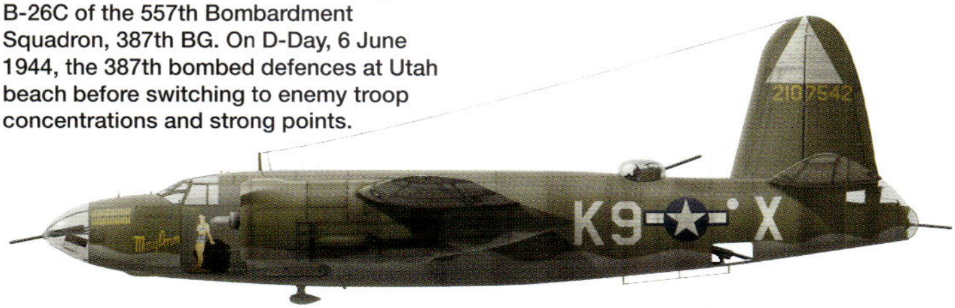

Above:
'Mary Ann' was a B-26C of the 494th BS, 344th BG, based at Stansted, Essex, in early 1944. Mary Ann eventually completed an impressive 111 missions and survived the war.

Below:
Several B-26s received shark's mouth decorations, one such was this B-26C of the 495th BS, 344th BG. In full invasion stripes for Operation Overlord, this aircraft bombed coastal batteries at Cherbourg in support of the D-day landings.

design featuring a tricycle undercarriage and notably small wing. No prototype was built and before the first production example was flown in November 1940, no fewer than 1131 B-26s were on order.

Service entry began in February 1941 and the first B-26 bombing mission was flown against the Japanese base at Rabaul on 5 April 1942. In operations Marauders usually flew unescorted and gave a good account of themselves against Japanese fighters, gaining a reputation for high speed and ruggedness. However, over Western Europe the B-26 had a disastrous combat debut, losing 10 of 11 aircraft committed to its first mission. A switch to medium-level operations proved successful, and the aircraft again gained a reputation for great accuracy as well as achieving an astonishingly low loss rate below 0.5 per cent, the lowest of any US bomber in Europe. However, while the B-26 was being successfully flown in combat overseas, it was gaining a sinister reputation in the USA due to its high accident rate during training. The problems were not caused by the aircraft itself but largely resulted from rushed training under wartime pressure.

Martin 167 Maryland

After losing out to the Douglas A-20 to supply a new light bomber for the Air Corps, Martin found a ready market for its high performance Model 167 overseas.

France was the first export customer for Martin's light bomber, ordering 200 Model 167Fs, although delivery was temporarily delayed by a US arms embargo. Officially designated the Glenn Martin 167 A-3 by the Armee de l Áir, the aircraft entered service in early 1940 and was therefore available during the German assault on France. Four squadrons equipped with the 'Glenn', as they were nicknamed by

A British Maryland shows off the type's distinctive fuselage profile. The aircraft was fast but cramped.

Martin 167 Maryland

Weight: 7624kg (16,809lb)
Dimensions: Length 14.2m (45ft 8in), Wingspan 18.7m (61ft 4in), Height 5m (16ft 3in)
Powerplant: Two 783kW (1050hp) Pratt & Whitney R-1830-S1C3-G Twin Wasp 14 cylinder air cooled radial piston engines
Maximum speed: 489km/h (304mph)
Range: 2100km (1300 miles)
Ceiling: 8991m (29,500ft)
Crew: 3
Armament: Four 7.7mm (0.303in) Browning Mk II machine guns fixed forward firing in outer wings, one 7.7mm (0.303in) Vickers K machine gun in dorsal and ventral positions; up to 907kg (2000lb) of bombs

Opposite:
This Free French Maryland was based in Aleppo, Syria, in 1944. French examples fought against the Germans in 1940, then as part of Vichy forces against British forces in Syria before rejoining the Allies.

Right:
Two French aircrew board their Martin 167A-3 in 1940. Against the Germans, the Martin bombers suffered a 4 per cent loss rate, which compared favourably to the 16 per cent loss rate suffered by the equally modern LeO 451.

Below:
This Maryland I was one of three such aircraft that formed No. 431 Flight on Malta in August 1940.

the French, proved effective as the aircraft possessed high speed and excellent manoeuvrability and losses were markedly lower than similar types. After the armistice, surviving French aircraft were transferred to North Africa, where some were used to bomb British Commonwealth forces, notably during the Syrian-Lebanon campaign of 1941.

The remaining 75 aircraft on the French order were transferred to the RAF, which named the aircraft Maryland Mk I, and re-engined it with Pratt & Whitney Twin Wasps. The Maryland was successful in service, prompting the British to order a further 150 Maryland Mk IIs. Most RAF Marylands saw action in North Africa and the Middle East, mainly in the photo reconnaissance role. A Maryland supplied detailed information on Italian ships in Taranto Harbour in a daring low-level reconnaissance flight in poor weather, contributing to the success of the Taranto raid by carrier-based aircraft in November 1940. In the hands of at least one pilot, the Maryland also proved surprisingly successful in aerial combat: reconnaissance pilot Adrian Warburton managing to score five confirmed victories in the type but by mid-1941 Martin had created the improved Model 187 Baltimore from the Maryland design and as a result only 450 Model 167s were built.

Martin 187 Baltimore

Derived from the Maryland, the Baltimore was an enlarged design that never saw service with the USAAF, although it saw sustained wartime use with other nations.

The overly cramped fuselage of the slender Martin 167 Maryland was the only serious problem with an aircraft that had otherwise proved highly effective in service, leading Martin to develop the Model 187 with a deeper fuselage and more powerful engines. Initially intended for French use, 400 were ordered for the Armee de l'Air but the aircraft appeared too late to see action with the French and the

From this angle the family resemblance to the slender Maryland is clear, but the Baltimore was a far more capable aircraft.

Martin 187 Baltimore

Weight: 23,001lb (10,433kg)
Dimensions: Length 14.8m (48ft 6in), Wingspan 18.7m (61ft 4in), Height 4.32m (14ft 2in)
Powerplant: Two 1268kW (1700hp) Wright GR-2600-A5B Twin Cyclone 14-cylinder air-cooled radial piston engines
Maximum speed: 488km/h (305mph)
Range: 1577km (980 miles)
Ceiling: 7315m (24,000ft)
Crew: 3
Armament: Four 12.7mm M2 Browning machine guns in wings, two or four 7.7mm (0.303in) Browning machine guns in dorsal turret, two 7.7mm (0.303in) Browning machine guns in ventral position; up to 910kg (2000lb) of bombs

Opposite top:
Named 'Redwing', this Baltimore V served with 13 Squadron RAF in Italy. The tally on the nose records that it had undertaken 80 missions, 66 by night.

Above:
Photographed on 14 June 1941, this factory-fresh Baltimore I would soon be delivered to the RAF.

order was taken on by the RAF, who named the aircraft Baltimore Mk I. The aircraft changed little over its production life and later variants differed from the Mk I only in terms of relatively minor improvements to its firepower and engines. Used exclusively in the Middle East, North Africa and the Mediterranean, the Baltimore represented a huge improvement over the Bristol Blenheim that was the RAF's predominant light bomber when the Baltimore began to arrive in combat units. The aircraft was praised for its heavy armament, strength, manoeuvrability, bombing accuracy and relatively high performance. Ironically, the only serious complaint, despite the enlarged fuselage, was that the aircraft was still seen as cramped. Committed to low-level attacks without fighter escort against advancing Axis forces in the Western Desert, losses were initially heavy. However, when operating at medium level the Baltimore enjoyed a low loss rate, with more aircraft lost to non-combat causes than enemy action.

Other users received Baltimores passed on from RAF stocks, notably the Free French and Italian Co-belligerent Air Force as well as Greece, Australia, South Africa and neutral Turkey. The Italians were particularly enthusiastic operators of the Martin bomber, naming one of their squadrons the 'Stormo Baltimore' in honour of the type. As well as bombing, the Baltimore was used, like the Maryland before it, as a reconnaissance aircraft, as well as a nocturnal intruder, target tug, (cramped) high speed transport and maritime patrol aircraft, credited with eight U-boats sunk during its career.

North American B-25 Mitchell

The B-25's place in military aviation history was assured by the 1942 Doolittle Raid, and the reliable, easy to fly Mitchell served many Allied nations.

The NA-62 was designed to replace the B-18 Bolo, and the Air Corps ordered 184 NA-62s 'off the drawing board' in September 1939 as the B-25. The first example flew in August 1940 and the first B-25 was accepted in February of 1941. Twenty-four B-25s were built before production moved to the B-25A, adding self-sealing fuel tanks and more crew armour, followed quickly by the B-25B with a dorsal turret. Few B-25Bs

The RAAF operated 50 B-35s. This natural metal example was photographed in flight over the outskirts of Brisbane, Australia.

North American B-25H Mitchell	
Weight: 15,876kg (35,000lb) **Dimensions:** Length: 15.49m (50ft 10in), Wingspan: 20.6m (67ft 7in), Height: 4.98m (16ft 4in) **Powerplant:** Two 1268 kw (1700hp) Wright R-2600- 13 Twin Cyclone 14-cylinder air-cooled radial piston engines **Maximum speed:** 441km/h (275mph) **Range:** 2173km (1350 miles) **Ceiling:** 7560m (24,800ft)	**Crew:** 5 **Armament:** One 75mm T13E1 cannon in nose, four 12.7mm (0.5in) Browning M2 machine guns in nose, four 12.7mm (0.5in) machine guns in blisters on starboard and port sides of aircraft, two 12.7mm (0.5in) Browning M2 machine guns in dorsal turret, two 12.7mm (0.5in) machine guns in waist position, two 12.7mm (0.5in) machine guns flexibly mounted in tail turret; up to 1450kg (3200lb) bombload

Opposite, right and below: Based at Catania, Sicily, in 1943, this B-25C served with the 487th BS, 340th BG. Note the RAF fin flashes, adopted as an identification aid, and the red surround to the national markings, which was officially used for only two months in mid-1943. The overhead view reveals evidence of battle damage, with patches liberally covering the elevator and starboard aileron.

saw combat in US hands but 16 aircraft were used to perform the Mitchell's first, and most famous mission: the Doolittle Raid, in which B-25s flew from the aircraft carrier USS *Hornet* on a one-way mission to bomb targets in Japan before flying on to land in China. The damage inflicted by the raid was insignificant, but as a propaganda exercise the mission was a huge success.

The more powerful B-25C and B-25D, identical except for being built in different factories, were the first of the truly mass-produced variants, with 1619 and 2290 made respectively. The B-25G, however, featured a new, shorter 'solid' nose armed with two 12.7mm (0.5in) Browning guns and a 75mm (3in) cannon, the largest calibre gun to be used by any operational aircraft during the war. Combat results with the B-25G proved the 75mm gun was a powerful and accurate weapon, but the weapon's rate of fire was slow, requiring a long straight approach to the target, and rendering the aircraft vulnerable to return fire. The final variant, the B-25J, of which 4318 were built, returned to a glazed nose design. The Mitchell was widely used with large numbers employed by the USA, UK and Soviet Union, and smaller numbers flown by France, the Netherlands, Australia and China during the war.

Vultee A-31 Vengeance

The Vengeance saw considerable action with Allied air forces in Burma (Myanmar), India and New Guinea and proved to be a highly accurate dive bomber.

Vultee developed its V-72 as a private venture to meet a specification issued by the French Armee de l'Air. France later ordered 300 examples of the aircraft but had surrendered before the order could be fulfilled. The UK ordered 200 V-72s in July 1940, naming it the 'Vengeance'. Flying for the first time on 30 March 1941, the V-72 was large for a single-engined aircraft and featured an unusual W-plan wing design. The

The Vengeance was noted for its pronounced nose-up attitude in flight, here demonstrated by an A-35B target tug.

Vultee Vengeance

Weight: 6486kg (14,300lb)
Dimensions: Length 12.12m (39ft 9in) Wingspan 14.63m (48ft), Height 4.67m (15ft 4in)
Powerplant: One 1193kW (1600hp) Wright R-2600- 19 Twin Cyclone 14-cylinder air-cooled radial piston engine
Maximum speed: 443km/h (275mph)
Range: 2253km (1400 miles)
Ceiling: 6860m (22,500ft)
Crew: 4
Armament: Four 7.62mm (0.3in) Browning machine guns fixed forward firing in wings, two 7.62mm (0.3in) Browning machine guns flexibly mounted in rear cockpit; up to 460kg of bombs in bomb bay, 220kg (500lb) bomb on wing racks

Opposite:
Free French forces briefly used the Vengeance in North Africa. This A-35B was used by Groupe de Bombardment I/32 in late 1943, based at Meknes, Morocco.

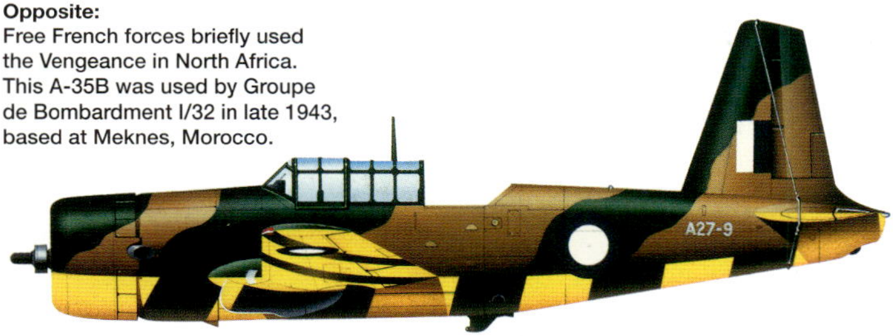

Above:
The striking black and yellow stripes denote this RAAF Vengeance I is in use as a target tug following the type's withdrawal from combat. Operating with No. 7 Operational Training Unit (OTU) in 1944, the Vengeances towed targets for training Liberator gunners.

Below:
This RAF Vengeance Mk III was serving with 1583 Calibration Flight at Chittagong, India, in 1944. Note the roundel with no red central dot, adopted in the Far East to avoid friendly fire incidents.

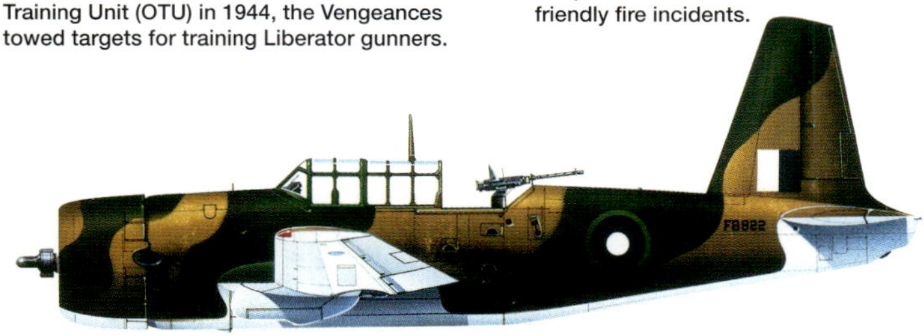

wing was also set at a neutral angle of incidence, optimized for performance in the dive but led to the aircraft assuming a pronounced nose-up attitude in level flight, restricting pilot view. After America entered the war, the USAAF commandeered 243 examples of the Vengeance and designated it the A-31.

By the time the Vengeance was available, the RAF had become disenchanted with the dive-bomber concept, primarily due to the vulnerability of this type of aircraft to enemy fighters. Units equipped with the Vengeance would not therefore be used in action in Europe or the Mediterranean but it was felt that the aircraft would be of use in the Far East, where fighter opposition was less intense. British and Indian squadrons flew the Vengeance against Japanese targets during heavy fighting on the India/Burma frontier in 1943 and 1944. Meanwhile, Australia used the Vengeance in New Guinea and against targets in the Netherlands East Indies (modern-day Indonesia), achieving considerable success before the aircraft was replaced by more versatile fighter bombers.

Axis

All of the Axis powers regarded bomber aircraft primarily as a tactical force to support their armies in the field. Although Germany spent considerable effort developing the He 177 heavy bomber, it was never built in large numbers. This did not prevent the Luftwaffe from attempting a strategic bombing campaign, using its fleets of medium bombers against British targets during the Blitz and later in the Soviet Union. Italy similarly targeted a campaign against Malta, while Japan bombed northern Australia. Japan was also the only Axis nation with operational aircraft carriers, and during the first two years of the war its carrier-based dive bombers and torpedo aircraft achieved notable success.

Opposite: A Dornier Do 17Z being prepared for a mission at Tiiksjärvi airfield in January 1942. Finland received 15 Dornier Do 17Zs in late 1941, using them for nocturnal bombing before relegating them to training; the last remained in service until 1952.

Letov Š.328

Seemingly anachronistic, the biplane S.328 proved highly versatile and was retained in frontline service as late as 1944.

Derived from the Š.28 of 1929, an improved version of which was built for Estonia as the Š.228, the Š.328 flew for the first time in February 1933. Originally commissioned by Finland, the Š.328 ultimately never served with that nation, although it performed sufficiently well that the Czech Army ordered the Š.328 for its own use as a reconnaissance bomber and the aircraft saw brief action in Czech hands

The Š.328 was widely used by Germany as a training aircraft. This Luftwaffe example was photographed at Markersdorf airfield in Austria.

Letov Š.328

Weight: 2640kg (5820lb)
Dimensions: Length 10.35m (34ft), Wingspan 13.7m (44ft 11in), Height 3.3m (10ft 11in)
Powerplant: One 430kW (580hp) Walter Pegasus II M2 nine-cylinder air-cooled radial piston engine
Maximum speed: 280km/h (174mph)
Range: 700km (435 miles)
Ceiling: 7200m (23,600ft)
Crew: 2
Armament: Two 7.92mm (0.31in) Ceska-Zbrojovka vz.30 machine guns fixed, forward firing in upper wing and two 7.92mm (0.31in) Ceska-Zbrojovka vz.30 machine guns flexibly mounted in rear cockpit; up to 500kg (1102lb) of bombs

Above:
Wearing the markings of the Slovak Resistance Air Force, this Š.328 operated against German forces as a reconnaissance bomber during the Slovak National Uprising of 1944.

Opposite top:
Bulgaria purchased 32 ex-Czech Air Force Š.328s and 30 new build examples in 1939. This aircraft was used on Black Sea coastal patrol duties during 1941 and 1942.

Above:
Most Luftwaffe Š.328s were finished in dark green but this light grey example, utilized as a trainer, was based at Olomouc-Holice airfield, Czechoslovakia in 1940.

against Hungarian forces in October 1938. When Czechoslovakia was occupied by Germany in 1939, production of the Š.328 was allowed to continue and the last examples rolled out in early 1940. The aircraft were divided between the Luftwaffe, which initially used the Š.328 primarily as a trainer, and the Slovak Air Force, which employed the aircraft in combat against Hungary in the week-long Slovak-Hungarian War before it was used as part of the Slovak contribution to the invasion of Poland, flying reconnaissance and ground-attack missions.

Slovak Š.328s subsequently participated in the invasion of the Soviet Union in 1941. German Š.328s were also used in action against the Soviet Union as tactical night-attack aircraft to harass ground units, following the highly successful example of Soviet Po-2s. Sixty-two Š.328s were also purchased from Germany by Bulgaria and were used for anti-submarine patrols over the Black Sea.

Arado Ar 234 Blitz

A revolutionary design, the Ar 234 was the first purpose-built jet-powered bomber to enter service. Although virtually immune from interception, very few saw operational use.

First flown in June 1943, the Ar 234 was an incredibly advanced design, combining the new technology of the jet engine with a pressurized cockpit for the pilot. As the only occupant of the aircraft, the pilot also had to act as bomb aimer and the bombsight was linked to the autopilot by a primitive computer system to aid in this task. In addition the pilot also acted as rear gunner, sighting two fixed rearward-firing cannon by a

Such a radical aircraft as the Ar 234 attracted considerable interest from its opponents. This example was photographed during testing in the United States.

Arado Ar 234B-2

Weight: 9800kg (21,605lb)
Dimensions: Length 12.64m (41ft 6in), Wingspan 14.41m (47ft 3in), Height 4.29m (14ft 1in)
Powerplant: Two 8.83kN (1990lbf) thrust Junkers Jumo 004B-1 turbojet engines

Maximum speed: 742km/h (461mph)
Range: 1556km (967 miles)
Ceiling: 10,000m (33,000ft)
Crew: 1
Armament: Up to 1500 kg (3309lb) bombload, carried externally

Opposite top:
Kampfgeschwader 76 (KG 76) began to convert to the Ar 234 in June 1944 and ultimately operated around a quarter of all Ar 234s built. This Ar 234B-2 was the first to fall into Allied hands when it crash-landed near Aachen in February 1945.

Above:
The Ar 234 had no bomb bay and carried its payload externally, including the 1000kg (2200lb) SC 1000 bomb fitted to this aircraft. This Ar 234B-2 was the personal aircraft of *Oberstleutnant* Robert Kowalewski, commander of KG 76.

periscope sight, although this system was found to be essentially useless and was deleted in nearly all production aircraft. To minimize weight, initial aircraft dispensed with landing gear and took off from a three-wheeled trolley, landing on retractable skids, although production Ar 234Bs featured a conventional tricycle undercarriage, greatly improving ground handling of the aircraft. The Ar 234 was also one of the first production aircraft to be fitted with an ejection seat.

The first operational use of the jet was as a reconnaissance platform in August 1944, utilizing prototype aircraft, and the speedy jet proved that it could penetrate British airspace with impunity, becoming the first German jet to appear over the UK. Bombing missions began in late 1944 with tactical attacks in support of the Ardennes Offensive, but the most famous operation was a series of attacks on the Ludendorff Bridge at Remagen across the Rhine during March 1945, which were ultimately successful but did little to stem the Allied advance.

Dornier Do 17

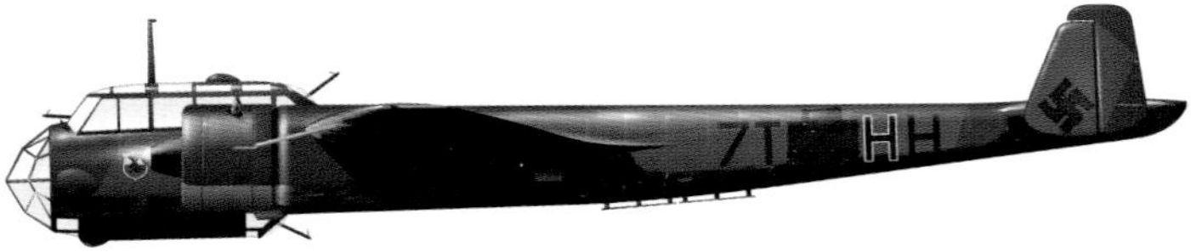

The slender Do 17, nicknamed the 'Flying Pencil', was a reliable and efficient medium bomber during the early war period and initially its high speed rendered it difficult to intercept.

Designed for Deutsche Luft Hansa as a fast six-passenger airliner and flown in 1934, the Do 17's fuselage was too cramped to be effective. Despite this, the military potential of the type was obvious and a modified prototype flew in mid-1935. Twin tails replaced the original single fin, a weapons bay was added, and although it was assumed the aircraft's speed would be sufficient defence against fighters,

Although from this angle virtually identical to the radial-powered Do 17, this is in fact one of the 102 examples of the Do 215 with Daimler Benz V-12 engines.

Dornier Do 17Z-2

Weight: 8837kg (19,482lb)
Dimensions: Length 15.8m (51ft 10in), Wingspan 18m (59ft 10in), Height 4.56m (15ft)
Powerplant: Two 746kW (1000hp) Bramo 323P 9-cylinder air-cooled radial piston engines
Maximum speed: 410km/h (255mph)
Range: 660km (410 miles)
Ceiling: 8200m (26,900ft)
Crew: 4
Armament: Six 7.92mm (0.312in) Rheinmetall MG 15 machine guns: one fixed firing forward through windscreen, the remainder on manual mounts in the lower nose, beam windows, dorsal position and rear ventral position; up to 1000kg (2205lb) bombload

Opposite:
Serving with 1./KüFlGr 606, this Do 17Z-5 was one of six that bombed industrial targets around Liverpool on 11 October 1940.

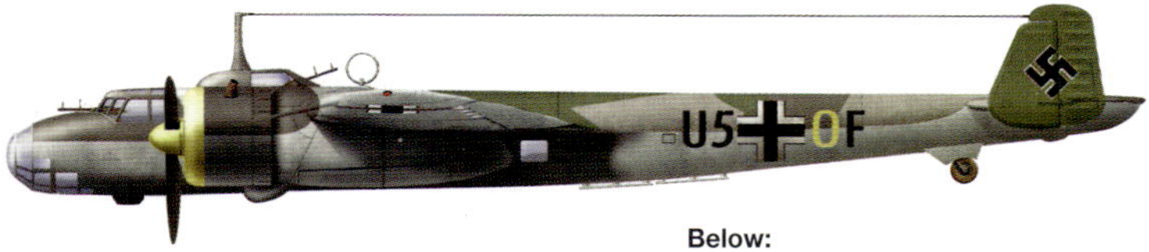

Above:
Operated by 6./Kampfgeschwader 2, this Do 17M-1 was involved in the campaign in Poland in September 1939.

Below:
Operating along the Polish Soviet border in the first half of 1941, this Do 215B-1 of 3./Aufklärungsgruppe Oberbehlshaber der Luftwaffe was used for clandestine reconnaissance of Soviet defences prior to the German invasion.

a single dorsal machine gun was fitted. The first production variant was the V-12 BMW VI-powered Do 17E, which had proved highly effective during the Spanish Civil War. By the start of World War II, production was underway of the definitive Do 17Z, the most numerous variant, which utilized a new, deeper cockpit area with more extensive glazing, incorporating a ventral position for a defensive rearward-firing gun operated by a prone gunner. A trainable gun was also provided in the lower nose firing forward. Initially powered by Bramo 323A-1 radial engines, the aircraft proved somewhat underpowered, but a switch to the 75kW (100hp) more powerful Bramo 323P led to a useful increase in performance and bombload, as well as allowing a fixed gun to be fitted, firing through the windscreen.

The aircraft was popular with crews as it was fast, rugged and manoeuvrable but during the Battle of Britain it proved vulnerable to modern fighters. An export variant, the Do 215, was also produced for Sweden. Delivery of this variant, featuring inline DB 601 engines, was embargoed and the 100 or so produced all served the Luftwaffe.

Dornier Do 217

Retaining only the basic layout of the Dornier Do 17, Dornier's larger and more powerful Do 217 proved formidable in a variety of roles, especially as a maritime bomber.

The first prototype of the Do 217 flew as early as August 1938, powered by DB 601 V-12 engines. However, the preferred engine was the radial BMW 801 and this powered the first major production variant, the Do 217E, which entered service in the reconnaissance role in late 1940. The standard E-1 could carry a 3000kg (6615lb) bombload, representing a colossal improvement over the 1000kg (2205lb)

Despite closely resembling its Do 17 predecessor, the Do 217, such as this Do 217E, was a far more effective machine.

Dornier Do 217E-4

Weight: 15,290kg (33,700lb)
Dimensions: Length 17.25m (56ft 6in), Wingspan 19m (62ft 4in), Height 4.8m (15ft 8in)
Powerplant: Two 1147kW (1539hp) BMW 801L 14-cylinder air-cooled radial piston engines
Maximum speed: 535km/h (332mph)
Range: 2400km (1400 miles)
Ceiling: 8200m (26,900ft)
Crew: 4
Armament: One 13mm (0.51in) MG 131 machine gun in dorsal turret, two 7.92mm MG 15 machine guns manually aimed in beam positions and one in extreme nose, one 15mm (0.59in) MG 151/15 cannon fixed firing forward in nose and one manually aimed from ventral position, up to 3000kg (6615lb) bombload

Opposite:
One of the aircraft used in the German attack on the Dieppe Raid in August 1942, this Do 217E-4 served with 9./Kampfgeschwader 2 based at Gilze-Rejen in the Netherlands.

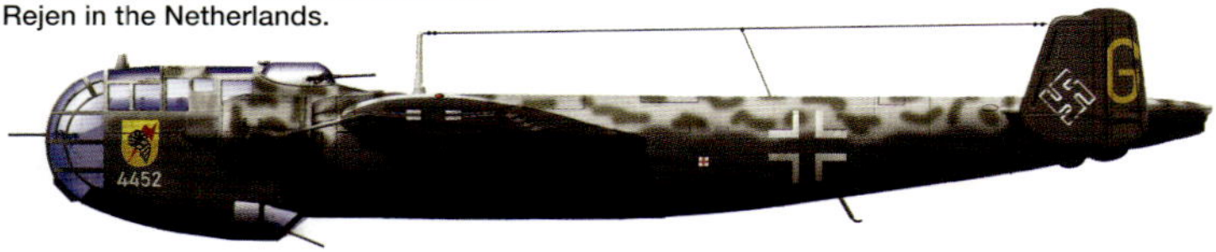

Above:
Based in France during 1943–44 for attacks against the United Kingdom, this Do 217K-1 'Yellow G' was on the strength of 3./KG 2.

Below:
Another KG 2 aircraft, this Do 217K was piloted by Major Walter Bradel, commander of the unit, and was based at Soesterburg in the Netherlands in mid-1943.

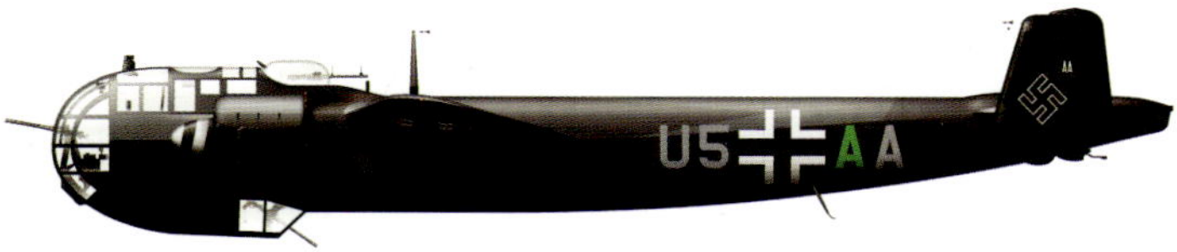

carried by the Do 17Z. It was also faster than the earlier aircraft and boasted an improved defensive armament. Bombing operations began in the spring of 1941 with the aircraft making its combat debut in anti-shipping missions against British vessels.

By late 1942, the Do 217K had entered service with its distinctive, extensively glazed, unstepped nose and, in K-2 and K-3 form, with provision to operate as a guided missile carrier, armed with two SD 1400X 'Fritz-X' guided bombs under the wings. This weapon yielded the type's most spectacular success when Do 217K-2s sank the Italian battleship *Roma* on 14 September 1943 as she was breaking out of La Spezia to join the Allies following Italy's capitulation. The Do 217M series was near-identical to the 217K but featured inline Daimler-Benz DB 603 engines in place of the BMW 801s. Before production of the Do 217 ceased in late 1943, Dornier had built three examples of the pressurized Do 217P for high altitude operations as well as the further-developed Do 317 bomber, intended to replace the Ju 88 and He 111. This design was rejected but the five examples constructed went into service, with pressurization equipment removed, as the Do 217R.

Focke-Wulf Fw 189 Uhu

Primarily a tactical reconnaissance aircraft, the Fw 189 was a tough and versatile aircraft, prompting its use in a variety of roles, including as a light bomber.

The twin-boom Fw 189 was a highly unconventional design by the standards of the late 1930s and its radical appearance initially drew a lukewarm reception from RLM (Reichsluftfahrtministerium) officials. The prototype's excellent performance could not be ignored, however, and resulted in the order of a small batch of production aircraft. Introduction of the Fw 189 into Luftwaffe service was

The twin-boom layout of the Fw 189 was radical for its era and provided an excellent view for its crew.

Focke-Wulf Fw 189 Uhu

Weight: 3950kg (8708lb)
Dimensions: Length 11.9m (39ft 1in), Wingspan 18.4m (60ft 4in), Height 3.1m (10ft 2in)
Powerplant: Two 342kW 459hp Argus As 410A-1 inverted V-12 air-cooled piston engines
Maximum speed: 344km/h (214mph)
Range: 940km (580 miles)
Ceiling: 7000m (23,000ft)
Crew: 3
Armament: Two 7.92 (0.31in) MG 17 machine guns fixed, forward firing in wing roots and one 7.92mm (0.31in) MG 15 machine gun flexibly mounted in dorsal and rear positions; up to 200kg (440lb) bombload

Opposite:
The majority of the Fw 189's service took place on the Eastern Front. This example was based at Dniepropetrovsk in Ukraine in 1943.

Above:
On the strength of Aufklärungsgruppe 32 (AufklGr. 32), this Fw 189 was based at Petsamo in Finland in the spring of 1943.

Below:
The liberal use of black in the finish of this Fw 189A-1 reflects its nocturnal role with Nachtkette/ NAGr.15 (Night Reconnaissance Group 15) in southern Poland during 1944.

slow and it was only by 1942 that meaningful numbers of the aircraft were available. The Fw 189 made its operational debut on the Eastern Front and although not particularly fast, the aircraft was highly manoeuvrable and could out-turn most Soviet fighters. It was well armed, especially in later production form, with two defensive machine guns in its dorsal turret and a further two in the tailcone supplementing the two fixed guns operated by the pilot. Despite its delicate appearance, the Fw 189 was a highly robust design with great structural strength.

These qualities saw the aircraft pressed into more offensive roles than had originally been intended and the Fw 189 was widely employed as a light bomber to attack partisan units with four 50kg (110lb) bombs mounted under the wings. The design initially envisioned interchangeable fuselage pods for different missions. The Fw 189C variant, featuring a heavily armoured but very cramped, fuselage pod, was flown but proved overweight and disappointing, and did not enter service. The Fw 189A-4 variant, however, retained the standard fuselage and introduced heavier armour as well as two 20mm (0.79in) cannon in the wing roots for the ground-attack role.

Focke-Wulf Fw 200 Condor

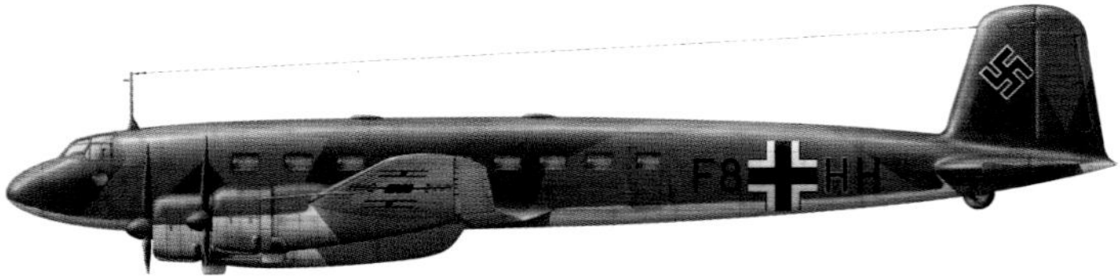

The Condor gained considerable notoriety as an anti-shipping aircraft during the Battle of the Atlantic.

The Fw 200 began life as a long-range airliner and the prototype became the first heavier-than-air aircraft to fly nonstop from Berlin to New York in August 1938; examples of the Fw 200A were operated by Deutsche Luft Hansa, Danish Airlines and Syndicato Condor in Brazil. The type's exceptional range prompted the Japanese Navy to order an example adapted for maritime patrol.

The second Fw 200C-1 to be built was rolled out from Focke Wulf's Bremen factory on a snowy January day in 1940.

Focke-Wulf Fw 200C-3

Weight: 22,714kg (50,067lb)
Dimensions: Length 23.45m (76ft 11in), Wingspan 32.85m (107ft 9in), Height 6.3m (20ft 8in)
Powerplant: Four 708kW (950hp) Bramo 323R-2 Fafnir nine-cylinder air-cooled radial piston engines
Maximum speed: 380km/h (240mph)
Range: 3560km (2210 miles)
Ceiling: 6000m (20,000ft)
Crew: 5
Armament: One 20mm (0.79in) MG 151 cannon in forward ventral position and one 7.92mm (0.31in) in rear ventral and two dorsal positions; up to 1000kg (2200lb) bombload in bomb bay or 5400kg (11,900lb) externally

Opposite:
The Condor served as both a transport and a patrol bomber. This example, formerly the Luft Hansa airliner D-AHMC, was later adopted by the Luftwaffe as a troop transport.

Above:
Based at Wesendorf, Germany, in 1943, by which time it was being used for training, this Fw 200C-3 has two ship silhouettes on the rudder signifying vessels sunk.

Although completed, it was never delivered due to the outbreak of war. Instead it formed the basis for the Luftwaffe's maritime variant, the Fw 200C, equipped with defensive armament and carrying a 1000kg (2200lb) bombload.

The Fw 200C patrolled the Atlantic searching for Allied convoys and reported their position to U-boats as well as directly attacking ships themselves. Initially highly successful, it sank 331,122 tonnes (365,000 tons) of shipping between June 1940 and February 1941, prompting Winston Churchill to call the aircraft 'the Scourge of the Atlantic'.

Later production examples featured ASV radar and were fitted with underwing racks to allow up to 5400kg (11,900lb) of bombs to be carried, including the Hs 293 guided glide bomb. However, a legacy of the Fw 200's civil origins was its comparatively weak structure: several examples broke their back on landing, leading to later aircraft receiving significant structural strengthening. The Condor was vulnerable to interception; for example, an Fw 200 became the first German aircraft shot down by US fighters during the war and Allied escort carriers soon greatly reduced its effectiveness.

Much of the aircraft's later career was as a transport aircraft, notably supplying the encircled Sixth Army at Stalingrad, as well as being used to parachute agents into enemy territory. It also served as a VIP transport for high-ranking Nazis, with Hitler's personal aircraft named *Immelmann III*. True to its airliner origins, a Condor flew the last scheduled Deutsche Luft Hansa service on 14 April 1945, flying from Barcelona to Berlin.

Heinkel He 111

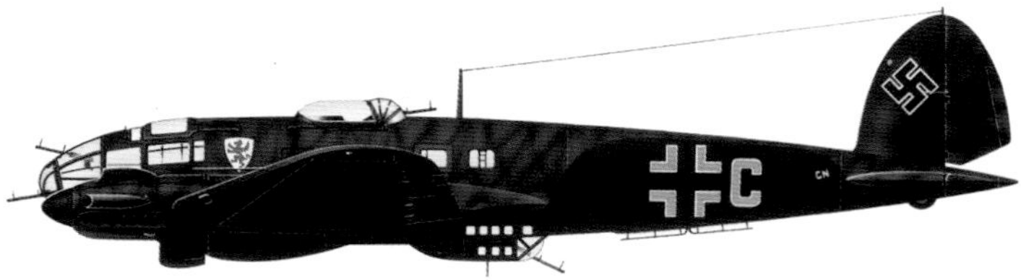

The distinctive He 111 became the iconic Luftwaffe bomber of the early war period. Despite increasing obsolescence, lack of an effective replacement saw it serve until the end of the conflict.

Developed simultaneously as an airliner and a bomber, the He 111 flew for the first time in February 1935 and demonstrated excellent performance and handling. When it entered service as an airliner with Deutsche Luft Hansa, the He 111 was touted as the fastest passenger aircraft in the world. The original cockpit with a conventional stepped windscreen lasted for a while, but was replaced in

Photographed over Rotherhithe, London, on the evening of 7 September 1940, this He 111 took part in the first raid of what became known as 'the Blitz'.

Heinkel He 111H-6

Weight: 14,000kg (30,865lb) **Dimensions:** Length 16.4m (53ft 9in), Wingspan 22.6m (74ft 2in), Height 3.4m (11ft 2in) **Powerplant:** Two 990kW (1320hp) Junkers Jumo 211F-1 liquid-cooled inverted V-12 piston engines **Maximum speed:** 436km/h (271mph)	**Range:** 2300km (1400 miles) **Ceiling:** 6500m (21,300ft) **Crew:** 5 **Armament:** One 7.92mm (0.31in) MG 15 or MG 81 machine guns flexibly mounted in nose, dorsal, ventral and two waist positions and one fixed, rearward firing in tailcone; up to 2000kg (4400lb) bombload in bomb bay

Opposite:
With large portions of the airframe painted black, this He 111P-2 of Kampfgeschwader 55, based at Villacoublay in France, was employed on the 'Night Blitz' of British targets in late 1940 and early 1941.

Right:
The distinctive broad and tapering wing shape of the He 111 inspired its German nickname of *der Spaten* (the Spade).

Below:
A much earlier aircraft, this He 111H-4 was on the strength of III./KG26 based at Stavanger, Norway.

the Daimler-Benz DB 601–powered He 111P and all later variants by a stepless, extensively glazed 'greenhouse' nose, giving the aircraft a highly distinctive appearance. The He 111H series was effectively identical to the He 111P but featured Junkers Jumo 211 engines in place of the DB 601s and became the most numerous variant, produced in a bewildering array of subvariants.

Initial operations in the Spanish Civil War were highly successful and the He 111 proved effective throughout World War II's early campaigns. However, in the Battle of Britain, the He 111's defensive armament proved inadequate and the type suffered heavy losses, leading to a switch to nocturnal operations in the West. With limited fighter opposition in the Balkans and early stages of the Soviet campaign, the He 111 operated extensively by day on both strategic and tactical bombing missions. By 1943, however, the faster Ju 88 and Do 217 had largely supplanted the older Heinkel, which continued to serve reliably in night bombing over the USSR.

Heinkel He 115

The He 115 was primarily used by the Luftwaffe for minelaying but achieved considerable success as a torpedo bomber against Allied convoys in the Arctic Ocean.

The He 115 flew for the first time in August 1937, having been ordered as a replacement for the biplane He 59. In March 1938, the prototype He 115 set a series of closed circuit floatplane speed records and deliveries to the Luftwaffe began in the same year. By 1939, production had shifted to the He 115B-1, featuring a fuel capacity increased by more than 50 per cent, while the B-2 had strengthened

A training torpedo is loaded into the weapons bay of an He 115B-1 of the Luftwaffe Lufttorpedoschule (Torpedo School).

Heinkel He 115B-1

Weight: 10,400kg (22,928lb)
Dimensions: Length 17.3m (56ft 9in), Wingspan 22.2m (73ft 1in), Height 6.6m (21ft 8in)
Powerplant: Two 710kW (950hp) BMW 132K nine-cylinder air-cooled radial engines
Maximum speed: 327km/h (203mph)
Range: 2100km (1300 miles)
Ceiling: 5200m (17,100ft)
Crew: 3
Armament: One 7.92mm (0.31in) MG 17 machine gun flexibly mounted in nose and one 7.92mm (0.31in) MG 15 flexibly mounted in dorsal position; up to 1000kg (2200lb) bombload

Above:
This cannon armed He 115C-1 served, like the aircraft opposite, with 1./KüFlGr 406. During 1942 it was involved in attacking British convoys in the Arctic Ocean transporting equipment to the Soviet Union.

Opposite:
The prominent steel skids under the floats reveal that this is an He 115B-2 strengthened for operations in snow and ice. This example was flown by 1./Küstenfliegergruppe (Coastal Flying Group) 406 in Norway.

Above:
Operating over the North Sea in 1940, this He 115A was on the strength of 1./KüFlGr 106 when it was based at Schellingwoude in the Netherlands.

floats, allowing the aircraft to operate from snow or ice when needed. By this time export He 115s had been supplied to Norway and Sweden. Norwegian He 115s saw action against German forces in early 1940 and four examples that escaped were subsequently flown in RAF service on clandestine missions. In the Luftwaffe, the He 115 saw extensive use delivering parachute mines, usually by night, in the approaches to British ports, including on the River Thames. Even more spectacular, however, was the He 115's role as a torpedo bomber, striking Allied convoys en route to Russian ports through the Arctic. The He 115C-4 was the dedicated torpedo variant, and aircraft based in Norway inflicted heavy losses on Allied shipping – most notably during Convoy PQ-17 in July 1942, when eight merchant ships were sunk by air attack out of a total of 23 lost. Improved air defences saw the He 115 withdrawn from this role, but the aircraft persisted in service as a minelayer and for reconnaissance.

Heinkel He 177 Greif

The He 177, the only heavy bomber to enter Luftwaffe service, was an impressive aircraft but plagued by a troubled development and a persistent reputation for engine fires.

Despite looking like a twin-engined aircraft, the He 177 actually featured two pairs of engines, each driving a single huge propeller. This configuration was chosen because the specification bizarrely required the aircraft to be capable of dive bombing. Using two propellers instead of four reduced drag and instability, improving dive performance and manoeuvrability. However, when the

This is the seventh prototype He 177, used for flight testing and later for crew training with KG40.

Heinkel He 177A-5/R-6

Weight: 31,000kg (68,300lb)
Dimensions: Length 22m (72ft 2in), Wingspan 31.44m (103ft 2in), Height 6.4m (21ft)
Powerplant: Two 2133kW (2860hp) Daimler-Benz DB 610 liquid-cooled 24-cylinder piston engines
Maximum speed: 565km/h (351mph)
Range: 1540km (960 miles)
Ceiling: 8000m (26,000ft)
Crew: 6
Armament: One 7.92mm (0.31in) MG 81 machine gun mounted in nose, one MG 151 20mm (0.79in) MG 151 cannon in forward ventral and tail positions, two 13mm (0.51in) MG 131 machine guns in rear dorsal turret and one in forward dorsal turret and rear ventral positions; 7000kg (15,000lb) bombload in bomb bay and 2500kg (5500lb) underwing

Left and below:
This He 177A-5/R2 was on the strength of II./KG 100 based at Bordeaux Mérignac in 1944. It took part in Operation Steinbock (Capricorn), known as the 'Baby Blitz', the Luftwaffe's final bombing campaign against the British Isles.

Opposite:
This He 177A-5/R6 was flown by 5./KG 1 in East Prussia during June 1944.

prototype made its first flight in November 1939, overheating engines forced a return to base after only a few minutes and ultimately four of the eight prototypes were lost to engine fires, which remained a major problem during the aircraft's initial service life. Early instability issues were cured by lengthening the fuselage, resulting in the He 177A-3, the first variant to be built in quantity. Although the flying qualities had been much improved, engine fires resulted in greater losses than enemy action. For example, in just 13 missions flown by early He 177s at Stalingrad, seven aircraft were lost to engine fires.

Modifications eventually cured the fire situation although the aircraft never completely shed its combustible reputation and mechanical issues persisted with the engine gearing systems, but the He 177A-5, the most produced variant, proved generally reliable in service. Most of the He 177's service took place on the Eastern Front where losses to Soviet fighters were light due to the aircraft's excellent performance at high altitude.

Junkers Ju 86

Although its Luftwaffe career was coming to a close by the start of World War II, the Ju 86 gained a new lease of life as a pressurized high-altitude bomber.

Designed both as a high-speed airliner and medium bomber, the Ju 86 made its maiden flight in November 1934. Operations over Spain with the Condor Legion demonstrated the general superiority of the He 111 over the Junkers aircraft and consequently only one Gruppe remained equipped with the Ju 86D when Germany invaded Poland in 1939. Most Luftwaffe Ju 86s were used for

This neat lineup of Ju 86 bombers was photographed in 1937 when the type was at the height of its career.

Junkers Ju 86

Weight: 8200kg (18,078lb)
Dimensions: Length 16.46m (54ft), Wingspan 22.5m (73ft 10in), Height 5.06m (16ft 7in)
Powerplant: 2 × Junkers Jumo 205 six-cylinder liquid-cooled two-stroke opposed-piston diesel engines
Maximum speed: 420km/h (260mph)

Range: 1500km (932 miles)
Ceiling: 12,800m (42,000ft)
Crew: 4
Armament: One 7.92mm (0.31in) MG 15 machine guns flexibly mounted in nose, dorsal and retractable ventral positions; up to 800kg (1764lb) bombload

Opposite:
Named 'Fumo 2', this Ju 86D was operated by KG 88, of the German Condor Legion in support of Franco's forces in Spain in late 1937.

Above:
Seen here with its ventral 'dustbin' gun position retracted, this Ju 86D-1 served with II.KG 254, based at Eschwege, central Germany, in 1937.

Below:
Hungary was a major operator of the Ju 86, receiving more than 60 of the Ju 86K-2 and using them during the first months of Operation Barbarossa. This aircraft served with the 1st Bomber Proficiency Squadron in summer 1939.

training, although many were pressed into the transport role in 1942 due to a shortage of more suitable aircraft, suffering heavy losses while resupplying encircled German forces at Stalingrad. In conventional bomber form, the Ju 86 continued in service with Hungary, which used the aircraft in support of the German invasion of the Soviet Union into 1942 when surviving aircraft were withdrawn from combat use due to increasingly heavy losses. Curiously, the Ju 86 also saw service with the Allies in the form of 18 Ju 86K airliners of South African Airlines, adapted in 1939 with machine guns and external bomb racks for coastal patrol and employed on bombing missions during the East African campaign.

A different role was undertaken by Luftwaffe Ju 86s following the successful tests of a high-altitude variant, the Ju 86P. Forty existing airframes were converted into Ju 86Ps for high-altitude bombing and reconnaissance missions, operating with impunity over the British Isles, North Africa and the Soviet Union for around two years until modified Supermarine Spitfires were coaxed to a sufficient altitude to make an interception.

Junkers Ju 87 'Stuka'

The Ju 87 dive bomber, the most notorious aircraft of the Blitzkrieg campaigns, was exceptionally accurate but, like other contemporary dive bombers, highly vulnerable to modern fighters.

The dive-bombing concept was embraced with enthusiasm by the technical director of the Luftwaffe, Ernst Udet, and the Ju 87 ultimately prevailed over the rival Heinkel He 118 to become Germany's standard dive bomber. Its nickname, 'Stuka', was a contraction of the German *Sturzkampfflugzeug* 'dive bomber', and the Ju 87 became so ubiquitous that the name became inseparably

Photographed over Rhodes in 1941, these aircraft are the long-range Ju 87R-2 variant, carrying 300 litre (66 gallon) external fuel tanks under the wings.

Junkers Ju 87B-2

Weight: 4250kg (9370lb)
Dimensions: Length 11m (36ft 1in), Wingspan 13.8m (45ft 3in), Height 3.77m (12ft 5in)
Powerplant: One 883kW (1200hp) Junkers Jumo 211Da liquid-cooled inverted V-12 pison engine
Maximum speed: 350km/h (217mph)
Range: 600km (373 miles)
Ceiling: 8100m (26,570ft)
Crew: 2
Armament: Two 7.92mm (0.31in) MG 17 machine guns fixed, firing forward in wings and one 7.92mm (0.31in) MG 15 machine gun flexibly mounted in rear cockpit; up to 1000kg (2200lb) bombload

Opposite:
The Ju 87 proved popular with Germany's allies. This Ju 87B-2 served with the Hungarian Air Force based at Jasionka, Poland, for operations against the Soviet Union in late 1943.

Right and below:
This aircraft flew with the Staff flight (Stab) of Sturzkampfgeschwader 77 (Dive bomber squadron 77), which painted a yellow nose for quick recognition during the Battle of Britain. Seen head-on, the sharply gull-winged Stuka design is evident, allowing short landing gear while providing adequate propeller and bomb clearance.

associated with it by both friend and foe. Initial operations in Spain validated the design and during the Polish campaign the Stuka proved both accurate and decisive. Surprisingly, a Ju 87 scored the first air-to-air victory of World War II, shooting down a PZL P.11c as it took off on the morning of 1 September 1939. By then, the Ju 87B was in production, featuring a much more powerful engine as well as Lärmgeräte ('noise device') sirens in the wings, intended to terrify those on the ground.

The campaigns in Norway, France and the Low Countries further cemented its reputation as an effective weapon. However, the Battle of Britain, which saw the Stuka face organized fighter defences for the first time, exposed the vulnerability of this slow, unmanoeuvrable aircraft. Subsequently Ju 87s would only operate in areas of German air superiority. The Ju 87D of 1941 featured a streamlined airframe and a more powerful Jumo engine, improving performance and allowing a much larger payload to be carried.

Junkers Ju 88

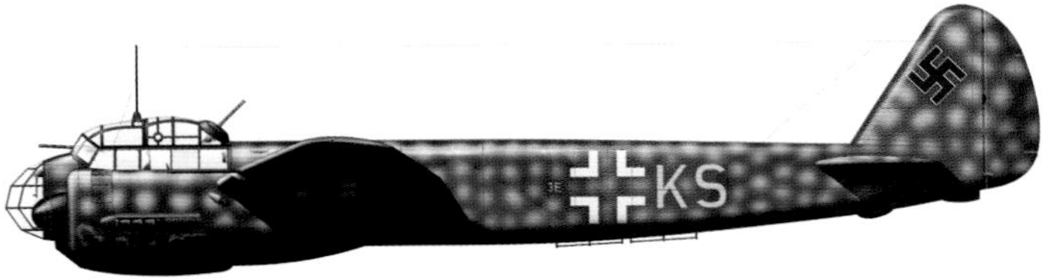

One of World War II's outstanding aircraft, the Ju 88 was the Luftwaffe's best medium bomber at the war's start and evolved into a successful multirole platform.

The Ju 88 first flew in December 1936 and displayed outstanding performance culminating in the fifth prototype setting a 1000km (620 mile) closed-circuit record while carrying a 2000 kg (4400 lb) payload at a speed of 517 km/h (321 mph) in early 1939. Service entry was delayed by modifications made to allow the aircraft to operate as a dive bomber and initial production was painfully

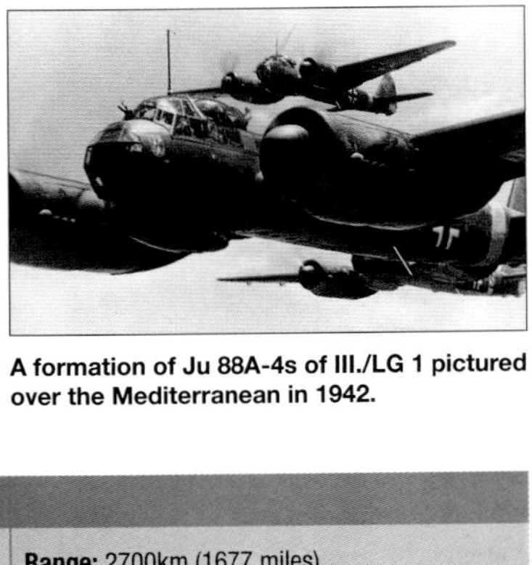

A formation of Ju 88A-4s of III./LG 1 pictured over the Mediterranean in 1942.

Junkers Ju 88A-4

Weight: 14,000kg (30,860lb)
Dimensions: Length 14.4m (47ft 3in), Wingspan 20m (65ft 8in), Height 4.8m (15ft 8in)
Powerplant: Two 1051kW (1410hp) Junkers Jumo 211J-2 liquid-cooled inverted V-12 piston engines
Maximum speed: 470km/h (292mph)
Range: 2700km (1677 miles)
Ceiling: 8200m (26,900ft)
Crew: 4
Armament: One 7.92mm (0.31in) MG 81 flexibly mounted in cockpit windscreen, lower cockpit glazing, and rear ventral positions, two 7.92mm (0.31in) MG 81Z in double mount in dorsal position; up to 1400kg (3100lb) bombload

Opposite:
Based at Melsbroek, Belgium, in 1944, KG 6 was in the process of converting to the Ju 188 but still retained a substantial number of Ju 88s.

Above:
Hungary operated more than 160 Ju 88s during the war. This Ju 88A-14 served with 1/3 *Bombázó század* (Bomber squadron) in the USSR during 1943.

Below:
Serving on the Eastern Front in 1944, this Ju 88A-4 served with 10./KG I 'Hindenburg'.

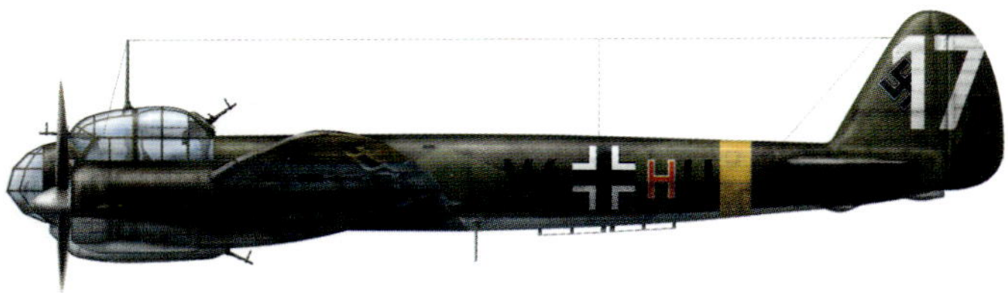

slow, but the Ju 88 was available just in time to participate in the invasion of Poland. The Ju 88A-1 was the first to be built in large numbers and was the variant committed in the largest numbers to the Battle of Britain, during which the Ju 88 was generally considered to be the most effective of the Luftwaffe's bombers. The A-series included most bomber variants and was produced in 17 subvariants, the most numerous being the A-4. With a longer-span wing, the A-4 saw widespread service over the Balkans, Mediterranean, North Africa and Russia, forming the backbone of the Luftwaffe's bombing force at the start of the invasion of the Soviet Union.

Later development of the original bombing role led to the Ju 88S – S standing for *Schnell* ('fast') – a high-speed derivative of the Ju88A-4 with the ventral gondola deleted and a more aerodynamic nose coupled with the GM-1 nitrous-oxide boost system, enabling the already swift bomber to attain more than 610km/h (380mph), the fastest of all Ju 88s.

Junkers Ju 188

A derivative of the highly successful Ju 88, the Ju 188 offered only a modest improvement in performance over its illustrious predecessor and was built in comparatively small numbers.

During 1940, Junkers flew the B variant of the Ju 88, which differed from the A model most obviously in its adoption of an extensively glazed egg-shaped stepless cockpit. The B-0 was powered by two BMW 801 radials each delivering 255kW (340hp) more than the Jumo 211B-1 engines fitted to the Ju 88A-1 and a pre-production batch of ten aircraft was built. Despite pilot enthusiasm, the design was

The Ju 188 was distinguished from its Ju 88 predecessor by its extended-span wing with pointed wingtips.

Junkers Ju 188E-1

Weight: 14,510kg (31,989lb)
Dimensions: Length 14.9m (49ft 1in), Wingspan 22m (72ft 2in), Height 4.45m (14ft 7in)
Powerplant: Two 1290kW (1730hp) BMW 801D-2 14-cylinder air-cooled radial piston engines
Maximum speed: 500km/h (310mph)
Range: 3400km (2110 miles)
Ceiling: 9350m (30,665ft)
Crew: 4
Armament: One 20mm (0.787in) MG 151/20 cannon flexibly mounted in nose and one 13mm (0.51in) MG 131 in dorsal turret, and one MG 131 flexibly mounted in rear dorsal and rear ventral positions; up to 3000kg (6600lb) bombload

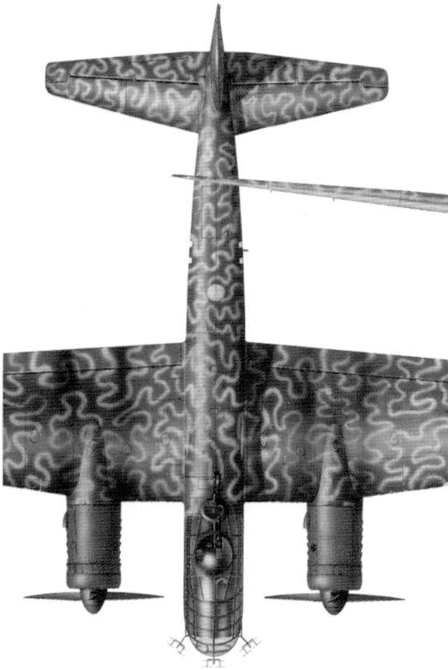

Opposite top and above:
The Ju 188A-3s of III./KG 26 were based in Norway when the war ended. The antennae on the nose reveal that this example was fitted with FuG 200 maritime patrol radar. This aircraft features the distinctive 'Arabesken' (Arabesques) freehand camouflage pattern adopted for its maritime role.

deemed insufficiently superior to the standard Ju 88A and production did not go ahead. However, delays afflicting the Ju 288 – a higher performance bomber intended to replace all the Luftwaffe's medium bombers – prompted the RLM to revisit the Ju 88B design as a stopgap and the aircraft entered production as the Ju 188. With more powerful Jumo 213A or BMW 801 G-2 engines powering the Ju 188A and Ju 188E respectively, the first combat operation flew in August 1943 when Ju 188E-1s attacked industrial targets in Lincoln, UK. Although production of Ju 188As did proceed, problems with the Jumo 213 meant that the majority of aircraft were BMW-powered Ju 188E-1s, the standard medium bomber variant.

In service, the Ju 188 offered better performance than the Ju 88 but this was offset by its small bomb bay, requiring most of the payload to be carried externally with a detrimental effect on speed. Nonetheless, the aircraft was popular with Luftwaffe aircrew due to its excellent flying qualities and the improvement in performance and armament. The Ju 188's main flaw was timing: the aircraft only appeared in the latter half of 1943, by which time Allied fighter opposition dominated the skies of Europe.

Junkers Ju 290

A large aircraft of impressive capability, the Ju 290 was designed as a military transport before being adapted for roles including long-range patrol.

Junkers had constructed a small number of the Ju 90 airliner for Deutsche Luft Hansa in the late 1930s and its large size and excellent performance prompted the RLM to order a military version in April 1939. On the outbreak of war the airliners were pressed into Luftwaffe service along with other military transport prototypes and saw considerable service, beginning their operational

In July 1945, this captured Ju 290A-4 was flown across the Atlantic and photographed during testing in the United States.

Junkers Ju 290A-5

Weight: 44,969kg (99,140lb)
Dimensions: Length 28.64m (94ft), Wingspan 42m (137ft 10in), Height 6.83m (22ft 5in)
Powerplant: Four 1300kW (1700hp) BMW 801D 14-cylinder air-cooled radial piston engines
Maximum speed: 439km/h (273mph)
Range: 6148km (3820 miles)
Ceiling: 6000m (19,685ft)
Crew: 9
Armament: One 20mm (0.79in) MG 151/20 cannon flexibly mounted in each dorsal turret, tail position, each side of fuselage, and forward ventral gondola position and one 13mm (0.51in) MG 131 flexibly mounted in rear of ventral gondola; up to 3000kg (6600lb) bombload

Opposite:
The Ju 290A-5 variant was more combat worthy than earlier variants due to its upgraded armour protection and heavier armament. This example served with Fernaufklärungsgruppe 5 in France.

Below (both images):
This Ju 290A-5 was based at Mont-de-Marsan in southern France when it was on the strength of Fernaufklärungsgruppe 5 (FAGr. 5).

career during the invasion of Norway. The last two Ju 90 prototypes were an improved version, which subsequently became the Ju 290, a larger aircraft with more powerful engines. Intended as a replacement for the Fw 200 Condor, the Ju 290 flew for the first time in July 1942 and entered service in transport form the following month, such was the urgent need for heavy cargo aircraft.

The Ju 290 introduced a hydraulically powered rear ramp, called the *Trapoklappe*, which raised the fuselage of this taildragger aircraft to a horizontal position and allowed vehicles to be driven straight into or out of the aircraft, becoming the forerunner of all modern military transports.

In early 1943 a heavily armed maritime patrol variant appeared, capable of remaining aloft for 18 hours at a time. It was equipped to carry three Fritz-X or Hs 293 guided missiles for anti-shipping strikes. Although the Kriegsmarine demanded that all Ju 290 production be allocated to support U-boat operations, in the event only 20 were ever assigned to this mission before production was halted in early 1944 to concentrate on fighters.

A pressurized heavy bomber variant remained unfinished when the war ended although a single example of a stretched variant – the huge six-engined Ju 390 – was built and flown as the Junkers entry in the Luftwaffe's 'Amerikabomber' programme, capable of flying across the Atlantic and back from bases in France.

Breda Ba.65

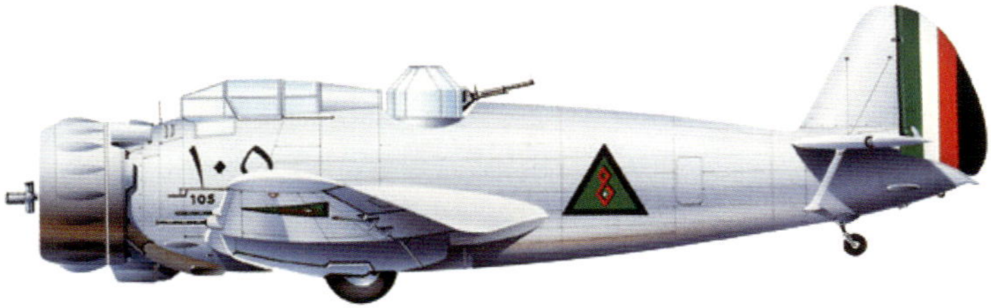

Developed as a dedicated attack aircraft in the early 1930s, the Ba.65 proved highly effective in Spain but was outdated by the time it saw action in North Africa.

The concept of a high-speed ground attack aircraft, capable of striking targets around 300km (186 miles) behind the front line, and possessing sufficient performance and agility to fend off enemy fighters was formulated in Italy in the early 1930s. Breda produced a modern monoplane aircraft to fulfill this role, the Ba.64, of which 42 were built. However, more power was required and the Ba.65

The Ba.65 was slow but tough and reliable and performed well in the early years of the war. These Fiat A.80 powered examples were photographed over Rome in 1939.

Breda Ba.65 A.80

Weight: 3150kg (6945lb)
Dimensions: Length 9.3m (30ft 6in) Wingspan 12m (39ft 4in) Height 3m (9ft 10in)
Powerplant: One 746kW (1000hp) Fiat A.80 R.C.41 18-cylinder air-cooled radial piston engine
Maximum speed: 430km/h (270mph)

Range: 550km (340 miles)
Ceiling: 7450m (24,440ft)
Crew: 1
Armament: Two 12.7mm (0.5in) and two 7.7mm (0.303in) Breda-SAFAT machine guns fixed, forward firing in the wings; up to 340kg (880lb) bombload in bomb bay and up to 600kg (1325lb) externally

Opposite:
The Royal Iraqi Air Force operated 12 turret-equipped Ba.65s. These aircraft performed the final combat operations of the Ba.65 when they attacked British forces in the brief Anglo-Iraqi war of 1941.

Above:
The Ba.65 proved effective in Spain. This Ba.65K-14 serving with the Aviazione Legionaria was based at Puig Moreno in northeastern Spain during 1938.

was produced with a 656kW (880hp) Gnome-Rhône engine in place of the 485kW (650hp) Alfa Romeo of the earlier aircraft.

Both a single seater and a two-seater variant were produced with an observer/gunner occupying a position level with the wing's trailing edge, and some subtypes featured a turret. Twenty-three examples of the Ba.65 formed part of Italy's contribution to the fighting in the Spanish Civil War, where they proved highly effective. At the decisive Battle of the Ebro, the Bredas attacked pontoon bridges over the Ebro River, destroying three after conventional bombers flying at medium altitude had failed to score a single hit.

By 1940 and Italy's entry into World War II, however, the Ba.65 was considered obsolete, despite the performance improvement delivered by a switch to the 746kW (1000 hp) Fiat A.80 engine. Most aircraft were in storage at this point but the sudden requirement for air power in Libya to fight the British prompted the urgent reactivation of as many Ba.65s as possible. The aircraft was involved in fierce fighting for the remainder of 1940, notably inflicting heavy losses on British ground forces at Sidi Rezegh.

In combat in Africa, the Ba.65 proved effective when unchallenged by enemy fighters, but it was becoming increasingly vulnerable and in January 1941 the Italian Ba.65s flew their last sorties. This was not quite the end of the Breda's combat career, however, as 17 Ba.65s had been acquired by Iraq in 1937 and were used in the short Anglo-Iraqi war of 1941.

CANT Z.1007 Alcione

Arguably the best bomber fielded in numbers by Italy, the trimotor Z.1007 flew for the first time in March 1937 and was used for bombing and reconnaissance.

Unusually derived from a floatplane, the Z.506, the Z.1007 Alcione ('Kingfisher') was an aerodynamically efficient aircraft but reflected an earlier era with its all-wood construction. Initial production aircraft were powered by Isotta Fraschini Asso inline engines, but these were replaced with far more reliable Piaggio P.XI radials, a licence-built Gnome-Rhône Mistral Major 14K, in the Z.1007bis.

Another Co-belligerent Alcione, this Z.1007bis was photographed over southern Italy in late 1944.

CANT Z.1007 Alcione

Weight: 13,621kg (30,029lb)
Dimensions: Length 18.35m (60ft 2in), Wingspan 24.8m (81ft 4in), Height 5.22m (17ft 2in)
Powerplant: Three 745kW (999hp) Piaggio P.XI R.C.40 14-cylinder air-cooled radial piston engines
Maximum speed: 458km/h (285mph)
Range: 1795km (1115 miles)
Ceiling: 7500m (24,600ft)
Crew: 5
Armament: Two 12.7mm (0.5in) Isotta Fraschini-Scotti or Breda-SAFAT machine guns in dorsal turret and ventral position, two 7.7mm (0.303in) Breda-SAFAT machine guns in fuselage sides; up to 1200kg (2645lb) of bombs in bomb bay and 1000kg (2200lb) carried under wings

Opposite:
After the 1943 armistice, surviving Z.1007s were grouped into the Raggruppamento Bombardamento Trasporti (Transport and Bombing Unit) of the Italian Co-belligerent Air Force. This aircraft was based at Lecce, southeastern Italy, during October 1944.

Above:
This Z.1007bis served with the 230ª Squadriglia of the 95° Gruppo for operations in Greece during February 1941.

Below:
Another example serving with the 230ª Squadriglia in Greece, this Z.1107bis is one of the single-tailed examples; units frequently operated both types simultaneously.

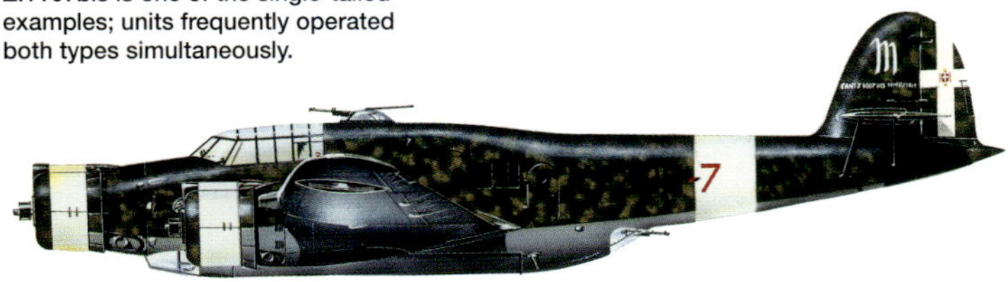

The Z.1007bis variant began to enter service in late 1939 and accounted for the majority of Z.1007 production. Later production aircraft featured a twin tail to allow the turret to fire directly to the rear but there was no change in designation between Z.1007bis aircraft with the two tail types. The aircraft entered combat during August 1940 when it was used to bomb targets in Malta. Later the same year a handful of aircraft were tested under operational conditions at the tail end of the Battle of Britain, but the first large-scale use of the Z.1007 took place in Greece.

In service, the Z.1007 proved popular due to its excellent handling and decent performance, although its slim fuselage forced pilot and copilot to sit in tandem rather than side by side. Their seats were offset to the left allowing crew access to the bombardier's position directly behind the nose engine. Like all Italian bombers, the Alcione suffered from poor defensive armament and after experiencing heavy losses to fighters, was used almost exclusively at night.

CANT Z.506 Airone

One of the largest floatplanes to operate during World War II, the remarkably successful Z.506 remained in service for more than 20 years.

The Airone ('Heron') first flew in August 1935 and began its career as a 15-passenger civil aircraft, setting a swathe of floatplane records in the late 1930s. The initial batch of 15 Z.506A airliners were used by the airline Ala Littoria on Mediterranean routes, proving successful enough that a larger, improved Z.509 model was developed. However, only three were built due to the outbreak of war.

This Z.506B was photographed landing in Allied territory after the Italian armistice in September 1943.

CANT Z.506 Airone

Weight: 12,705kg (28,010lb)
Dimensions: Length 19.24m (63ft 1in) Wingspan: 26.5m (86ft 11in) Height: 7.45m (24ft 5in)
Powerplant: Three 560kW (750hp) Alfa Romeo 126 R.C.34 nine-cylinder air-cooled radial piston engines
Maximum speed: 350km/h (220mph)
Range: 2000km (1200 miles)
Ceiling: 7000m (23,000ft)
Crew: 5
Armament: One 12.7mm (0.50in) Isotta Fraschini-Scotti machine gun in dorsal turret, three 7.7mm (0.303in) machine guns in ventral and beam positions; 1200kg (2645lb) of bombs or one 816kg (1800lb) torpedo

Opposite top:
Based at Majorca in 1939, this Z.506B of 73° Gruppo was part of the Nationalist Agrupación Española.

Above:
Pictured in its hangar on 5 January 1941, this Z.506B of 31° Stormo da Bombardamento Marittimo (Maritime Bombardment Wing) was based at Cagliari-Elmas on Sardinia.

The Z.506B, a militarized version that entered service in 1939, was built in large numbers, and demand was so high that Piaggio built it under licence. The biggest external change to the aircraft was the addition of a long ventral gondola, housing a bomb bay, a bomb aimer and a defensive rear gun. Unusually for a late 1930s design, the aircraft's construction was entirely of wood except for the floats, which were metal but skinned with an early plastic called 'Chitonal' for waterproofing.

A few Z.506Bs served in Spain during the latter stages of the Spanish Civil War in the patrol and torpedo bombing role . They operated in a similar fashion during the early stages of World War II, as well as conducting bombing raids on shore targets during the campaigns against France and Greece. As more capable combat aircraft became available, the Z.506 was used for less demanding duties such as convoy escort and anti-submarine patrol, as well as becoming a vital air-sea rescue (ASR) aircraft. As an ASR aircraft, the Airone was used by both sides following the 1943 armistice and continued in this role into the Cold War, the last only being withdrawn in 1959.

Caproni Ca.133

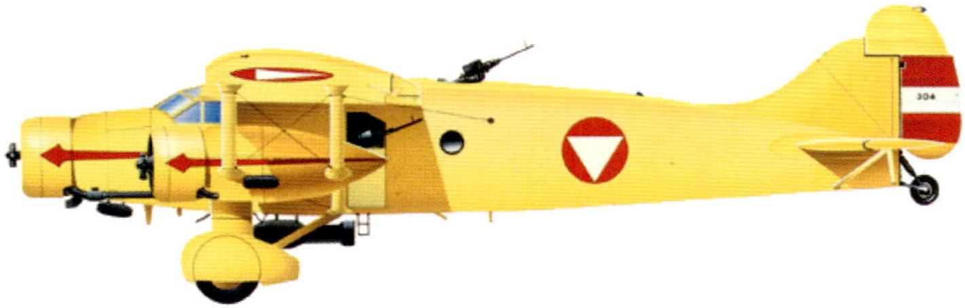

Intended to act as both a bomber and transport in Italian colonies, the Ca 133 was reliable, simple, and comparatively cheap to operate.

Beginning as an airliner design, the Ca.133 first flew in 1934 and was essentially an aerodynamically and structurally improved version of the earlier trimotor Ca.101. For military use, the aircraft was equipped with two small bomb bays allowing it to carry up to 500kg (1100lb) of bombs. Four manually aimed machine guns were provided for defence in dorsal and ventral positions as well as one

Many Ca.133s were adapted for use as air ambulances, such as this example being pushed across the tarmac in 1941.

Caproni Ca.133

Weight: 6500kg (14,330lb)
Dimensions: Length 15.35m (50ft 5in), Wingspan 21.3m (69ft 8in), Height 4m (13ft 1in)
Powerplant: Three 343kW (460hp) Piaggio Stella P.VII C.16 7-cylinder air-cooled radial piston engines
Maximum speed: 230km/h (140mph)
Range: 1350km (840 miles)
Ceiling: 5500m (18,000ft)
Crew: 5
Armament: Four flexible 7.7 mm (0.303 in) Breda-SAFAT machine guns, manually aimed in dorsal, ventral and beam positions; up to 1000kg (2200lb) bombload carried in bomb bay and on external racks

Opposite top:
With bombload suspended under the fuselage, this Ca.133 was one of five on the strength of Fliegerregiment 2 of the Austrian Air Force, based at Zeltweg in 1937.

Above:
The Ca.133 was specifically intended for use in Italian colonial territories. This example was photographed undergoing maintenance in a hangar in Addis Ababa, Ethiopia, in 1937, shortly after the end of the Second Italo-Ethiopian War.

fired from each side of the fuselage. The aircraft first saw combat in the Second Italo-Ethiopian War (1935–36), carrying out conventional bombing missions and, more controversially, dropping mustard gas in violation of the Geneva Protocol, drawing widespread international condemnation. The Ca.133 had enjoyed total air superiority over Ethiopia but when committed to the Spanish Civil War its vulnerability to fighters became starkly apparent. Its subsequent use in Europe was limited to transport duties, although its performance was deemed sufficient for use in Africa and on the outbreak of World War II 14 squadrons were still equipped with the Caproni trimotor.

The Ca.133 undertook missions against British forces during the East African campaign in the summer of 1940, bombing the port of Aden and Khormaksar airfield, as well as attacking advancing British columns. Remarkably, one of these quite elderly and only modestly capable aircraft scored an air-to-air victory on 23 January 1941, when a Ca.133 shot down a South African Air Force Avro Anson over Somalia. The aircraft's later career saw it primarily used as a transport aircraft as well as an air ambulance, in its Ca.133S ('Sanitario') variant. A few examples survived to the 1943 armistice.

Caproni Ca.135

Although it never served operationally with its country of origin, the Ca.135 saw considerable action with the Hungarian Air Force on the Eastern Front.

The Ca.135's life in Italian service was brief, first flying in April 1936, 204 examples were ordered for the Regia Aeronautica but the first examples were delivered late, entering service in January 1938, a year after the Br.20, which had been ordered at the same time. The Ca.135s proved underpowered and unpopular with pilots and the first 32 were withdrawn from frontline squadrons and assigned

A Ca.135 Mod shows off its unusual nose. Later production aircraft featured more extensive nose glazing.

Caproni Ca.135

Weight: 9548kg (21,050lb)
Dimensions: Length 14.4m (47ft 1in), Wingspan 18.75m (61ft 8in), Height 3.4m (11ft 2in)
Powerplant: Two 746kW (1000hp) Piaggio P.XI R.C.40 14-cylinder air-cooled radial piston engines
Maximum speed: 440km/h (273mph)
Range: 1200km (746 miles)
Ceiling: 7000m (22,966ft)
Crew: 4 or 5
Armament: One or two 12.7 mm (0.500 in) Breda-SAFAT machine guns manually aimed in dorsal turret, ventral and nose positions; up to 1600kg (3527lb) bombload

Opposite top:
Hungary was the only nation to use the Ca.135 in combat during World War II. This example served on the Eastern Front in late 1941 in the hands of 4/III Bombázó század.

Above:
Early Ca.135s were powered by a pair of Isotta-Fraschini Asso ('Ace') liquid cooled V-12 engines, such as this Regia Aeronautica example pictured in 1937.

to training units less than a year after entering service. Seven were earmarked for operational tests in Spain but only two arrived (three crashed en route and two had to return to Italy) and were never used in combat. Despite their poor performance, a second batch of 32 Ca.135s was ordered and delivered straight to flying schools before being sold to Hungary, although the first batch was scrapped by the end of 1941.

Despite its dismal Regia Aeronautica career, the Caproni proved satisfactory in Hungarian service and a further 36 Ca.135s were ordered. The Ca.135 made its combat debut on the same day that Hungary declared war on the Soviet Union and subsequently operated as part of the Hungarian Rapid Corps until September 1941. On the Eastern Front, although the aircraft performed acceptably in combat, the Ca.135's serviceability proved problematic and the aircraft's structure, much of which was wooden, suffered in the rigours of the Soviet climate. A single squadron supported Hungarian forces on the Don in the summer of 1942 and endured intense action for around six months before the survivors were relegated to training. Meanwhile, on the other side of the world, Caproni had succeeded, surprisingly, in selling six Ca.135s to Peru and these were used in combat during the Ecuadorian-Peruvian war in 1941–42.

Caproni Ca.308 and derivatives

A prolific family of closely related designs, Caproni's twin-engined light bombers grew increasingly powerful and, by Italian standards, were built in large numbers.

All of Caproni's light bombers derived from the Ca.306 airliner that appeared in 1935 and, although it did not enter serial production, formed the basis for the Ca.308 Borea ('North Wind'). Five examples were built as an airliner and two as a general purpose aircraft for the colonial administration in Libya. The Ca.309 Ghibli (named after a Libyan desert wind) followed, of which more than 240 served with the Regia

A Caproni Ca.309 Ghibli pictured in Sicily in 1943. By this time the aircraft's primary role was liaison.

Caproni Ca.313

Weight: 5900kg (13,007lb)
Dimensions: Length 11.79m (38ft 8in), Wingspan 16.11m (52ft 11in), Height 3.7m (12ft 2in)
Powerplant: Two 540kW (730hp) Isotta Fraschini Delta R.C.35 I-DS air-cooled inverted V12 piston engines
Maximum speed: 436km/h (271mph)
Range: 1200km (750 miles)
Ceiling: 7300m (24,000ft)
Crew: 3
Armament: One 12.7mm (0.5in) Isotta Fraschi-Scotti machine gun fixed, forward firing in wing root, one flexibly mounted in dorsal turret and one flexibly mounted in ventral fuselage step; up to 400kg (880lb) bombload

Opposite top:
A Ca.310 Libeccio of the Italian Aviazione Legionaria supporting rebel forces in Spain. The Ca.310 was the first of the family to be fitted with a retractable undercarriage.

Above:
A Ca.310 of Norway's Hærens flyvåpen (Army Air Service). This example was based at Sola airfield, near Stavanger.

Left:
This Ca.313 was one of 84 examples acquired by Sweden in 1940 and 1941 that were utilized for the duration of the war.

Aeronautica. The Ca.309 served well as a reconnaissance and light bombing aircraft during the early stages of the war in North Africa. Re-engined with more powerful Piaggio Stella radial engines in place of the 6-cylinder Alfa Romeo inline units of the Ghibli and equipped with retractable undercarriage, the aircraft later became the Ca.310 Libeccio ('Southwest Wind'). Introduced into service in 1938, 16 examples of the Ca.310 were delivered to Spain for operational trials, but by the outbreak of World War II the Ca.310 was considered vulnerable and was used only for reconnaissance where aerial opposition was unlikely to be encountered. The aircraft was further developed into the Ca.311, which introduced a heavily glazed, unstepped nose and relocated the small dorsal turret to a position immediately behind the cockpit.

The Ca.313 followed, powered by Isotta Fraschini Delta V-12 engines that more than doubled the power of the Gypsy six engines of the original Ca.308. A total of 271 were built, which enjoyed considerable export success with sales to Sweden, France and Croatia, along with a large order from the United Kingdom. However, Italy's entry into the war prevented these deliveries being fulfilled. The most numerous variant of the whole family was the Ca.314, which differed from the 313 only in reverting to a conventional stepped windscreen. These aircraft were employed by Italy for maritime patrol, torpedo bombing and ground attack.

Fiat BR.20 Cicogna

First flown in February 1936, the stressed-skin cantilever BR.20 was the most advanced bomber in service in the world when it was introduced into the Regia Aeronautica later the same year.

Unfortunately, the pace of aviation development in the late 1930s meant that by 1940 the BR.20, while still capable, was not as impressive as it had been when it made its combat debut during the Spanish Civil War. A total of 13 aircraft were sent to Spain and were heavily used on both bombing and reconnaissance missions, proving almost impossible to intercept by opposing fighters.

BR.20s of the Italian Aviazione Legionaria cruise over rugged territory during the Spanish Civil War.

Fiat BR.20M

Weight: 10,100kg (22,267lb)
Dimensions: Length 16.68m (54ft 9in), Wingspan 21.56m (70ft 9in), Height 4.75m (15ft 7in)
Powerplant: Two 746kW (1000hp) Fiat A.80 R.C.41 18-cylinder air-cooled radial piston engines

Maximum speed: 440km/h (270mph)
Range: 2750km (1710 miles)
Ceiling: 8000m (26,000ft)
Crew: 5
Armament: One 7.7mm (0.303in) Breda-SAFAT machine gun in dorsal turret and one manually aimed in flexibly mounted nose and ventral positions; up to 1600kg (3500lb) bombload

Opposite:
Shown with its ventral gun position deployed, this BR.20M of 1ª Squadriglia, 43° Gruppo was based at Bir Dufan, Libya, in February 1942. The squadron adopted the emblem of Donald Duck, seen here painted on the rear fuselage.

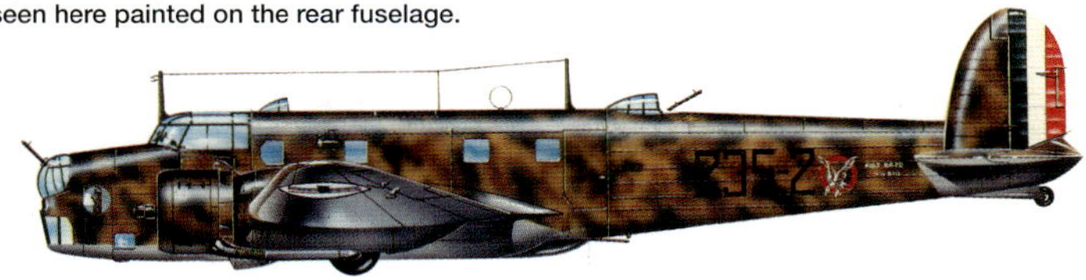

Above:
Based at Jesi, near the Adriatic coast, in 1939, this BR.20 of 41° Stormo Bombardamento Terrestre features the earlier, blunter nose with gun turret of earlier production machines.

Below:
The BR.20M (for 'Modificato') adopted a more streamlined nose design. This example was operating on the Greco-Albanian front in late 1940 with 277ª Squadriglia of 116° Gruppo.

Japan acquired 82 BR.20s in 1937 and used them on long-range bombing missions in China until September 1939. Despite having been withdrawn before Japan entered World War II, the Fiat received the Allied reporting name 'Ruth'. When Italy declared war on the UK and France on 10 June 1940, 172 BR.20s were in service and the aircraft was in action within days, attacking targets during the brief French campaign and suffering light losses. Committed to attacking British targets from Belgium, however, the limitations of the BR.20 force became apparent; although only three Fiats were shot down by RAF fighters, a quarter of the 80-strong BR.20 force were lost over the course of the brief campaign. The aircraft performed better in the Mediterranean and North Africa, attacking the contested port of Tobruk, as well as regularly bombing Malta in force, suffering heavy losses in the process. BR.20s also formed part of the Italian Expeditionary Force on the Eastern Front, but by the time of the 1943 armistice virtually all BR.20s had been relegated to the training role.

Piaggio P.108

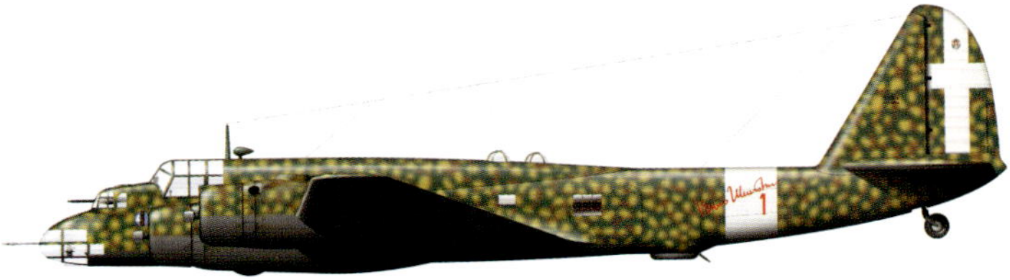

Arguably the best heavy bomber fielded by the Axis, the Regia Aeronautica's formidable Piaggio P.108 was produced in only very small numbers.

First flown in November 1939, one of the P.108's test pilots was Benito Mussolini's son Bruno, who later lost his life in the 1941 crash of a brand new P.108B. Despite this mishap, the P.108 proved to be an impressive aircraft, reaching a top speed of 475km/h (295mph) and, unlike other Italian aircraft, featuring powerful, advanced defensive armament, including remotely controlled turrets

The powerful P.108 boasted an impressive performance, yet its impact was limited by the small number produced.

Piaggio P.108B

Weight: 29,885kg (65,885lb)
Dimensions: Length 22.29m (73ft 2in), Wingspan 32m (105ft), Height 6m (19ft 8in)
Powerplant: Four 1120kW (1500hp) Piaggio P.XII R.C.35 18-cylinder air-cooled radial piston engines
Maximum speed: 475km/h (295mph)
Range: 3295km (2047 miles)
Ceiling: 10,500m (34,400ft)
Crew: 6 or 7
Armament: Two 12.7mm (0.5in) Breda-SAFAT flexibly mounted in each remotely aimed turret located in the outboard engine nacelles and one manually aimed in dorsal, ventral and beam positions; up to 3500kg (7700lb) bombload

Opposite top and above:
A Piaggio P.108B of 274° Squadriglia, Bombardamento a Grande Raggio (Long Range Bombardment) in March 1942. This aircraft has the name of Bruno Mussolini, son of Benito, inscribed on the rear fuselage.

Right:
A press shot taken at Guidonia airfield, Italy, shows the large number of air and ground crew needed to keep a Piaggio P.108 operational.

on the outer wings. The aircraft was also extremely strong, being built to a 6G load factor, a level more usual for contemporary fighters, but only 24 examples of the P.108B bomber variant were ever constructed.

These were used sporadically from June 1942, when P.108s repeatedly bombed Gibraltar, until the final missions to attack Allied forces during the invasion of Sicily in July 1943. Flown nearly exclusively at night, the aircraft proved successful but given the miniscule numbers available, material damage was understandably limited and in total, only six of the P.108Bs were ever lost to fighters and flak.

The aircraft was also produced as a transport, the P.108T capable of carrying 60 troops or 12 tonnes of cargo, and, oddly, as the P.108C pressurized 32-passenger transatlantic airliner. Production of the transport variants continued after the armistice under German control and most of the 12 P.108C and Ts constructed saw extensive use until the end of the war with Transportfliegerstaffel 5 of the Luftwaffe.

Savoia Marchetti SM.79 Sparviero

The archetypal Italian bomber of World War II, the trimotor Sparviero ('Sparrowhawk') served throughout the conflict, gaining particular fame later in its career as a torpedo bomber.

The Sparviero prototype announced its appearance in fine style by setting a swathe of speed with payload records during September 1935, having flown for the first time a year earlier. Like many Italian aircraft, the initial combat deployment of the SM.79 occurred during the Spanish Civil War where the aircraft proved highly successful. More than 100 examples were committed to the conflict and only four were lost

Although a very fast bomber when introduced, this advantage had faded by 1940; nonetheless, the Sparviero remained valued for its reliability and robustness.

Savoia-Marchetti SM.79-I Sparviero

Weight: 10,500kg (23,100lb)
Dimensions: Length 16.2m (53ft 2in), Wingspan 21.2m (69ft 7in), Height 4.1m (13ft 6in)
Powerplant: Three 582kW (780hp) Alfa-Romeo 126 R.C.34 nine-cylinder air-cooled radial piston engines
Maximum speed: 430km/h (267mph)
Range: 2000km (1243 miles)
Ceiling: 7000m (22,970ft)
Crew: 4–6
Armament: One 12.7mm (0.5in) Breda-SAFAT machine gun fixed, firing forward in fuselage above cockpit, one flexibly mounted in dorsal position and one in ventral position, one 7.7mm (0.303in) Lewis gun flexibly mounted in each waist position; up to 1000kg (2200lb) bombload

Opposite top:
Four SM.79Bs were acquired by the Iraqi Air Force in 1938. Powered by a pair of Fiat A.80 radial engines, all were destroyed during the 1941 uprising against the British.

Left and below:
This SM.79 was flown by Capitano Emilio Verrascina of 192ª Squadriglia, 81° Gruppo, based at Sciacca on Sicily in August 1940. The full extent of the distinctive dorsal gun position is revealed in this overhead view. The SM.79's defensive armament was more than adequate over Spain but proved severely lacking against modern fighters.

during combat, mainly due to the aircraft's speed, which rendered it virtually impossible for fighters to intercept. This was fortunate as the SM.79 was also too fast for contemporary Fiat CR.32s to escort. This invulnerability had evaporated by the time the SM.79 was committed to operations, and although the robust and reliable aircraft remained popular with crews, the Sparviero suffered heavy losses during the bombing campaign against Malta.

However, from 1940 onwards, the aircraft began to be used in the torpedo bomber role, resulting in considerable success against Allied shipping in the Mediterranean, sinking many vessels and seriously damaging others, the aircraft carrier *Indomitable*, for example, was put out of action by SM.79s for several months in 1943. After the armistice, the pro-German RSI continued to fly the Sparviero in the torpedo role, although with ever increasing losses, until the end of 1944.

Savoia-Marchetti SM.81 Pipistrello

The rugged SM.81 was essentially obsolete when Italy entered the war, but its versatility and reliability resulted in the Pipistrello ('Bat') remaining in service until the end of the conflict.

Flown in February 1934, a few months before the more famous (and much faster) SM.79, the SM.81 was destined to become a true workhorse of the Regia Aeronautica. It made its combat debut during 1935 in Ethiopia and was used, like the contemporary Ca.133, to drop poison gas, in contravention of international accords. Large numbers were committed to the Spanish Civil War in the following year and the

A lineup of SM.81s prepares to take part in celebrations for the 13th anniversary of the Regia Aeronautica on 28 March 1936.

Savoia Marchetti SM.81b Pipistrello

Weight: 10,450kg (23,040lb)
Dimensions: Length 17.8m (58ft 5in), Wingspan 24m (78ft 9in), Height 4.45m (14ft 7in)
Powerplant: Three 485kW (650hp) Alfa Romeo 125 R.C.35 9-cylinder air-cooled radial piston engines
Maximum speed: 340km/h (210mph)
Range: 1500km (930 miles)
Ceiling: 7000m (23,000ft)
Crew: 6
Armament: Two 7.7mm (0.303in) Breda-SAFAT machine guns in dorsal turret, two in retractable ventral turret, and one each flexibly mounted in waist positions: up to 1000kg (2200lb) bombload

Opposite:
This SM.81 of XXV Gruppo, 21° Stormo was based at Talavera de la Reina in Central Spain in 1936.

Below:
Used as a transport, this SM.81 was serving with Gruppo Trasporto 10 of the German allied Aeronautica Nazionale Repubblicana at Riga, Latvia in 1944.

Below:
Flown by the 202ª Squadriglia, 40° Gruppo, this SM.81 served on missions over Albania in 1941 and wears yellow cowls as a quick recognition aid.

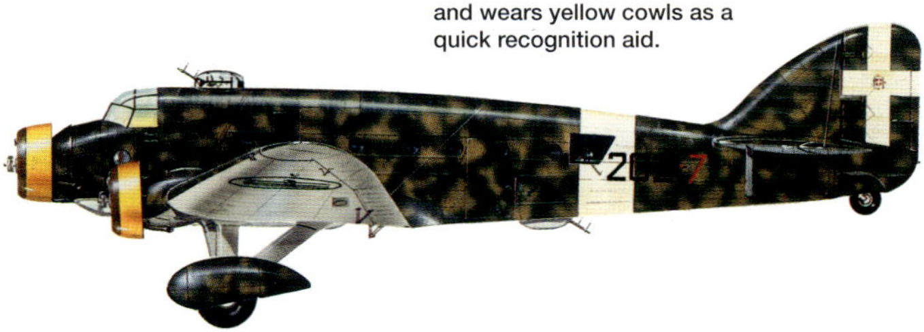

Pipistrello was one of the most important aircraft available to the Nationalist rebels. Around 100 aircraft served in Spain, initially proving capable of defending themselves from fighters until the more potent Polikarpov I-15 and I-16 began to arrive from the Soviet Union.

By the time Italy entered World War II, the SM.81 was slow and vulnerable, but around 300 remained in frontline service with Regia Aeronautica units. The aircraft was the main bomber type operating in the East African campaign and a single example opened hostilities in that theatre when it bombed Port Sudan on 11 June 1940. The SM.81 proved vulnerable, even when operated by night, and by March 1941 only 10 of an initial strength of 59 remained. The worsening losses suffered by the Pipistrello when committed to the North African campaign saw it increasingly used as a transport aircraft. Its robust, fixed undercarriage configuration rendered it eminently suitable for use in austere conditions such as those encountered at Stalingrad, where the SM.81 suffered heavy losses while contributing to the combined effort to resupply the encircled Sixth Army.

Aichi B7A Ryūsei 'Grace'

With exceptional performance and handling, the B7A never had the chance to operate from the carriers it was designed for, as none were afloat by the time it became available.

Designed to a challenging specification calling for an aircraft with manoeuvrability comparable to the Mitsubishi A6M 'Zero' fighter, a maximum speed of at least 550km/h (340mph), and a normal range of 1800km (1120 miles), the multirole Ryūsei ('Shooting Star') comfortably exceeded these requirements. Intended to replace both the Nakajima B6N torpedo bomber and

This forlorn unfinished B7A2 was photographed in the wreckage of the Omura manufacturing plant in 1945.

Aichi B7A2 Ryūsei

Weight: 5625kg (12,401lb)
Dimensions: Length 11.49m (37ft 8in), Wingspan 14.4m (47ft 3in), Height 4.08m (13ft 5in)
Powerplant: One 1361kW (1825hp) Nakajima Nk9C Homare 12 18-cylinder air-cooled radial piston engine
Maximum speed: 565km/h (351mph)
Range: 3040km (1889 miles)
Ceiling: 11,250m (36,910ft)
Crew: 2
Armament: Two 20mm (0.79in) Type 99 cannon fixed, forward firing in wings and one 0.92mm (0.31in) Type 1 machine gun flexibly mounted in rear cockpit; up to 800kg (1764lb) bombload or one 848kg (1870lb) Type 91 torpedo

Opposite top:
Seen here fitted with its torpedo armament, this was one of the few operational B7A2s, serving with the Yokosuka Kōkūtai at Yokosuka naval base in 1945.

Above:
Only two units ever used the B7A operationally, the Yokosuka Kōkūtai and the 752nd Kōkūtai. This aircraft belonged to the latter unit.

Right:
Pictured postwar while undergoing testing in the USA, the B7A impressed its new owners with its high speed and 'fighterlike' manoeuvrability.

the Yokosuka D4Y dive bomber, the B7A was specifically designed for the Imperial Navy's new *Taihō*-class carriers, the first of which had been laid down in July 1941. The aircraft was notably larger than its predecessors, as the larger deck lifts of the new carriers meant that previous size restrictions could be lifted and it became the largest and heaviest Japanese carrier aircraft to enter production. The Navy had specified that the new aircraft use the promising Nakajima Homare, rated at 1357kW (1820hp), but this was a brand new design and suffered from prolonged teething troubles, delaying the service entry of the new aircraft. In April 1944 the new Homare 12 became available delivering much improved reliability and the Ryūsei entered production fitted with this engine as the B7A2, the only production model.

Unfortunately for the B7A, the carrier *Taihō*, lead ship of its class and the only one to be completed, was sunk in November 1944. As a result the only combat use of the B7A took place from land with the aircraft seeing intense action at Okinawa. A single B7A was also likely the single aircraft (misidentified as a 'Judy' by US personnel) that crippled the carrier *Franklin* with two 250kg (550lb) bombs in a spectacular solo attack and knocked her out for the rest of the war. Only 114 B7As were built before an earthquake ended production in 1945.

Aichi D3A 'Val'

A profoundly accurate dive bomber, the D3A earned its place in history by spearheading the Pearl Harbor raid and is credited with sinking more Allied shipping than any other Axis aircraft.

Aichi maintained a close relationship with Heinkel during the 1930s and the influence of the German manufacturer is clear in the D3A's elegant elliptical wing form. The D3A was otherwise a conventional aircraft. Retractable undercarriage was seen as unnecessary for the comparatively slow flying aircraft, easily identifiable by its large wheel spats. Designed to meet a 1936 call for a monoplane

This D3A was serving with the 33rd Kōkūtai in mid-1942, based at Surabaya in Java.

Aichi D3A Val

Weight: 8407kg (3650lb)
Dimensions: Length 10.2m (33ft 6in), Wingspan 14.37m (47ft 2in), Height 3.35m (11ft)
Powerplant: One 802kW (1075hp) Mitsubishi Kinsei 44 14-cylinder air-cooled radial piston engine
Maximum speed: 389km/h (242mph)
Range: 1820km (1131 miles)
Ceiling: 9500m (31,170ft)
Crew: 2
Armament: Two 7.7mm (0.303in) Type 97 machine guns, fixed in forward fuselage decking and one 7.7 mm (0.303 in) Type 92 machine gun flexibly mounted in rear cockpit; one 250kg (550lb) bomb carried under the fuselage and two 60kg (130lb) bombs under the wings

Above and right:
One of the aircraft that took part in the 7 December 1941 Pearl Harbor attack, this D3A1 was part of the 2nd Kōkūsentai aboard the carrier *Soryu*.

Opposite top:
This D3A1 was serving with the Yokosuka Kōkūtai in 1940, at Yokosuka naval base, for testing and trials work.

dive bomber, the aircraft first flew in January 1938. It made its debut in November 1939, a month before its official acceptance by the Navy, in the Second Sino-Japanese War, dive bombing targets in support of the Imperial Army.

By the start of the Pacific war, the D3A1 was a proven weapon operated by experienced crews and the first 10 months of its involvement in World War II saw the aircraft attain the zenith of its career. 'Vals' sunk HMS *Hermes*, three cruisers, two destroyers and a corvette in the Indian Ocean in April 1942, an action that saw 80 per cent of the D3A's bombs hit their targets – an incredible level of accuracy for the era. In 1942, the D3A was fast and manoeuvrable enough to act as a fighter when necessary, but improvements in Allied fighters saw it become ever more vulnerable, despite the introduction of a more aerodynamic model, the D3A2 in late 1942, and it was replaced by the faster Yokosuka D4Y. The D3A continued to operate until the end of the conflict, often in the kamikaze role, sinking its last victim, the destroyer USS *William D. Porter*, on 10 June 1945.

Kawasaki Ki-48 'Lily'

Typical of many light bombers designed in the early stages of World War II, the Ki-48 was fairly fast but highly vulnerable to fighters once it lost the speed advantage it enjoyed during its early career.

Inspired by the high-speed Soviet Tupolev SB – which had shocked the Japanese by outpacing their Ki-27 fighters over China – the Ki-48 drew on Kawasaki's experience developing the Ki-45 heavy fighter. Speed was intended to be the Ki-48's primary defence and it was capable of exceeding 500km/h (310mph), but it was also provided with three defensive machine gun positions,

These Ki-48-Is were photographed in 1940, the same year the Ki-48 entered service.

Kawasaki Ki-48 Lily

Weight: 6750kg (14,881lb)
Dimensions: Length 12.75m (41ft 10in), Wingspan 17.45m (57ft 3in), Height 3.8m (12ft 6in)
Powerplant: Two 858kW (1150hp) Nakajima Ha-115 14-cylinder air-cooled radial piston engines

Maximum speed: 480km/h (289mph)
Range: 2400km (1491 miles)
Ceiling: 10,100m (33,135ft)
Crew: 4
Armament: One 7.7mm (0.303in) Type 89 machine gun, flexibly mounted in nose, dorsal and ventral positions; up to 800kg (1764lb) bombload

Opposite:
Operating in Thailand in April 1943, this Ki-48-Ib was on the strength of the 1st Chutai, 34th Sentai.

Above:
This Ki-48-I of the 3rd Chutai, 8th Hikosentai, was based in China in late 1940.

Left:
The Ki-48 continued to be used on trials work after it became too vulnerable for the frontline. This example was used to flight test the Ishikawajima Ne-20, Japan's first turbojet, which can be seen mounted under the bomb bay.

typical for the era but soon to prove inadequate. First flown in the summer of 1939, the Ki-48-Ia and near identical -Ib entered service in May the following year, beginning combat operations in China in the autumn of 1940. A little over a year later, in the first month of World War II, Ki-48s were heavily employed in the fighting in the Philippines and then in Malaya and Singapore, proving highly effective.

By early 1942, Japanese success in Burma allowed Ki-48s to bomb Assam airfield in India and in early 1943 the Ki-48-IIa appeared in units, with more powerful engines, more armour and a larger bombload alongside the Ki-48-IIb equipped with wing dive brakes and stressed for the dive-bombing role. In practice, however, the dive-bombing equipment was generally discarded to save weight. By this time, Allied air superiority compelled the Ki-48 to operate mostly by night, although the difficult terrain prevalent in Burma (modern-day Myanmar) prevented the construction of Allied airbases, allowing the Ki-48 to continue operating successfully by day in the theatre until early 1945.

Towards the end of the war, many aircraft were converted to the Ki-48-II KAI model fitted with 800kg (1760lb) of explosives for the kamikaze role.

Mitsubishi G3M 'Nell'

Although it was coming to the end of its career by the time of Pearl Harbor, the G3M was involved in several important operations during the early stages of the Pacific War.

Despite being flown for the first time as early as July 1935, the G3M was an all-metal cantilever monoplane with retractable undercarriage and when it entered service possessed unprecedented speed and range. Intended specifically for the anti-shipping mission, its impressive performance stemmed from a prescient specification issued by Admiral Yamamoto, later the commander in

These G3M2s of the Mihoro Kōkūtai were stationed on Tinian in the Mariana Islands during early 1942.

Mitsubishi G3M2

Weight: 8000kg (17,637lb)
Dimensions: Length 16.45m (54ft), Wingspan 25m (82ft), Height 3.69m (12ft 1in)
Powerplant: Two 791kW (1061hp) Mitsubishi Kinsei 14-cylinder air-cooled radial piston engines
Maximum speed: 375km/h (233mph)
Range: 4400km (2700 miles)
Ceiling: 9200m (30,200ft)
Crew: 7
Armament: One 20mm (0.79in) Type 99 cannon flexibly mounted in dorsal position, one 7.7mm (0.303in) Type 92 machine gun in retractable forward dorsal turret and one in each fuselage waist blister; up to 800kg (1800lb) bombload or one 848kg (1870lb) Type 91 torpedo

Above and right:
T-342 was a G3M2 on the strength of the Takao Kōkūtai, of the 21st Kōkūsentai operating from Hanoi, in Indochina (modern-day Vietnam), in March 1941.

Opposite top:
This G3M2 was based at Hankow for operations over the Szechwan Province, China, during April and May 1940.

chief of the Imperial Navy. Mitsubishi's winning design could carry either bombs or a torpedo but in order to meet the challenging range and speed requirements, the G3M was not equipped with any armour or self-sealing fuel tanks, rendering it vulnerable if hit by enemy fire – a fact that became apparent during the G3M's earliest operations over China during 1937, where Chinese fighters inflicted serious losses. When Japan entered World War II, the G3M was considered obsolescent but more than 200 were still in frontline service with the Imperial Navy and 54 aircraft were flown from bases in Formosa to bomb targets in the Philippines while others attacked Singapore. The G3M's single most important mission took place on 10 December 1941 when G3Ms, in concert with its successor aircraft, the G4M, attacked and sank the British battleship *Prince of Wales* and the cruiser *Repulse* off the coast of Malaya. Early 1942 saw G3Ms form part of the force that bombed Darwin and as late as January 1943 the aircraft torpedoed and hit the American cruiser *Chicago*. Subsequently, the G3M was withdrawn from frontline service and the aircraft served as glider tugs, as VIP transports for high-ranking officers, and as trainers for aircrew and paratroops.

Mitsubishi G4M 'Betty'

The Japanese navy's most important land-based bomber, the G4M was built to replace the G3M. Like the earlier aircraft, it delivered exceptional range but was prone to catching fire when hit.

The specification for a G3M replacement was issued just two months after the aircraft entered service, calling for a range of 3,700 km (2300 miles), an 800kg (1764lb) payload, and a top speed of 398 km/h (247mph). As with its predecessor, the design was intended for conventional bombing as well as torpedo attack and included neither armour nor self-sealing fuel tanks to save weight and meet the

An anonymous G4M in flight. Despite the aircraft's flammable reputation, it possessed excellent range and performance.

Mitsubishi G4M1

Weight: 12,860kg (28,351lb)
Dimensions: Length 19.97m (65ft 6in), Wingspan 24.89m (81ft 8in) Height 4.9m (16ft 1in)
Powerplant: Two 1140kW (1530hp) Mitsubishi MK4A Kasei 11 14-cylinder air-cooled radial piston engines
Maximum speed: 428km/h (266mph)
Range: 2852km (1772 miles)
Ceiling: 9144m (30,000ft)
Crew: 7
Armament: One 20mm (0.79in) Type 99 cannon in tail position, one 7.7mm (0.303in) Type 92 machine gun in dorsal turret, nos and ventral positions; up to 1000kg (2200lb) bombload or one 848kg (1870lb) Type 91 torpedo

Opposite:
Painted in an unusual finish of overall forest green, this G4M1 was serving with the 761st Kōkūtai at Kanoya, southern Kyushu, in 1943.

Above:
A G4M3 of the Yokosuka Kōkūtai in September 1945. By this juncture the G4M had acquired a powered dorsal turret and armour protection but still proved vulnerable if intercepted.

Below:
Based at the major Japanese stronghold of Rabaul in New Britain, this G4M1 belonged to the 705th Kōkūtai.

specification. Aerodynamic design of the G4M was excellent, the engine cowling design was superior to contemporary Western aircraft and the overall fuselage shape was extremely efficient. The shape also led to the Japanese nickname for the aircraft, 'Hamaki' meaning 'Cigar', a name that became grimly appropriate when the aircraft met determined fighter opposition.

The first flight occurred in October 1939 and the first production aircraft appeared in April 1941 with combat operations beginning in September 1940 in China. The aircraft was very successful in the first year of the Pacific war, with G4Ms contributing to the loss of HMS *Prince of Wales* and *Repulse* only two days after bombing Clark Field in the Philippines and attacking Singapore and Darwin. Weak fighter opposition meant losses were light but as Allied defences became more effective the vulnerability of the G4M became apparent and its propensity to burst into flames when hit led to its nickname of the 'One Shot Lighter' by Allied pilots. Losses increased despite the introduction of self sealing tanks and armour protection on later models, but the lack of a successor saw the G4M produced until the end of hostilities, becoming the most produced twin-engined aircraft in Japanese service.

Mitsubishi Ki-21 'Sally'

Built to an ambitious specification issued by the Imperial Army in 1936, the Ki-21 flew for the first time in December 1936 and was in action over China by late 1938.

The Ki-21 was conceived specifically for use in the vast areas seized by Japan in the early 1930s. Manchuria bordered the Soviet Union and the Army required a bomber that could deliver tactical bombloads over great distances of mostly uninhabited territory. Mitsubishi's bomber beat a rival design from Nakajima to obtain a production contract and small numbers of the initial production Ki-21-Ia were

A Ki-21-I of the 60th Sentai photographed in flight over China.

Mitsubishi Ki-21-IIb

Weight: 10,600kg (23,369lb)
Dimensions: Length 16m (52ft 6in), Wingspan 22.5m (73ft 10in), Height 4.85m (15ft 11in)
Powerplant: Two 1100kW (1500hp) Mitsubishi Ha-101 14-cylinder air-cooled radial piston engines
Maximum speed: 485km/h (301mph)
Range: 2700km (1700 miles)
Ceiling: 10,000m (33,000ft)
Crew: 5–7
Armament: One 12.7mm (0.5in) Ho-103 machine gun flexibly mounted in dorsal position and one 7.7mm (0.303in) Type 92 machine gun flexibly mounted in nose, ventral, beam, and tail positions; up to 1000kg (2200lb) bombload

Opposite top:
This Ki-21-Ia of the 2nd Chutai, 60th Sentai, was operating in Manchuria in 1939 and boasts an unusual wraparound green and brown camouflage scheme encircling the entire fuselage.

Above:
This Ki-21-IIb of an unknown unit in 1944 shows the later production standard with the dorsal turret replacing the earlier extensive 'greenhouse'. The crude camouflage scheme was likely applied at unit level.

Right:
Another anonymous Ki-21 shows off its distinctive dorsal canopy and the unusually large and prominent aerial mast.

introduced to operations supplementing Fiat BR.20s on raids over China. Crews soon expressed a preference for the Ki-21 over the Italian aircraft, as it boasted a generally superior performance, although it carried a smaller bombload – a legacy of the specific operational requirement for which it was designed. The Ki-21 subsequently saw action in 1939 against the very opponent it was intended to face during the intense four-month war with the Soviet Union, known in Japan as the Nomonhan Incident, operating as intended in the long-range tactical bombing role. Losses to Soviet fighters were heavy and prompted the introduction of some armour and self-sealing fuel tanks in the Ki-21-Ib.

By the outbreak of the Pacific War, IJAAF units were re-equipping with the improved Ki-21-IIa with more powerful engines and larger tail surfaces but the aircraft was being met by ever more effective Allied fighters and losses began to increase to alarming levels, resulting in the introduction of the Ki-21-IIb with a power operated dorsal turret and further armour provided for pilot and dorsal gunner. This made little difference to the aircraft's survivability and the Ki-21 was gradually withdrawn from frontline units.

Mitsubishi Ki-30 'Ann'

Designed to replace the last biplane bomber of the Japanese Army, the highly conventional Ki-30 performed well until its vulnerability to fighter opposition became starkly apparent.

The Ki-30 was developed to supersede the Kawasaki Ki-3, the last biplane bomber ordered by the IJAAF (Imperial Japanese Army Air Service), and first flew in February 1937. Despite the Ki-3's obsolescent configuration, it proved satisfactory in service apart from its Kawasaki Ha-2 V-12 engine (a licence-built BMW VI), which was highly unreliable. The specification for its replacement therefore required either

This Ki-30 was photographed crossing the Ordos Desert during a mission to bomb the town of Shenmu, China, on 24 January 1941.

Mitsubishi Ki-30 'Ann'

Weight: 3322kg (7324lb)
Dimensions: Length 10.34m (33ft 11in), Wingspan 14.55m (47ft 9in), Height 3.65m (12ft)
Powerplant: One 708kW (950hp) Mitsubishi Ha-5 Zuisei 14-cylinder air-cooled radial piston engine
Maximum speed: 423km/h (263mph)
Range: 1700km (1056 miles)
Ceiling: 8570m (28,117ft)
Crew: 2
Armament: One (sometimes two) 7.7mm (0.303in) Type 97 machine gun fixed, forward firing in wing(s) and one 7.7mm (0.303in) Type 92 machine gun flexibly mounted in rear cockpit; up to 400kg (882lb) bombload

Opposite top:
Flying with the 2nd Chutai of the 10th Hikosentai in 1942, this Ki-30 was operating in China.

Above:
The Ki-30 saw much action in China; these examples are shown en route to bomb Yan'An in Shaanxi Province on 7 November 1939 during the Sino-Japanese War.

a Mitsubishi Ha-6 or Nakajima Ha-5 radial engine and Mitsubishi's Ki-30 proved successful in competition against Kawasaki's rival Ki-32. Despite this, several hundred examples of the Ki-32 were subsequently produced due to its excellent flying characteristics, but it was withdrawn from combat service before the end of 1941. Mitsubishi's Ki-30 meanwhile saw considerable service in the early stages of Japan's involvement in World War II.

Initially deployed in China, the Ki-30 was reliable and possessed sufficiently high performance that losses were comparatively light. By the beginning of 1941 the Ki-30 was numerically the most important bomber in IJAAF service and saw action during the campaigns in the Philippines and into Burma (Myanmar). Operating in the absence of fighter opposition, the Ki-30, like equivalent light bombers such as the Su-2 and Fairey Battle, was capable and effective but when faced with modern fighters it proved appallingly vulnerable. By the end of 1942 most Imperial Army Ki-30s had been relegated to training.

However, the aircraft saw further service with the Royal Thai Air Force, with whom it proved popular and efficient, seeing combat with Thai forces against the French in early 1941 and later flying as a component of the Northern Air Wing of the IJAAF against the Allies in Burma.

Mitsubishi Ki-51 'Sonia'

Resembling a scaled-down Ki-30, the Ki-51 was a multirole aircraft, capable of performing reconnaissance, observation, artillery spotting, low-level attack and dive bombing.

First flown in mid-1939, flight testing of the Ki-51 proved largely trouble-free. In contrast to the preceding Ki-30, the Ki-51 disposed of an internal bomb bay, all payloads being carried externally. Although this approach caused an inevitable penalty in drag, it allowed for a wider variety of stores to be carried and dispensed with the hydraulically operated bay doors that on the Ki-30 had proved troublesome

This damaged Ki-51 was discovered abandoned on Hollandia airfield, northwestern New Guinea, in April 1944.

Mitsubishi Ki-51 'Sonia'

Weight: 2920kg (6437lb)
Dimensions: Length 9.2m (30ft 2in), Wingspan 12.1m (39ft 8in), Height 2.73m (9ft)
Powerplant: One 701kW (940hp) Mitsubishi Ha-26-II 14-cylinder air-cooled radial piston engine
Maximum speed: 425km/h (264mph)
Range: 1060km (659 miles)
Ceiling: 8270m (27,130ft)
Crew: 2
Armament: Two 7.7mm (0.303 in) Type 89 machine guns or two 12.7mm (0.5in) Ho-103 machine guns fixed, firing forward in wings and one 7.7 mm (.303 in) Te-4 machine gun flexibly mounted in rear cockpit; up to 200kg (440lb) bombload

Opposite top:
By the end of the conflict, virtually all aircraft apart from the latest fighters were being used in suicide attacks. This Ki-51 belonged to the 64th Shinbutai Kōkūtai 'special attack unit' from Hokkota Air Base, April 1945.

Above:
Like most wartime Japanese aircraft, the Ki-51 first saw combat in China. These aircraft were photographed warming up before a mission on 28 November 1941, just days before the Pacific War began.

in service. Unusually for a Japanese aircraft, the design incorporated some armour protection from the start and the aircraft was notable for its outstanding manoeuvrability: in mock combat against a Ki-27 during testing, the Ki-51 proved broadly equivalent to the fighter, itself noted for its exceptional agility, and later analysis revealed that the Ki-27's gun camera had scored not a single hit on the bomber.

In action from June 1941, the comparatively simple Ki-51 was reliable, and during the winter in northwest China it stood up to the harsh conditions far better than the Ki-32 aircraft it replaced. Committed to operations during World War II, the aircraft proved vulnerable to faster Allied fighters but in the hands of an experienced crew could cause problems due to its manoeuvrability. It saw much action over the vast areas of the Chinese and Burmese fronts, proving effective as a ground-attack aircraft and in its ability to operate from austere forward airfields. Later in the war, the aircraft was increasingly used for kamikaze attacks, although a Ki-51 was responsible for sinking the final US warship of the war by conventional attack when on 6 August 1945 a single aircraft depth charged the *Balao*-class submarine USS *Bullhead* off the coast of Bali.

Mitsubishi Ki-67 Hiryū 'Peggy'

The superlative Ki-67 had the misfortune to appear only once Japan had lost air supremacy, but in just over a year of operations it proved to be the finest bomber developed in Japan.

The Ki-67 was designed to meet a 1941 specification for a much faster bomber than any previous design, yet it also possessed remarkable agility. Fitted with self-sealing fuel tanks and decent armour from the start, it gained a unprecedented reputation for toughness among Japanese designs. The aircraft first flew in December 1942 and was developed concurrently as a bomber and as a heavy escort

The same aircraft in the profile above, with ground crew sitting in the shade of the aircraft's wings.

Mitsubishi Ki-67 'Peggy'	
Weight: 13,765kg (30,347lb) **Dimensions:** Length 18.7m (61ft 4in), Wingspan 22.5m (73ft 10in), Height 7.7m (25ft 3in) **Powerplant:** Two 1417kW (1900hp) Mitsubishi Ha-104 18-cylinder air-cooled radial piston engines **Maximum speed:** 537km/h (334mph)	**Range:** 3800km (2361 miles) **Ceiling:** 9470m (31,070ft) **Crew:** 6–8 **Armament:** One 20mm (0.79in) Ho-5 cannon in dorsal turret, one 12.7mm (0.5in) machine gun flexibly mounted in nose, tail and each waist position; up to 800kg (1764lb) bombload or one 848kg (1870lb) Type 91 torpedo

Opposite, above and right: Operating with the Imperial Army Air Force's 74th Sentai, this Ki-67-Ib was based at Matsumoto Airfield in 1945. The yellow leading edges prominent in this head-on view of the Ki-67 were an identification feature applied to all Japanese military aircraft after early 1943.

fighter, the Ki-69, although the latter was abandoned when delays to the bomber became unacceptable. The first production examples appeared in the spring of 1944 but initial deliveries were slow and it was only in October that the first combat missions flew with Ki-67s attacking US forces in Formosa and the Ryukyu Islands.

In service the *Hiryū* ('Flying Dragon') proved immensely popular with its crews thanks to its easy flying characteristics, performance and impressive manoeuvrability, all of which contributed to its comparative survivability. Many projects were schemed for the Ki-67 but only two bomber variants were produced in numbers, the Ki-67-Ia, most of which served as torpedo bombers, and the Ki-67-Ib, which differed only in possessing an upgunned tail turret with two 20mm (0.79in) cannon. Its excellent performance also resulted in the construction of 22 examples of a fighter variant, the Ki-109, sporting an enormous 75mm (2.95in) cannon in the nose. Built to combat B-29 raids, the aircraft did not possess sufficient altitude performance to succeed in this role. A tiny number of specialized suicide attackers were also built, the most notable being the nine *Sakura-Dan* ('Cherry Blossom') conversions with a 2900kg (6400lb) shaped charge behind the cockpit.

Nakajima B5N 'Kate'

Japan's standard carrier-borne torpedo bomber for most of the conflict, the B5N achieved notoriety due to its considerable success in the early stages of the Pacific War.

Notably superior to its US torpedo bomber equivalent, the TBD Devastator, the B5N was nonetheless nudging obsolescence by late 1941. Despite this, its career was outstanding, with the B5N responsible for sinking five battleships at Pearl Harbor. Operating alongside Aichi D3As, the B5N sent many other vessels to the bottom, most notably the fleet carriers *Lexington* and *Hornet* in May

Two B5N2s cruise over Japanese shipping moored in the major naval base at Truk (modern-day Chuuk) in the Caroline Islands.

Nakajima B5N2

Weight: 4100kg (9039lb)
Dimensions: Length 10.3m (33ft 10in), Wingspan 15.52m (50ft 11in), Height 3.7m (12ft 2in)
Powerplant: One 746kW (1000hp) Nakajima NK1B Sakae 11 14-cylinder air-cooled radial piston engine

Maximum speed: 378km/h (235mph)
Range: 1990km (1237 miles)
Ceiling: 8260m (27,100ft)
Crew: 3
Armament: One 7.7mm (0.303in) Type 92 machine gun flexibly mounted in rear cockpit; up to 500kg (1100lb) bombload or one 848kg (1870lb) Type 91 torpedo

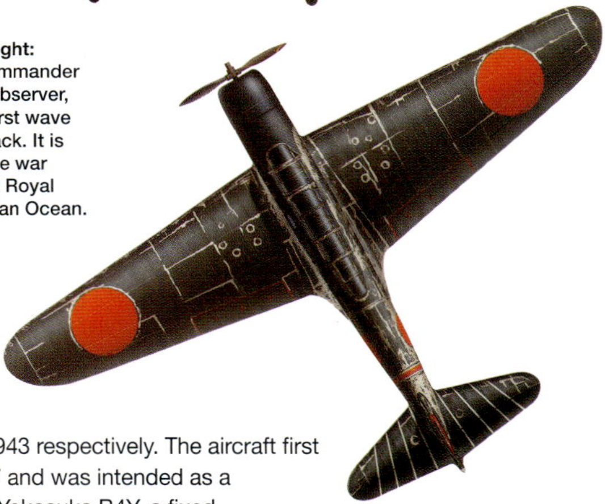

Opposite, above and right: This aircraft carried Commander Mitsuo Fuchida as its observer, who commanded the first wave of the Pearl Harbor attack. It is pictured here later in the war while operating against Royal Navy targets in the Indian Ocean.

1942 and January 1943 respectively. The aircraft first flew in January 1937 and was intended as a replacement for the Yokosuka B4Y, a fixed undercarriage biplane, representing a considerable technological leap with its cantilever monoplane structure and retractable undercarriage. Like most Japanese aircraft in service at the outbreak of World War II, the B5N had already seen combat during the Second Sino-Japanese War, which revealed several deficiencies in the initial B5N1 production variant. The Navy was concerned about the lack of protection for the fuel tanks and crew, but Nakajima resisted adding armour and self-sealing tanks due to the detrimental effect on performance, instead proposing to increase speed so the aircraft could outrun enemy fighters.

In the new B5N2 version, a more powerful Nakajima Sakae 11-cylinder engine replaced the Hikari 9-cylinder unit of the B5N1 in an aerodynamically clean cowl. However, performance was only marginally improved and the aircraft remained vulnerable to modern fighters. Nonetheless, the B5N2 was put into production and became the most numerous wartime variant. Progressively withdrawn from carrier use as the B6N entered service, the B5N continued to operate as an anti-submarine aircraft.

Nakajima B6N Tenzan 'Jill'

Nakajima's successor to its own supremely successful B5N, the Tenzan ('Heavenly Mountain') was a more formidable aircraft, but its service entry was delayed by protracted development issues.

The B6N first flew in March 1941, before Japan entered the war with the Allies. Intended to replace the B5N on Japanese carriers, its troubled development meant that by the time it became available most of Japan's fleet carriers had been sunk, and the Tenzan operated largely from shore bases. Problems with handling immediately afflicted the new B6N, but the main issue with the aircraft

Probably photographed during training aboard *Zuikaku,* this torpedo-armed B5N2 is shown taking off in 1944.

Nakajima B6N2

Weight: 5650kg (12,456lb)
Dimensions: Length 10.87m (35ft 8in), Wingspan 14.9m (48ft 11in), Height 3.8m (12ft 6in)
Powerplant: One 1380kW (1850hp) Mitsubishi MK4T Kasei 25 14-cylinder air-cooled radial piston engine
Maximum speed: 480km/h (298mph)
Range: 3045km (1892 miles)
Ceiling: 9040m (29,660ft)
Crew: 3
Armament: One 7.7mm (0.303in) Type 92 machine gun flexibly mounted in rear cockpit and another flexibly mounted in ventral tunnel; up to 800kg (1764lb) bombload or one 848kg (1870lb) Type 91 torpedo

Opposite top:
A B6N2 shows off its distinctive slightly forward-swept tail, adopted to allow sufficient clearance on the standard deck lifts of Japanese carriers.

Above:
Graphically illustrating the immense defensive firepower faced by torpedo aircraft attacking a US carrier, this B6N2 was photographed in the final stages of its attack on USS *Yorktown* off Truk in April 1944.

was its engine. Although the Navy had requested the use of the proven Kasei 14-cylinder radial, a product of Nakajima's arch-rival Mitsubishi, the B6N1 was instead fitted with Nakajima's own 14-cylinder Mamoru engine. Although it delivered more power, the Mamoru was unreliable, prone to excessive vibration and overheating, and rarely delivered its rated power. Eventually considered reliable enough for production, only 133 B6Ns were built with the Mamoru before the Navy ordered its production stopped and specified the originally requested Kasei engine; consequently, the vast majority of B6Ns were Kasei-powered and designated B6N2.

The aircraft first went into action in November 1943, from shore bases on Rabaul, attacking Allied shipping off the Solomon Islands. The first carrier-based combat took place during the Battle of the Philippine Sea in June 1944, by which time the US had established convincing air superiority and the aircraft suffered heavy losses from F6F Hellcats. Subsequently, virtually all B6N operations took place from land, especially over Okinawa in 1945.

Nakajima Ki-49 Donryū 'Helen'

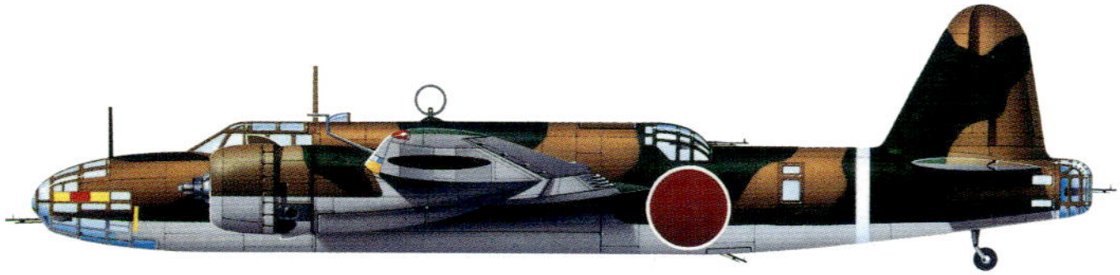

Intended to replace the Ki-21, the Donryū ('Storm Dragon') was a more formidable aircraft, capable of penetrating enemy airspace without requiring a fighter escort.

As early as 1938, it became clear that the Ki-21 could not operate without fighter protection, prompting the Army to require its replacement to have the speed and defensive armament necessary to function independently. Meanwhile, Nakajima had been undertaking design studies for just such an aircraft following their loss to Mitsubishi's Ki-21 in the design competition of 1937. Mitsubishi

Caught in the gun camera of an American fighter, this Ki-49 is shown left smoking from a strafing attack.

Nakajima Ki-49 Donryu 'Helen'

Weight: 11,400kg (25,133lb)
Dimensions: Length 16.5m (54ft 2in), Wingspan 20.42m (67ft), Height 4.25m (13ft 11in)
Powerplant: Two 1119kW (1500hp) Nakajima Ha-109 14-cylinder air-cooled radial piston engines
Maximum speed: 492km/h (306mph)
Range: 2950km (1833 miles)
Ceiling: 9300m (30,150ft)
Crew: 8
Armament: One 20mm (0.79in) Ho-1 cannon in dorsal position and one 7.7mm (0.303in) Type 89 machine gun flexibly mounted in nose, tail, ventral and each waist position; up to 1000kg (2200lb) bombload

Opposite:
Devoid of unit marking, this Ki-49-I was serving in China in early 1944.

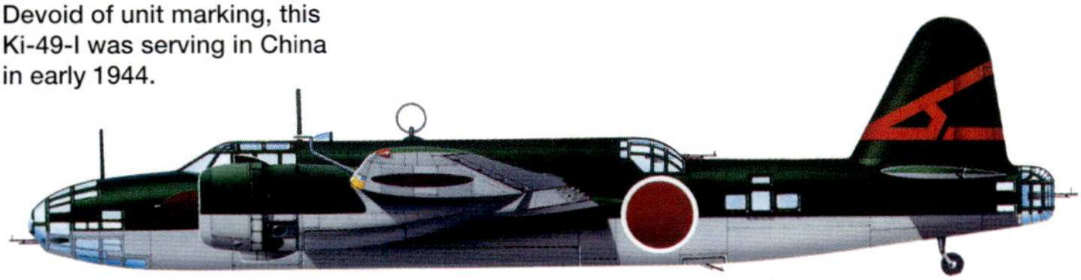

Above:
A Ki-49-II-Ko of the 61st Sentai based in Taiwan during 1945. The red tail marking of the Sentai consists of an abstracted representation of the Arabic numerals 61.

Below:
Operated over Burma, the Dutch East Indies (modern-day Indonesia), and New Guinea in 1944, this Ki-49-II-Ko of the 62nd Sentai displays rather loosely applied camouflage.

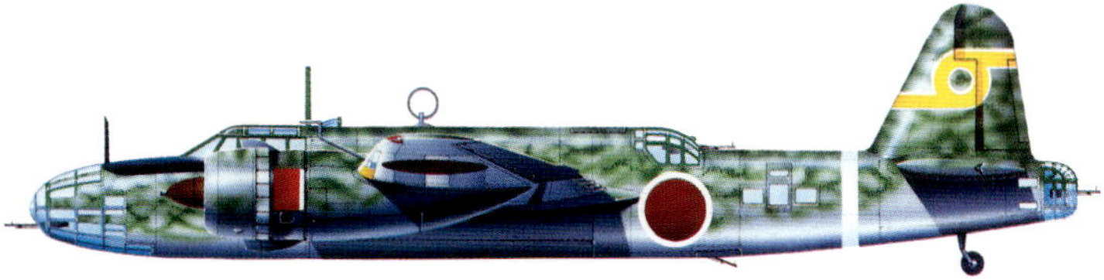

withdrew their own Ki-50 design from consideration when they realized how far advanced Nakajima's Ki-49 design was and the aircraft proceeded through testing and into production without any competitor. First flown in 1939, the Ki-49 was the first Japanese bomber to feature self-sealing tanks and armour protection for the crew from the outset.

The aircraft entered service in the autumn of 1941 and only saw a few months of action before being committed to the Pacific War. Early production aircraft were underpowered, leading to the introduction of the improved Ki-49-IIa version in early 1942, fitted with more powerful Ha-109 engines in place of the original Ha-5 KAIs. Despite the aircraft's armament and comparatively high performance, the Ki-49 still suffered high losses when faced with Allied fighters, a situation that the upgrading of three of the machine guns to 12.7mm (0.5in) calibre and improvements to the armour and self-sealing tanks did little to ameliorate. The futility of attempting to operate the Ki-49 as a conventional daylight bomber in the face of overwhelming Allied fighter strength resulted in the use of the Donryū as an anti-submarine warfare patrol aircraft and troop transport as well as in the kamikaze role.

Yokosuka D4Y Suisei 'Judy'

Designed to replace the Aichi D3A, the D4Y was a notably faster aircraft and was one of very few Japanese wartime aircraft produced with a liquid-cooled engine.

The Japanese equivalent to the US Navy's SB2C Helldiver, the D4Y was faster, handled better and was generally a notably less problematic design, although initial production aircraft suffered from engine unreliability. The aircraft derived from a specification calling for a long-range dive bomber able to match the performance of the A6M Zero fighter. To meet this challenging requirement,

YA D4Y1 is sen taking off from the carrier *Junyo* during the Battle of the Philippine Sea. Note the inline engine of this early model.

Yokosuka D4Y2

Weight: 4250kg (9370lb)
Dimensions: Length 10.22m (33ft 6in), Wingspan 11.5m (37ft 9in), Height 3.74m (12ft 3in)
Powerplant: One 1044kW (1400hp) Aichi Atsuta 32 liquid-cooled inverted V-12 piston engine
Maximum speed: 550km/h (342mph)
Range: 1465km (910 miles)
Ceiling: 10,700m (35,105ft)
Crew: 2
Armament: Two 7.7mm (0.303in) Type 97 machine guns, fixed forward firing in wings and one 7.92mm (0.31in) Type 1 machine gun flexibly mounted in rear cockpit; up to 800kg (1764lb) bombload

Opposite top:
This D4Y3, assigned to the 601st Kōkūtai, was stationed at Hyakurihara naval base when hostilities ceased.

Above:
This D4Y3, abandoned at Clark Field in the Philippines in January 1945, was restored to airworthy condition and tested by the Technical Air Intelligence Unit, South West Pacific Area, as shown here.

a liquid-cooled engine, the Aichi Atsuta, a licence-built Daimler-Benz DB 601, was selected due to its low drag, although this would prove an unhappy choice. Making its maiden flight in December 1940, the first D4Ys operated in the carrier reconnaissance role, as the D4Y1-C, with two acting in this capacity during the Battle of Midway in June 1942. The D4Y1 dive bomber saw extensive action at the Battle of the Marianas but suffered appalling losses, as its speed advantage over the F4F Wildcat did not extend to the faster F6F Hellcat. As was normal for Japanese combat aircraft, the D4Y did not possess self-sealing fuel tanks or armour and tended to catch fire when hit by gunfire.

Meanwhile, the poor reliability suffered by the engine resulted in a switch to the proven Mitsubishi Kinsei radial engine in the D4Y3, completely transforming the aircraft's serviceability although cruising speed and range were somewhat reduced. By the time the D4Y3 entered service virtually all of Japan's carriers had been sunk and the aircraft operated almost entirely from shore bases. Despite the lack of experienced aircrew and the overwhelming numerical superiority of Allied airpower, the Suisei still managed a few successes, seriously damaging several ships and sinking the carrier USS *Princeton*.

Yokosuka P1Y Ginga 'Frances'

A potentially outstanding aircraft, the fast and nimble P1Y had to contend with unreliable engines and problematic hydraulics while facing near-total Allied air supremacy.

The Ginga ('Galaxy') first flew in August 1943 and, while partly intended to replace the G4M bomber, also led a new class of Imperial Navy aircraft: a fast, multi-engine bomber capable of conventional, torpedo or dive-bombing missions. As a result the aircraft became the first, and ultimately only, aircraft to receive the Navy's 'P' designation. In performance it was similar to the Army's popular Ki-67.

Mid-1945, this P1Y1 is caught in an exceptionally clear gun-camera image for the period.

Yokosuka P1Y1a

Weight: 13,500kg (29,762lb)
Dimensions: Length 15m (49ft 3in), Wingspan 20m (65ft 7in), Height 4.3m (14ft 1in)
Powerplant: Two 1,361kW (1,825hp) Nakajima NK9C Homare 12 18-cylinder air-cooled radial piston engines
Maximum speed: 547km/h (340mph)
Range: 5370km (3340 miles)
Ceiling: 9400m (30,400ft)
Crew: 3
Armament: One 20mm (0.79in) Type 99 cannon flexibly mounted in nose, one 13mm (0.51in) Type 2 machine gun flexibly mounted in dorsal position; up to 1000 kg (2200lb) bombload or one 848kg (1870lb) Type 91 torpedo

Opposite and above:
A P1Y1 of the 762nd Kōkūtai, 5th Kōkū Kantai, was based at Kanoya, Japan. This aircraft was believed to be the lead aircraft of the kamikaze contingent in Operation Kikusui II (Floating Chrysanthemum II), targeting Allied landings on Okinawa on 12 April 1944.

Above:
The kanji character on this P1Y1's tail code identifies it as part of the Yokosuka Kōkūtai, where it was used for trial duties in August 1945.

Test pilots were highly enthusiastic about the new aircraft and production, which was to be handled by Nakajima, began swiftly. Unfortunately for the new aircraft, the pilots' enthusiasm was not shared by ground crew. Its Homare radial engines were notoriously unreliable and rarely delivered their rated power, requiring constant mechanical attention; its hydraulic systems also failed regularly. These problems delayed the Navy's acceptance of the aircraft, although a few pre-production examples were delivered to a service test unit in February 1943, proving unreliable even with highly experienced aircrew and the best maintenance personnel.

Eventually, however, the production aircraft was cleared for service use and the P1Y entered combat in the Marianas in June 1944. Shortages in experienced crew, fuel and spares crippled the aircraft's ability to operate as intended, however, even in its relatively brief service life, the P1Y demonstrated that it was a formidable opponent. Its most destructive use was as a suicide aircraft: a single P1Y sank the escort carrier *Ommaney Bay* in January 1945. A night fighter development, the P1Y-2S Kyokko ('Aurora') was also produced in numbers but its success against B-29s was compromised by its lack of altitude performance.

IAR 37, 38, 39

More than 300 examples of this light bomber and reconnaissance aircraft were produced and it was heavily used by the Romanian Air Force throughout the war and afterwards.

Conceptually obsolete when it entered service in 1939, the IAR 37 proved surprisingly successful. The aircraft enjoyed a long production life, with the last example of the IAR 39 variant only rolling out of the factory at the end of 1944. Developed in the late 1930s, the first prototype of this conventional biplane tactical bomber made its maiden flight in 1937 and entered production in the following year. Only

This IAR 37 was photographed in the spring of 1945 after Romania had joined the Allies.

IAR 39

Weight: 3085kg (6801lb)
Dimensions: Length 9.6m (31ft 6in), Wingspan 13.1m (43ft), Height 3.99m (13ft 1in)
Powerplant: One 716kW (960hp) IAR K.14-IV C32 14-cylinder liquid-cooled radial piston engine
Maximum speed: 336km/h (209mph)
Range: 1050km (652 miles)
Ceiling: 8000m (26,245ft)
Crew: 3
Armament: Two 7.92mm (0.31in) FN-Browning machine guns fixed, forward firing in upper wing and one flexibly mounted in rear cockpit; up to 288kg (635lb) bombload

Opposite top:
Wearing the Romanian roundels adopted after Romania switched sides in August 1944, this IAR 39 was serving in the army co-operation role during the autumn of 1945.

Above (both images):
This IAR 39 flew with the 4th Romanian Army at Stalingrad in late 1942 and features temporary white camouflage on its upper surfaces.

a relatively few of the initial variant were produced before the interim IAR 38 version, powered by a BMW 132 engine in place of the IAR K14 (a licence-built Gnome-Rhône Mistral Major) began to be built in 1939. Just 75 of this model were produced, however, before production switched to the IAR 39 with a more powerful version of the K14 and that made up the majority of aircraft produced.

When Romania joined Germany in its invasion of the Soviet Union, 15 squadrons were operating the IAR biplane, making their first attack on 22 June 1941 in a raid on a Soviet airfield near Izmail, Ukraine. Operations continued as Axis forces pressed further into the USSR, culminating in fierce activity around Stalingrad. By this time losses of the biplanes began to mount as Soviet fighters improved in quality, and the aircraft were withdrawn to perform coastal patrols over the Black Sea. However, despite obsolescence, the IAR bombers returned to frontline bombing missions in spring 1944, fighting in the Transylvanian campaign. The last combat sortie was flown on 8 May 1944, but the aircraft persisted in service as a trainer into the 1960s.

INDEX

Page numbers in **bold** refer to captions.

Aichi B7A Ryūsei 'Grace' 188–9
Aichi D3A 'Val' 190–1, **190**, 206–7, 212
  Aichi D3A1 'Val' 191, **191**
  Aichi D3A2 'Val' 191
Air France 20, 21
Air Guard Training Center **17**
Air Ministry 74–5, 84–5, 92, 95
Albert Canal **81**
Alfa Romeo 169, 179
Allied convoys **8**, 151, 154–5, **155**, 185, 190, 209
  Convoy PQ-17 155
Amiot 143 12–13, **12–13**
  Amiot 143M **13**
Anglo-Iraqi War 91, 169, **169**
Arado Ar 234 Blitz 9, 142–3, **142–3**
  Arado Ar 234B Blitz 143
  Arado Ar 234B-2 Blitz **143**
Ark Royal (aircraft carrier) 83, **83**
Arkhangelsky, Aleksander 50, 51
Arkhangelsky Ar-2 50–1, **50–1**
Armee de l'Air 20, 22, **117**, 130, 132, 136
Armstrong-Whitworth Albemarle 60–1, **61**
  Armstrong-Whitworth Albemarle ST Mk.V **60**
Armstrong-Whitworth Whitley 62–3, **62–3**
  Armstrong-Whitworth Whitley I **63**
  Armstrong-Whitworth Whitley V **63**
ASM-N-2 Bat guided missiles **106**, 107
Asmara 95
ASV radar 65, 79, 85, 151
Atlantic 103, **107**, 121, 151, 167
atomic weapons 7, 100, 101
Australia 71, 94, 133, 135, 137, 139
Austrian Air Force **175**
Avia 17
Avia B-33 37
Avro Anson 64–5, **64–5**, 122, 175
  Avro Anson I **65**
Avro Lancaster 11, 66–7, **67**, 68, 69, **69**, 75, 85, 89
  Avro Lancaster B.I 67
  Avro Lancaster B.II 67
  Avro Lancaster B.III 67
  Avro Lancaster I **66**, 67
Avro Manchester 66–7, 68–9, **69**, 84, 93
  Avro Manchester IA **68**
  Avro Manchester Mk III 67, 69

Belgium 17, 21, 23
Bismarck (battleship) **83**, 85
Black Sea Fleet (Russian) **31**, **41**
Blitz 139, **152**, **157**
Bloch MB.174 14–15, **15**
  Bloch MB.174A.3 **15**
Bloch MB.175 14–15, **14**
  Bloch MB.175B.3 15, **15**
Bloch MB.200 16–17, **16**
Bloch MB.210 16–17, **16–17**
BMW 46, 52, 145–7, 164–5, 217
Boeing B-17 Flying Fortress 11, 75, 98–9, 102, 114
  Boeing B-17B Flying Fortress 99
  Boeing B-17C Flying Fortress **98**, 99
  Boeing B-17E Flying Fortress 99
  Boeing B-17F Flying Fortress 99
  Boeing B-17G Flying Fortress 99, **99**
Boeing B-29 Superfortress 7, 11, 100–1, **100–1**, 104, 105, **105**, 125, 205, 215
Boeing Model 299 98
Boeing Model 345 100
Boeing Model XB-29 100–1
Bonn **113**
Bougainville campaign 121, **121**
'Bouncing Bomb' **67**
Breda Ba.64 168
Breda Ba.65 168–9, **168–9**
Bréguet 690 **18**
Bréguet 691 19
Bréguet 693 18–19, **19**
Brest 69, 71
Bristol Beaufighter 66–7, 73
Bristol Beaufort 70–1, **70–1**, 91
  Bristol Beaufort VIII **71**
Bristol Blenheim 11, **11**, 70, 72–3, 124, 133
  Bristol Blenheim Mk I **73**
  Bristol Blenheim Mk IV 72, **72**, **73**
  Bristol Blenheim Mk V 73, **73**
Bristol Centaurus 93
Bristol Hercules engine 67, 85, 92–3, 97
Bristol Jupiter engine 90
Bristol Pegasus engine **25**, 27, **90**, 97
Bristol Perseus engine **90**

Britain 7, 111, 169, 175
Britain, battle of 7, 145, 153, 161, **161**, 163, 171
British Overseas Airways Corporation **92**
Bulgaria 27, 29, 141, **141**
Bunker Hill (aircraft carrier) 109
Burma (Myanmar) **100**, 123, 137, 193, 201, 203

Canada **31**
CANT Z.506 Airone 170, 172–3
CANT Z.506A Airone 172
CANT Z.506B Airone **172–3**, 173
CANT Z.509 172
CANT Z.1007 Alcione 170–1, **171**
CANT Z.1007bis Alcione 170–1, **170**, **171**
Cape Matapan, battle of 77
Caproni Ca.101 174
Caproni Ca.133 174–5, **174–5**, 186
Caproni Ca.135 176–7, **176–7**
Caproni Ca.308 and derivatives 178–9
Caproni Ca.308 Borea 178
Caproni Ca.309 Ghibli 178–9
Caproni Ca.310 Libeccio 179, **179**
Caproni Ca.311 179
Caproni Ca.313 179, **179**
Caproni Ca.314 179
China 31, 37, 101, **108**, 127, 135, 192, 193, 197–9, 201, 203, **203**
Condor Legion 158, **159**
Consolidated B-24 Liberator 11, 102–3, 104, 107, 125
Consolidated B Mk.VI Liberator **103**
Consolidated B-24C Liberator 103
Consolidated B-24D Liberator 103, **103**
Consolidated B-24H Liberator 103
Consolidated B-24J Liberator **102**, 103
Consolidated B-32 Dominator 104–5, **104–5**
Consolidated Model 33 104
Consolidated PB4Y-1 Liberator 106–7, **107**
Consolidated PB4Y-2 Privateer 106–7, **106**
Consolidated XB-24 102–3
Consolidated XB-32 105
Continuation War 25
Coral Sea, battle of 119
Curtiss SB2C Helldiver 108–9, **109**, 117, 121, 212
Curtiss SB2C-1 Helldiver 109
Curtiss SB2C-1C Helldiver 109
Curtiss SB2C-3 Helldiver 109, **109**
Curtiss SB2C-4 Helldiver 109
Curtiss SB2C-5 Helldiver **108–9**, 109
Curtiss SBD Dauntless 108, 109
Curtiss XSB2C Helldiver 108
Czech Mixed Air Division **33**
Czechoslovakia 17, 37, **39**, 140–1
annexation, 1938 17

D-Day 61, **129**
Daimler Benz **144**, 145, 146, 147, 153, 213
Danish Airlines 150
de Havilland Mosquito 8–9, 11, 73, 74–5, 125
de Havilland Mosquito B Mk.IV **74**, 75, **75**
de Havilland Mosquito B Mk.VI **75**
de Havilland Mosquito B Mk.XVI 75
Deutsche Luft Hansa 144, 150–2, 166
Dieppe Raid **147**
Doolittle Raid 1942 134, 135
Dornier Do 17 144–5, 146
Dornier Do 17M-1 **145**
Dornier Do 17Z **139**, 145, 147
Dornier Do 17Z-5 **145**
Dornier Do 18 122–3
Dornier Do 215 **144**, 145
Dornier Do 215B-1 **145**
Dornier Do 217 146–7, 153
Dornier Do 217E **146**
Dornier Do 217E-1 146–7
Dornier Do 217E-4 **147**
Dornier Do 217K 147, **147**
Dornier Do 217K-1 **147**
Dornier Do 217K-2 147
Dornier Do 217K-3 147
Dornier Do 217P 147
Dornier Do 217R 147
Douglas A-20 Boston 110–11, 113, 130
Douglas A-20B Boston 111, **111**
Douglas A-20G Boston **110–11**, 111
Douglas A-20J Boston 111
Douglas A-24B **117**
Douglas A-26 Invader 112–13, **113**
Douglas A-26B Invader **112**, 113
Douglas B-10 **114**
Douglas B-10B **115**
Douglas B-18 Bolo 114–15, **115**, 134
Douglas B-18A Bolo 115
Douglas B-23 Dragon 115
Douglas B-24 115

Douglas B-26 115
Douglas Boston III 111
Douglas C-47 Skytrain **39**
Douglas DB-7 110–11
Douglas DC-2 114
Douglas DC-3 34–5, 38–9
Douglas Model 7B 110
Douglas SBD Dauntless 116–17
Douglas SBD-2 Dauntless **116**
Douglas SBD-4 Dauntless 117
Douglas SBD-5 Dauntless 117, **117**
Douglas TBD Devastator **7**, 118–19, **118–19**, 120, 206
Douglas XA-26 112
Douglas XTBD-1 118–19
Dutch (Netherlands) East Indies 25, 94, 113, 127, 137

East Africa 90, 91, 95, 159, 175, 187
Eastern Front **35**, 149, **149**, 157, 177, **177**, 181
Eder dam **67**
Enterprise (aircraft carrier) **116**, 117, **119**

Fairey Albacore 76–7, **76–7**, 83
Fairey Barracuda 78–9, **78**
Fairey Barracuda Mk I 78–9
Fairey Barracuda Mk II 79, **79**
Fairey Barracuda Mk III 79, **79**
Fairey Barracuda Mk IV 79
Fairey Battle 80–1, **80–1**, 201
Fairey Fulmar **91**
Fairey Seal 82
Fairey Swordfish 76, 77, 82–3, **82–3**
Fairey Swordfish Mk II 85
Far East 47, 103, 137
Far East Air Forces 113
Farman F.220 20
Farman F.221 20
Farman F.222 20–1, **20–1**
Farman F.223 (later NC.223) 21
Farman NC.223
Farman NC.223.3 21
Farman NC.223.4 21
Fiat BR.20 Cicogna 176, 180–1, **180–1**, 199
Fiat BR.20M Cicogna **181**
Fiat CR.32 185
Focke-Wulf Fw 189 Uhu 148–9, **148–9**
Focke-Wulf Fw 189A-1 Uhu **149**
Focke-Wulf Fw 189A-4 Uhu 149
Focke-Wulf Fw 189C Uhu 149
Focke-Wulf Fw 200 Condor **123**, 150–1, **151**, 167
Focke-Wulf Fw 200A Condor 150
Focke-Wulf Fw 200C-1 Condor **150**
Focke-Wulf Fw 200C-3 Condor **151**
Fokker C.V 24–5, **25**
Fokker C.X 24–5, **24–5**
Fokker F.VII 28
France 7, 11, 12–23, 81, 99, 102–3, 110, 130–3, 135–6, 161, 167, 173, 179, 181
fall of 13
Franklin (aircraft carrier) 189
Free French Forces 13, 23, **125**, **131**, 133, **137**

Galileo Galilei (submarine) 91
Garland, Donald **81**
George V (battleship) **101**
Germany 7–8, 13–14, **14**, 16–17, 19, 21, 23, 27, **27**, 29, 31, **37**, 43–5, **45**, 47, **51**, 59, 66, 71, 73, 77, 81–3, 87, 99, 111, **113**, 130, **131**, 139, **140–1**, 141, 142–67, 183, 190, 217
Glenn Martin 167 A-3 **131**
Glenn Martin 167 A-4 130
Glidden, Major Elmer G. **117**
Glorious (aircraft carrier) 82
Gneisenau (battlecruiser) 71
Gnome-Rhône engines 22, 27, 169, 170, 217
'Grand Slam' bomb 67
Greece 29, 133, 171, **171**, 173
Grumman F4F Wildcat 213
Grumman F6F Hellcat 209, 213
Grumman TBF Avenger 79, 120–1, **120–1**
Grumman XBTF-1 120–1

Handley Page Halifax 84–5, 89
Handley Page Halifax C.VIII **84**
Handley Page Halifax II Series IA **85**
Handley Page Halifax Mk III 85, **85**
Handley Page Hampden 63, 86–7, **86–7**, 96
Handley Page Hampden I **87**
Harris Lebus 61
Hawker Hart 80–1
Heinkel He 59 154
Heinkel He 111 **8**, **123**, 147, 152–3, **152–3**, 158
Heinkel He 111H 153
Heinkel He 111H-4 **153**
Heinkel He 111H-6 **8**
Heinkel He 111P 153
Heinkel He 111P-2 **153**

Heinkel He 115 154–5
Heinkel He 115A **155**
Heinkel He 115B-1 154, **154**
Heinkel He 115B-2 154–5, **155**
Heinkel He 115C-1 **155**
Heinkel He 115C-4 155
Heinkel He 118 160
Heinkel He 177 Greif 139, 156–7
Heinkel He 177A-3 Greif 157
Heinkel He 177A-3/R2 Greif **156**
Heinkel He 177A-5 Greif 157
Heinkel He 177A-5/R2 Greif **157**
Heinkel He 177A-5/R6 Greif **157**
Helsinki 39
Hermes (aircraft carrier) 191
Hiei (battleship) 121
Hiroshima 101
Hispano-Suiza 21, 22, 50–1
Hornet (aircraft carrier) 135, 206–7
Hungarian Air Force **161**
Hungarian Rapid Corps 177
Hungary 141, 159, **159**, **163**, 176, 177, **177**

IAR 37, 38, 39 216–17, **216–17**
Ilyushin DB-3 30–1, **30–1**, 34–5, **35**
Ilyushin DB-3F 34–5
Ilyushin DB-3T 31, **31**
Ilyushin IL-1 36
Ilyushin IL-2 Shturmovik 11, 32–3, **32–3**, 36–7
Ilyushin IL-2M3 Shturmovik **33**
Ilyushin IL-4 34–5, **34–5**
Ilyushin IL-8 37
Ilyushin IL-10 36–7, **36–7**
Ilyushin TsKB-26 30
Ilyushin TsKB-55 32
Immelmann III (Hitler's personal aircraft) 151
Imperial Japanese Army 191, 198, 200, 201, **205**, 210, 214
Imperial Japanese Army Air Service (IJAAF) 199, 200–1
Imperial Japanese Navy 150, 189, 191, 195, 196, 207, 209, 214, 215
Indomitable (aircraft carrier) 185
Iraqi Air Force **169**, **185**
Ishikawajima Ne-20 **193**
Isotta Fraschini Asso engines 170, **177**, 179
Italian Aviazione Legionaria **179**, **180**
Italian Co-belligerent Air Force 133, **170**, **171**
Italy 19, 63, 77, 83, 91, 95, 139, 147, 168–87

jamming equipment **85**, **103**, 107
Japan 31, 37, 79, 91, 99, 101, 105, **105**, 113, 117, **117**, 121, **121**, 125, 127, 129, 135, 137, 139, 181, 188–215
Junkers Ju 86 158–9, **158**
Junkers Ju 86D 158, **159**
Junkers Ju 86D-1 **159**
Junkers Ju 86K 159
Junkers Ju 86K-2 **159**
Junkers Ju 86P 159
Junkers Ju 87 'Stuka' 9, 160–1, **161**
Junkers Ju 87B 'Stuka' 161
Junkers Ju 87B-2 'Stuka' **161**
Junkers Ju 87D 'Stuka' 161
Junkers Ju 87R-2 'Stuka' **160**
Junkers Ju 88 40, 41, 55, 89, 147, 153, 162–3, **163**, 164, **164**, 165
Junkers Ju 88A 165
Junkers Ju 88A-1 163, 164
Junkers Ju 88A-4 **162–3**, 163
Junkers Ju 88A-14 **163**
Junkers Ju 88B 164, 165
Junkers Ju 88B-0 164
Junkers Ju 88S 163
Junkers Ju 90 166–7
Junkers Ju 188 164–5, **164**
Junkers Ju 188A 165
Junkers Ju 188A-3 **165**
Junkers Ju 188E 165
Junkers Ju 188E-1 165
Junkers Ju 288 165
Junkers Ju 290 166–7
Junkers Ju 290A-4 **166**
Junkers Ju 290A-5 **167**
Junkers Jumo engines 153, 164–5

Kaafjord **79**
kamikaze attacks 203, 205, 211, 215, **215**
Kawasaki Ki-3 200
Kawasaki Ki-32 201
Kawasaki Ki-48 'Lily' 192–3
Kawasaki Ki-48-I 'Lily' **192–3**
Kawasaki Ki-48-Ia 'Lily' 193
Kawasaki Ki-48-Ib 'Lily' 193, **193**
Kawasaki Ki-48-II KAI 'Lily' 193
Kawasaki Ki-48-IIa 'Lily' 193
Kawasaki Ki-48-IIb 'Lily' 193
Kenney, General George 113
Khalkhin-Gol, battle of 46
Klimov engines 42–3, 57, 59
Kowalewski, *Oberstleutnant* Robert **143**

Leningrad **33**, 39, 51
LeO 451 13, 22–3, **22–3**, **131**
Letov Š.28 140–1
Letov Š.328 140–1, **140–1**
Lexington (aircraft carrier) 117, 206–7
Leyte, battle of **109**
Lisunov Li-2 38–9, **38–9**
Lisunov Li-2NB 39
'Little Boy' (atomic bomb) 101
Lockheed A-28/A-29 Hudson 65, 72, 122–3, **122–3**, 124
Lockheed Model 14 Super Electra 122, 124
Lockheed Model 18 Lodestar 124
Lockheed PV-1 Ventura 124–5, **124–5**
Luftwaffe **11**, **35**, **85**, 87, 139, **140–1**, 141, 145, **145**, 148–9, 151–2, 154–6, **154**, 158–60, 162–3, 165–7, 183

Mariana Islands 101, **101**, 213, 215
Martin 167 Maryland 130–1, **130–1**, 132
Martin 167F Maryland 130
Martin Maryland Mk I 131, **131**
Martin Maryland Mk II 131
Martin 187 Baltimore 131, 132–3, **132**
Martin Baltimore Mk I 133, **133**
Martin Baltimore Mk V **133**
Martin B-10 126–7, **127**
Martin B-26 Marauder 113, 128–9, **128–9**
Martin Model 123 126
Martin Model 139 25, 126–7
Martin Model 166 126–7
Messerschmitt Bf 109 **11**, 23, 51
Messerschmitt Bf 109E 41
Messerschmitt Bf 110 23, 89
Midway, battle of 116, 117, 119, **119**, 213
Mikulin engines 32, 37, 43, 47, 52–3, 55
Mitsubishi A6M 'Zero' 188, 212
Mitsubishi G3M 'Nell' 194–5, **194**, 196–7
Mitsubishi G3M2 'Nell' **195**
Mitsubishi G4M 'Betty' 196–7, **196**
Mitsubishi G4M1 'Betty' **197**
Mitsubishi G4M3 'Betty' **197**
Mitsubishi Ki-21 'Sally' 198–9, **199**, 210
Mitsubishi Ki-21-I 'Sally' **198**
Mitsubishi Ki-21-Ia 'Sally' **199**
Mitsubishi Ki-21-IIa 'Sally' 199
Mitsubishi Ki-21-IIb 'Sally' 199, **199**
Mitsubishi Ki-27 203
Mitsubishi Ki-30 'Ann' 200–1, **200–1**, 202–3
Mitsubishi Ki-50 211
Mitsubishi Ki-51 'Sonia' 202–3, **202–3**
Mitsubishi Ki-67 Kiryū 'Peggy' 204–5, **204–5**, 214
Mitsubishi Ki-67Ia Kiryū 'Peggy' 205
Mitsubishi Ki-67Ib Kiryū 'Peggy' 205
Mitsubishi Ki-69 205

'Nachthexen' (Night Witches) 45, **45**
Nagasaki 101
Nakajima B5N 'Kate' 206–7, **206–7**, 208
Nakajima B5N1 'Kate' 207
Nakajima B5N2 'Kate' 207, **208**
Nakajima B6N Tenzan 'Jill' 188–9, 207, 208–9
Nakajima B6N1 Tenzan 'Jill' 209
Nakajima B6N2 Tenzan 'Jill' **209**
Nakajima Ki-49 Donryu 'Helen' 210–11, **210**
Nakajima Ki-49-I Donryu 'Helen' **211**
Netherlands 24, 24–5, **24**, 89, 127, 135
New Zealand 91, **91**, **121**, 123
North Africa 23, 117, 131, 133, 159, 163, 168, 179, 181, 187
North American B-25 Mitchell 134–5, **134**
North American B-25A Mitchell 134
North American B-25B Mitchell 134–5
North American B-25C Mitchell 135, **135**
North American B-25D Mitchell 135
North American B-25G Mitchell 135
North American B-25J Mitchell 135
North American NA-62 134
Northern Fleet Air Force **87**
Northrop BT-1 116
Norway 24, 71, 77, 79, **79**, 117, 155, 161, 167, **179**

Okinawa 189, 209
Operation Barbarossa 35, **57**, 63, **159**

Operation Leader 117
Operation Market Garden 61
Operation Millennium 67, 87
Operation Overlord **129**
Operation Steinbock **157**
Operation Torch 23, 77, 117
Operation Tungsten 79

Pacific War 116–17, 191, 194, 197, 199, 206, 211
Palestine **95**
Pearl Harbor 115, 119, 123, 190, **191**, 194, 206, **207**
Petlyakov ANT-42 42
Petlyakov Pe-2 11, 40–1, **40**, 51, **55**, 57
  Petlyakov Pe-2FT **41**
Petlyakov Pe-8 42–3, **42–3**
Petlyakov TB-7 42
Petlyakov VI-100 40–1
Philippine Sea, battle of 109, 117, 209, **212**
Piaggio 170, 173, 179
Piaggio P.108 182–3, **182–3**
  Piaggio P.108B 183, **183**
  Piaggio P.108C 183
  Piaggio P.108T 183
Ploieşti oil fields 41, 103
Poland 11, 26–9, **37**, 41, 47, 141, 158, 161, 163
Polikarpov, Nikolai 45
Polikarpov I-15 187
Polikarpov I-16 59, 63, 187
Polikarpov Po-2 44–5, 47, 141
Polikarpov R-5 46–7, **46–7**
  Polikarpov R-5Sh 47
  Polikarpov R-5SSS 47, **47**
Polikarpov R-Z 46–7, **47**
Polikarpov U-2 44–5, **45**
  Polikarpov U-2LNB 45
  Polikarpov U-2S **44**
Polish Air Force **37**
Potez 637 15
Pratt & Whitney 38, 71, **71**, 93, 97, 131
PZL.23 Karaś 26–7, **26–7**
  PZL.23A Karaś 26
  PZL.23B Karaś 26–7
PZL.37 Łoś 11, 28–9, **28–9**
  PZL.37A Łoś 29
  PZL.37B Łoś 29
PZL.43 27
PZL.46 Sum ('Catfish') 27
PZL P.11c 161

Rabaul 109, 129, 209
Regia Aeronautica 176–7, **177**, 178–9, 180, 186–7, **186**
Rolls-Royce Merlin engines 63, 66, 69, 81, 84–5, **85**, 97
Rolls-Royce Vulture engines 68–9, 84, 93
Romanian Air Force **29**, 216
Romanian Army **217**
Romanian oilfields 41, 103
Royal Air Force (RAF) 8, **11**, 23, 60–3, **61**, 66, 72, 77, 81, 84, **85**, 88, 90–1, **91**, 95–7, 99, 106, 111, 123, 131, 133, **133**, **135**, 155, 181
  Bomber Command 8, 62, 63, 65, 67, 87, **89**
  Coastal Command 63, 64–5, **65**, **71**, 72, **72**, 85, 87, **122**, 123, 125
Royal Australian Air Force (RAAF) 71, **85**, **134**, **137**
Royal Canadian Air Force (RCAF) 115
Royal Navy 76, 121, **207**
  Fleet Air Arm 82
Royal Netherlands Air Force 25
Royal Netherlands Naval Air Service **65**
Royal New Zealand Air Force (RNZAF) **87**, 121, **121**, 125
Royal Thai Air Force 201
Savoia Marchetti SM.79 Sparviero 184–5, **184–5**, 186
  Savoia Marchetti SM.79B Sparviero **185**
Savoia-Marchetti SM.81 Pipistrello 186–7, **186–7**
Short Stirling 88–9, **88–9**
Shvetsov engines 38, 43, 49, 55
Sicily 61, **135**, **178**, 183, **185**
Singapore 91, **101**, 127, 193, 195, 197
Sino-Japanese Wars 46, 127, **201**
  Second 191, 207
Slovak Air Force 141
Slovak Resistance Air Force **141**
Soviet Union 11, 24–5, 27, 29, 30–59, **61**, **87**, 111, **111**, 135, 141, 149, 153, **153**, 157, 177, 187, 198–9
Spain 16, 31, 47, 51, **67**, 91, 158, **159**, 161, 168, **169**, 173, 177, 179, **179**, **185**, 187
Spanish Civil War 7, 46, 91, 145, 153, 169, 173, 175, 180, **180**, 184, 186–7
Stalingrad 151, 157, 159, 187, 217, **217**
Sukhoi ANT-51 48–9
Sukhoi BB-1 49
Sukhoi Su-2 48–9, **48–9**, 201
Sukhoi Su-6 37
Sweden 145, 155, 179, **179**
Swedish Air Force **25**

Taranto 83, 131
Tirpitz (battleship) 77, 79, **79**
Tokyo 105, **105**
  fire-bombing 101
Trapoklappe rear ramp 167
Truk **117**, **206**, **209**
Tupolev, Andrei 50, 51, 54
Tupolev Aircraft 103 54–5

Tupolev ANT-40 50
Tupolev design bureau 48
Tupolev SB 192
Tupolev SB-2 30, 50–1, **51**, 57
Tupolev TB-3 31, 39, 42, 52–3, **52–3**
Tupolev Tu-2 54–5, **54–5**
Tupolev Tu-2S 55

United Kingdom 60–97, 103, 106, 135, 136, 181
United States 8, 34, **42**, 98–137, 151, 209
United States Air Force (USAF) 112
9th Air Force 111
Ninth Air Force 113, **113**
United States Army Air Corps (USAAC) 98, 100, 102, 104, 114, **114**, **115**, **126**, 127, 128, 130, 134
United States Army Air Forces (USAAF) 8, 11, 23, 99, 103, **110–11**, 111, 113, **117**, **123**, 125, 128, 132, 137
Eighth Air Force 98, 99, **99**, 103
United States Marine Corps 116–17, **117**, 125
United States Navy 106, 109, 118, 119, 123, 212

Vichy Air Force **19**, 23, **23**
Vichy France 13, **14–15**, 15, 17, 19, 21, 77, 127, **131**
Vickers Vildebeest 90–1
Vickers Vildebeest Mk III 90, **91**
Vickers Vildebeest Mk IV **90**
Vickers Vincent 90–1, **91**
Vickers Warwick 92–3
Vickers Warwick ASR **93**
Vickers Warwick C Mk.III **93**
Vickers Warwick GR Mk.V 93, **93**
Vickers Wellesley 94–5, **94–5**
Vickers Wellington 41, 96–7
Vickers Wellington I **97**
Vickers Wellington IA **96–7**
Vickers Wellington IC **97**
Vickers Wellington Mk.III 97
Victorious (aircraft carrier) **79**
Vultee A-31 Vengeance 136–7
Vultee A-35B Vengeance **136**, **137**
Vultee V-72 Vengeance 136–7

Yakovlev BB-22 57
Yakovlev BB-22b 57
Yakovlev Yak-2 56–7, **57**
Yakovlev Yak-4 56–7, **56–7**
Yakovlev Yak-9 55
Yermolaev DB-240 58–9
Yermolaev Yer-2 58–9, **58–9**
Yokosuka B4Y 207
Yokosuka D4Y Suisei 'Judy' 188–9, 191, 212–13
Yokosuka D4Y1 Suisei 'Judy' **212**, 213
Yokosuka D4Y1-C Suisei 'Judy' 213
Yokosuka D4Y3 Suisei 'Judy' 213, **213**
Yokosuka P1Y Ginga 'Frances' 214–15
Yokosuka P1Y1 Ginga 'Frances' **214–15**
Yokosuka P1Y-2S Kyokko 215

Photographic and Artwork Credits

Alamy: 16 (Vintage Mechanics), 20 (Maverick90), 26 (Vintage Mechanics), 28 (Hum Images), 60 (piemags), 138 (Niday Picture Library), 140 (piemags),144 (Sueddeutsche Zeitung Photo), 154 (Pictorial Press), 168 (The History Collection), 174 (Carlo Maggio), 179 (Art Collection), 180 (Sueddeutsche Zeitung Photo),182 & 183 (Vintage Mechanics), 186 (Interfoto), 202 (Vintage Mechanics)
Alamy/Chronicle: 12, 14, 25, 56, 61, 80, 90, 92, 113, 192, 204
Amber Books: 9, 10, 32, 54, 62, 64, 66, 68, 70, 71, 72, 74, 78, 79, 82, 84, 86, 88, 96, 98, 100, 102, 110, 122, 128, 134, 146, 148, 162, 164, 166, 184, 190, 196
ASL Photos: 31, 34, 40, 42, 52, 77, 142, 150, 156, 194, 198, 199, 206, 208, 209, 210
Getty Images: 13 (Albert Harlingue/Roger-Viollet), 76 (Print Collector), 93 (Keystone), 94 (Popperfoto), 95 (Royal Air Force Museum), 112 (Photo 12), 131 (Albert Harlingue/Roger-Viollet), 172 (Keystone), 173 (De Agostini), 200, 201 & 203 (The Asahi Shimbun)
Naval History & Heritage Command: 107, 108, 115, 116, 118, 120, 124
Public Domain: 6, 17, 18, 22, 23, 24, 36, 44, 46, 47, 48, 50, 58, 59, 104, 105, 106, 119, 126, 127, 130, 132, 133, 136, 152, 158, 160, 170, 175, 176, 177, 178, 188, 189, 193, 212, 213, 215, 216
Smithsonian National Air and Space Museum, Washington: 214
Stavka: 30, 35, 38, 45
U.S. Air Force: 114

All illustrations Amber Books Ltd, apart from:
ArtbyEdo: 30, 31, 35, 39 (both), 42, 45, 46, 47, 48, 50, 52, 56, 57, 60, 129 (both)
Rolando Ugolini: 82, 102, 150, 151, 160, 163 (both)
Teasel Studios: 22, 27 (both), 29 (both), 53 (both), 58, 59, 128, 162, 182, 183, 189, 193, 202, 214, 215, 217 (both)